Applying Model Cornerstone Assessments in K–12 Music

Applying Model Cornerstone Assessments in K–12 Music

A Research-Supported Approach

Edited by Frederick Burrack
and Kelly A. Parkes

Published in Partnership with the
National Association for Music Education

ROWMAN & LITTLEFIELD
Lanham • Boulder • New York • London

Published in partnership with the National Association for Music Education, 1806 Robert Fulton Drive, Reston, Virginia 20191; nafme.org

Published by Rowman & Littlefield
A wholly owned subsidiary of The Rowman & Littlefield Publishing Group, Inc.
4501 Forbes Boulevard, Suite 200, Lanham, Maryland 20706
www.rowman.com

Unit A, Whitacre Mews, 26-34 Stannary Street, London SE11 4AB, United Kingdom

British Library Cataloguing in Publication Information Available

Library of Congress Cataloging-in-Publication Data

Names: Burrack, Frederick. | Parkes, Kelly A.
Title: Applying model cornerstone assessments in K–12 music : a
  research-supported approach / [edited by] Frederick Burrack and Kelly A.
  Parkes.
Description: Lanham : Rowman & Littlefield, [2018] | Includes bibliographical
  references.
Identifiers: LCCN 2018017989 (print) | LCCN 2018018381 (ebook) | ISBN
  9781475837407 (Electronic) | ISBN 9781475837384 (cloth : alk. paper) |
  ISBN 9781475837391 (pbk. : alk. paper)
Subjects: LCSH: Music—Instruction and study—Evaluation. |
  Music—Instruction and study—Research.
Classification: LCC MT1 (ebook) | LCC MT1 .M75 2018 (print) | DDC 780.71—
  dc23 LC record available at https://lccn.loc.gov/2018017989

∞™ The paper used in this publication meets the minimum requirements of American National Standard for Information Sciences—Permanence of Paper for Printed Library Materials, ANSI/NISO Z39.48-1992.

Printed in the United States of America

We dedicate this book to Dr. Carla Maltas, who worked diligently with this Model Cornerstone Assessment project until her untimely passing during the first round of piloting—and to the music teachers and students who integrated the MCAs into their classrooms, provided student work for analysis, and whose feedback helped guide the revisions that led to the assessments as they currently are presented.

Contents

Acknowledgments   ix

Introduction   xi

Chapter One   Model Cornerstone Assessments   1
  Kelly A. Parkes

Chapter Two   The Pilot Study Process   9
  Frederick Burrack and Kelly A. Parkes

Chapter Three   Grade 2 Model Cornerstone Assessments   17
  Daniel C. Johnson

Chapter Four   Grade 5 Model Cornerstone Assessments   39
  Denese Odegaard, Michael J. Ruybalid, and Mary Kate Newell

Chapter Five   Grade 8 Model Cornerstone Assessments   53
  Ann Clements, Katherine Willow, and Kristina R. Weimer

Chapter Six   The Model Cornerstone Assessments for Ensembles   69
  Al D. Holcomb, Glenn E. Nierman, and Bret P. Smith

Chapter Seven   Harmonizing Instruments Model
                  Cornerstone Assessment   89
  Wendy K. Matthews and Daniel C. Johnson

Chapter Eight   Composition/Theory Model
                  Cornerstone Assessments   107
  Patricia Riley

Chapter Nine   Technology Model Cornerstone Assessment
                  for Creating   121
  Phillip Payne

Chapter Ten   Methodology for Qualitative Data   139
  Frederick Burrack

Chapter Eleven   Methodology for Examining the
                 Psychometric Qualities of the Model
                 Cornerstone Assessments   141
  Brian C. Wesolowski

Chapter Twelve   Examination of the Psychometric Qualities of
                 the Model Cornerstone Assessments   151
  Brian C. Wesolowski

Chapter Thirteen   A Case for Validity and Reliability   181
  Frederick Burrack

Chapter Fourteen   Connections to Higher Education in Music   185
  Phillip Payne and Jeffrey Ward

Chapter Fifteen   Curricular and Professional Implications   195
  Frederick Burrack and Kelly A. Parkes

About the Contributors   201

About the Editors   209

Acknowledgments

We wish to acknowledge the vision of Dr. Timothy Brophy for pursuing the involvement of assessment researchers in the development and piloting of the MCAs; the faith and support of Dr. Scott Shuler as we worked to reflect standard statements into classroom action; the guidance of all standards writers to help the assessment writers remain faithful to the educational intent of the standards; to Chris Urban for assisting in developing the platform that was used to sort and analyze qualitative data; the school administrators and parents who gave permission to pilot these MCAs in the schools and collect the data needed to progress with an effective project; and to the many teachers who adjusted their instructional plans to experience these MCAs.

Introduction

Educative assessment requires assessment designers to better honor the students' needs for engaging and useful work, and the teachers' needs for more direct, useful, and timely information. (Wiggins, 2015)

BACKGROUND BEHIND THE 2014 NATIONAL STANDARDS FOR MUSIC EDUCATION

Academic standards are public statements about what students should know and be able to do as a result of a formal learning experience (Burrack & Parkes, in press). They are intended to guide programs' curriculum development and focus instruction and assessment. According to Shuler (1995), music standards define expectations of achievement in skills and knowledge for all students reflective of high-quality programs. When implemented in schools' curricula, standards can focus instructional efforts to enhance student learning. Thus, standards and related assessments are intended and designed to improve teaching and learning. Nierman (2012) suggests that one primary purpose of standards is to bridge the gap between curriculum expectations, classroom instruction, and student learning assessment. He affirms that curriculum, instruction, and standards should be interdependent. Clarifying learning expectations that guide curriculum development and implementation of instruction is the purpose of standards. Assessments enable students to demonstrate how they apply what has been learned. To fulfill the purpose of standards, the revised National Standards for Music Education included assessments that can be integrated with instruction.

Staying at the Forefront

In 2010, responsive to current directions in education, the State Education Agency Directors of Arts Education (SEADAE, 2015a) gathered in Washington, DC, and voted to pursue revising the 1994 national arts standards. In spring 2011, the newly created National Coalition for Core Arts Standards (NCCAS)[1] involved consultants Jay and Daisy McTighe to guide the inclusion of an inquiry approach to higher-order thinking skills from *Understanding by Design* (McTighe & Wiggins, 2004).

Revising the National Standards

The 2014 National Core Arts Standards were developed, in part, through a desire to describe a new vision of goals for student learning in American school music classes. In the 20 years that separates them from the National Standards for Arts (1994), researchers and leaders in curriculum policy elaborated on the need for authentic curriculum goals that furthered student development relevant to the 21st-century global environment.

By January 2012, specific writing teams for dance, media arts, music, theatre, and visual arts were in place to unify arts standards across all the disciplines, supported by research, and attainable for preK–12 arts educators. During the first year of development, philosophical foundations and lifelong goals emerged that were used to articulate broad goals for learning. Two frameworks were particularly prominent in the development of the National Core Arts Standards. The first was the Arts Education Assessment Framework or *Three Artistic Processes* that served as the framework for the national arts assessment in the 1997 National Assessment of Educational Progress (Persky, Sandene, & Askew, 1998). The 2014 National Core Arts Standards use the framework for planning and assessing student engagement in musical processes designed to promote critical thinking, creativity, collaboration, and student independence in creating original music, performing music, and responding to music based on what students know and have experienced inside and outside the classroom.

The second framework was the planning and instructional process model elaborated by Jay McTighe and Grant Wiggins in a series of works titled *Understanding by Design* (2004). This model asks curriculum developers to engage in a process they call Backward Design, where standards are used to determine what learning outcomes and assessment evidence will be necessary to determine a student's achievement toward the Core Music Standards, and then develop learning activities, assessment tasks, and resources will optimize the student's opportunities for success. The major elements of the 2014 Core Standards include, in addition to the artistic processes, process components that are grouped by *Common Anchor Standards* across all grade levels, *Enduring Understandings*, *Essential Questions*, the *Performance Standards* themselves, and *Model Cornerstone Assessments* (SEADAE, 2015b).

Taken together, these frameworks guide a deep and careful rethinking of how and whether teachers in varying school music contexts have been able to fulfill their tenets and results. The desire to develop students' ability to create (compose, improvise) and respond (analyze, reflect, describe, interpret, evaluate) is not new to ensemble directors; the 1994 standards included them, as did other familiar curriculum models going back to the 1960s, such as the Manhattanville Music Curriculum (Thomas, 1970) and Harvard Project Zero (1992).

Artistic processes of creating, performing, and responding formed the pillars for the framework, which were more clearly delineated through their component parts. The important ideas of lasting value that are to be attained in the development of each component part of the artistic process (NCCAS, 2014) and the overall question(s) students should be asking themselves as they progress through the process components (essential questions) were included. The depth of understanding attained from all these considerations led to the development of grade-by-grade performance standards for music.

Each of the three artistic processes is divided into a sequence of component performance standards.

- Creating components—imagine, plan, make, evaluate, refine, present
- Presenting/performing components—select, analyze, interpret, rehearse, evaluate, refine, present
- Responding components—select, analyze, interpret, evaluate

When viewed individually, this appears to be a long list of performance standards. In reality, each sequence reflects a step taken by musicians in a singular process in which our students engage. So instead of considering 17 independent performance standards, we should see them as part of three processes in which students engage for affective musical experience. The primary difference from the former standards is the focus. The new standards emphasize processes through which students interact with music: creating music, performing music, and responding to music in contrast to products of musical interactions. The significant aspect of these new standards is that these artistic processes are already a focus of most general or performance classrooms, and applicable at every developmental level. These standards do not limit musical experience to traditional music-education settings, but encourage school music programs to allow student experience in creating, performing, and responding in nearly any format, genre, or style considered relevant (developmentally and culturally) for students. If embraced by music teachers, they will provide a framework that closely matches the goals unique to specialized classes as well as traditional music courses. For this reason, the new standards are presented in a grade-by-grade sequence from preK through grade 8 and through discrete strands associated with middle and high school music classes, such as traditional and alternative ensembles, harmonizing instruments (piano, guitar, etc.), music composition/theory, and technology.

By 2013, draft standards were released to the public for review and feedback. "During a series of three public reviews, the coalition received over 1.5 million comments from over 6,000 reviewers, all of which were meticulously studied by research teams, with results driving revisions and edits" (NCCAS, 2014). Responding to the suggestions through various revisions, the authors shared the final standards publicly in June 2014. Unique to this set of standards is that they are published online through an interactive website, allowing users to access, sort, and print the standards specific to the needs of each teacher.

Developing Assessments

New to the standards are assessment tasks and scoring devices that can be integrated into a music program's curriculum. The resulting assessments are the means through which students demonstrate development and achievement of the National Standard for Music. Because musicians engage in the artistic process in an unlimited variety of ways, the assessment structure in the Model Cornerstone Assessments is presented as a framework enabling students to demonstrate learning in the artistic processes of music as it relates to their personal and culturally relevant experiences and varied forms of musical literacy. Although the Model Cornerstone Assessments (MCAs) are focused on processes, the tasks are supported by and require appropriate development of knowledge and skills relevant to the expectations of music programs.

In this book, chapter 1 provides a thorough description of the concept behind and structure of a Model Cornerstone Assessment. In each chapter, there are clear descriptions of the standards for each artistic process associated with the particular grade level or strand. Links in each chapter will connect to additional documents of the artistic processes and performance standards for each. Chapter 2 describes the rationale behind the pilot study process implemented to confirm validity, the extent to which the tasks represent authentic learning as defined by the standards, usefulness and appropriateness for use in a variety of music classrooms, consistency of scoring student work among various schools' contexts, teacher perception of appropriateness for developmental levels of students, strategies for instructional integration, and adaptations implemented.

Chapters 3–9 are written to help music teachers understand the MCAs, describe how they were administered and adapted by teachers, report what was learned through the pilot study, and provide ideas for incorporating program curricula into the assessment framework.

Chapter 10 addresses the methodology for qualitative data analyses and teacher feedback. Chapter 11 describes the methodology used to investigate the evidence of reliability and validity, in addition to defining student ability, criterion difficulty, and scorer severity. Chapter 12 is a technical report of the the research findings and the psychometric qualities of the MCAs. Chapter 13 is designed to assist music teachers in understanding and explaining the rationale as to the validity and reliability of the MCAs and scoring devices.

Chapter 14 describes connections of the MCAs to preparation for higher education in music. The discussion explores current higher education expectations, considerations for school music programs to prepare students for success beyond secondary school, and suggestions to institutions of higher education to take full advantage of learning assessment through the MCAs. Chapter 15 is a chance for the book's editors to look to the future, considering next steps and some implications based on the cumulative work of the book's authors. Inference is offered as to possible futures of music education, the national standards, music assessment, and connections to lifelong music involvement.

Curriculum standards of any kind reflect an interpretation of the relative importance of the familiar domains of *Bloom's Taxonomy* (Anderson & Krathwohl, 2001): the cognitive (knowledge), psychomotor (skills and executive processes), and affective (attitudes, dispositions, and emotional responses). Each generation of educators, and hence the standards they develop, exists within a policy context driven by the needs and pedagogical preferences of the day—and our generation is no exception. Prior formulations of the desired results of formal music instruction have emphasized specific skill sequences formulated as behavioral objectives (Boyle, 1974) and, to some extent, aesthetic goals (Broudy, 1990).

NOTE

1. "Members included the American Alliance for Theatre and Education, the College Board, the Educational Theatre Association, the National Art Education Association, the National Association for Music Education, the National Dance Education Organization and the State Education Agency Directors of

Arts Education . . . Young Audiences Arts for Learning and Americans for the Arts, the John F. Kennedy Center for the Performing Arts and the Lincoln Center Education department." National Coalition for Core Arts Standards, "History: 2011—Building the Framework." Retrieved July 1, 2017 from http://nccas .wikispaces.com.

REFERENCES

Anderson, L. W., & Krathwohl, D. R. (Eds.). (2001). *A taxonomy for learning, teaching and assessing: A revision of Bloom's taxonomy of educational objectives.* New York: Longman.

Boyle, J. D. (Ed.). (1974). *Instructional objectives in music: Resources for planning instruction and evaluating achievement.* Reston, VA: Music Educators National Conference.

Broudy, H. S. (1990). The role of music in general education. *Bulletin of the Council for Research in Music Education, 105,* 23–43.

Burrack, F., & Parkes, K. (in press). The development of standards-based assessments in music. In T. S. Brophy (Ed.), vol. 1, *Policy, measurement, and teacher education* (chapter 30). New York: Oxford University Press.

McTighe, J., & Wiggins, G. (2004). *Understanding by design: Professional development workbook.* Alexandria, VA: Association for Supervision and Curriculum Development.

Music Educators National Conference (1994). *National Standards for arts education: What every young American should know and be able to do in the arts.* Reston, VA: Music Educators National Conference.

National Coalition for Core Arts Standards. (2011). History: 2011—Building the framework. Retrieved from http://nccas.wikispaces.com

National Coalition for Core Arts Standards (NCCAS). (2013). History: 2013—Revising and refining. Retrieved from http://nccas.wikispaces.com

National Coalition for Core Arts Standards (NCCAS). (2014). Enduring understandings and essential questions. In *National Association for Music Education.* Retrieved from www.nafme.org/wp-content/uploads/2014/06/Core-Music -Standards-EUs-EQs-Definitions.pdf

Nierman, G. (2012). Making a case for high-stakes assessment in music. In T. Brophy & A. Lehmann-Wermser (Eds.), *Music assessment across cultures and continents: The culture of shared practice. Proceedings of the 3rd International Symposium on assessment in music education* (pp. 97–107). Chicago, IL: GIA Publications.

Persky, H. R., Sandene, B. A., & Askew, J. M. (1998). *The NEAP 1997 arts report card* (NCES 1999-486). Washington, DC: U.S. Department of Education, Office of Educational Research and Improvement, National Center for Education Statistics.

Project Zero, Harvard Graduate School of Education. (1992). *Arts PROPEL: A handbook for music.* Cambridge, MA: Author.

Shuler, S. (1995). The impact of national standards on the preparation, in-service professional development, and arts education. *Policy Review, 96*(3), 2.

State Education Agency Directors of Arts Education. (2015a). *National core arts standards: dance, media arts, music, theatre and visual arts.* Retrieved from http://nationalartstandards.org

State Education Agency Directors of Arts Education. (2015b). *Model cornerstone assessments.* Retrieved from http://www.nafme.org/my-classroom/standards/mcas-information-on-taking-part-in-the-field-testing/

Thomas, R. B. (1970). *Manhattanville music curriculum program: Final report.* Purchase, NY: Manhattanville College. Retrieved from ERIC database (ED045865).

Wiggins, G. (2015). *Educative assessment: Designing assessments to inform and improve student State Education Agency Directors of Arts Education.* Retrieved from http://nationalartstandards.org

ONE

Model Cornerstone Assessments

Kelly A. Parkes

In 2012, the National Coalition for Core Arts Standards (NCCAS) tasked the professional organizations included in the revised arts standards (music, visual art, theatre, dance, and media arts) with creating Model Cornerstone Assessments (MCAs) that aligned with the criteria of the new performance standards to become content standards. A leader of the music standards writing team approached the chair of the National Association for Music Education (NAfME) Society for Research in Music Education (SRME) Assessment Special Research Interest Group (SRIG) to convene a team of researchers who would develop, test, and revise Model Cornerstone Assessments in collaboration with K–12 music teachers and the music standards writing team leaders. This was done in an effort to enrich the new national standards with research-based assessments that could answer the call in states and school districts for authentic and robust measures of student learning.

The focus of the MCA development centered on developmental readiness research that supported the writing of the new standards, as well as the most current educational psychology. The 2014 Core Arts Music Standards are intended to cultivate a student's ability to carry out the three artistic processes of creating, performing, and responding. Model Cornerstone Assessments are curriculum-embedded measures designed for music students to apply relevant knowledge and skills while demonstrating learning in the standards that define the artistic processes. They are meant to engage students in tasks authentic to a school's curriculum and honor the intent of the Music Performance Standards.

Model Cornerstone Assessments serve as more than just a means of gathering assessment evidence. They embody valuable learning goals and accomplishments of students becoming increasingly sophisticated across the grades. These assessments also provide a basis for teachers to collect and evaluate the student work that illustrates the nature and quality of student achievement as envisioned in the standards.

Model Cornerstone Assessments are not designed to be a means of gathering evaluative evidence of programmatic success, nor are they meant to compare students' content knowledge/skill attainment between classrooms, districts, or states. They do not follow the national trend to use standardized measures that narrow curricula, but instead they are structured to be authentically and contextually based. The use of the MCAs encourages students to demonstrate achievement of the standards in a variety of ways within and beyond the school curriculum. The tasks are designed to reflect experience with music in and beyond schools.

The structure for all MCAs provides a framework into which teachers integrate their curriculum content to match the unique goals of any music class, while using common learning expectations of process and rubrics. Each school program has a unique population and circumstances, so respecting the professional autonomy of teachers, who know their students and educational culture, is essential. Providing adaptable assessment tasks that will allow students to demonstrate the quality of learning associated with the performance standards is also important. The scoring rubrics have been designed to allow for task flexibility while measuring student learning according to the criteria in the performance standards. They are developed and tested, with the research methodology reported in this book, to be used in the classroom by teachers, thereby eliminating external evaluation of student learning with standardized and narrow testing. If administered with integrity by practicing teachers, the MCAs are valid measures of student achievement according to the criteria in the performance standards and can reliably illustrate the learning of students as they move through a music program. The MCAs are developed for grades 2, 5, and 8, and there are discrete strands for middle and high school music classes such as ensembles, composition/theory, harmonizing instruments such as piano and guitar, and technology.

DEVELOPMENT OF THE MCAS

The development occurred along the following time line:

Spring 2012	Chair (Tim Brophy) and chair-elect (Kelly Parkes) of NAfME Assessment SRIG attended standards writing meetings in an observatory capacity only. Then a team of research advisors (RAs) were contacted and invited to join the project.
Fall 2012	New SRIG chair (Parkes) and new chair-elect (Frederick Burrack) attended standards writing meetings in an observatory capacity only. RA roles were defined to work with standards writing team leaders in grade bands (second, fifth, eighth grade) and settings (ensembles—traditional and non-traditional, harmonizing instruments).
Spring 2013	Parkes and Burrack continued to observe standards writing team meetings. Orientation was provided for RAs on the standards still in development. RAs met with the leaders of the standards writing team subcommittees to fully comprehend intentions of the performance standards that would be used as the criteria for the assessment expectations. RAs reviewed the SRME-related literature on student learning compiled for the standards development and summarized inferences to make the information accessible and transferable for the standards writing team members.
Fall 2013	The RAs began conceptualizing assessment tasks and associated scoring devices that aligned with the artistic processes, process components, and the criteria of the performance standards to become the foundation for Model Cornerstone Assessments. Options developed were shared with the leaders of the standards writing team subcommittees and school music teachers aligned with the teams.
Spring 2014	RAs developed prototypes of Model Cornerstone Assessments within NCCAS guidelines/format. Subcommittees provided feedback. Finalized versions of the National Core Arts Standards were published.
Fall 2014	A prepilot of elementary and ensemble MCAs allowed teachers in the field to experience the drafted versions in their classrooms and provide valuable feedback to guide adjustments. Substantial revisions to the tasks, scoring devices, pilot protocol, and NCCAS format were implemented.

Spring 2015	A fully implemented pilot of the revised MCAs was administered in classrooms across the United States. Through this pilot, student work was collected and scored by the classroom teachers, peer teachers, and a panel of selected trained evaluators. Many-Facet Rasch analyses were performed to identify consistency of ratings and problems in the measures. These findings, along with teacher feedback, resulted in substantial revisions to the measures and tasks.
Fall 2015	Revised MCAs were piloted in schools across the United States (grades 2, 5, and 8; band chorus orchestra ensembles; theory/composition). Student work was collected and scored by teachers and peers. Feedback was collected through a postsurvey.
Spring 2016	Piloting continued for MCAs with the addition of an MCA for harmonizing instruments. Student work was collected and scored by teachers and peers. Feedback was collected through a postsurvey.
Fall 2016	Piloting continued for MCAs with the addition of technology. Student work was collected and scored by teachers and peers. Feedback was collected through a postsurvey.

(Note: All work conducted in this project was done voluntarily by the SRIG chairs, the RAs, and the teachers involved. No financial remuneration was provided by NCCAS or NAfME.)

The initial inclusion of RAs on the subcommittees of the NCCAS Music Standards Writing Teams was to inform the development of the standards relative to assessment processes and to guide the development of assessment frameworks for standards-aligned music classrooms. The RAs,[1] selected from higher education institutions, were researchers and teacher educators with specialized knowledge in the research on music development and assessment practices. Their work focused on creating Model Cornerstone Assessments that worked across grade bands and course strands aligned (K–2, 3–5, 6–8, traditional ensembles, emerging ensembles, harmonizing instruments, theory/composition, and technology).

Subcommittee participants of the standards writing teams met with the RAs to provide a fundamental knowledge of the *Understanding by Design* framework (McTighe & Wiggins, 2004), as well as the background aims of the new Arts Standards (NCCAS, 2014). To begin development of assessment tasks, a review of assessment scholarship and formally designed assessments was undertaken. This review revealed assessments from the Connecticut Common Arts Assessment Initiative (2016), the Washington State Performance Assessments (2017), and the assessments reviewed by the Colorado Content Collaborative (2018). These examples provided guidance in articulating assessment tasks useful for the Model Cornerstone Assessments. In the review of the assessments, content specifications were reviewed to determine if any of the tasks and/or rubrics could be appropriate for measuring student learning for the revised National Standards for Music Education.

Designing the models for assessment of the National Standards for Music required that the RAs and the subcommittee members carefully consider how students at each developmental level demonstrate expectations defined in the performance standards. Although not directly assessed, knowledge and skills necessary and relevant to successfully demonstrate the artistic process components were considered and defined for the tasks. The tasks were designed intentionally to require levels of skill and developmental understandings of knowledge without having to specify a predefined context. Structures of each Model Cornerstone Assessment had to be designed for each developmental level and needed to be appropriate for integration into current practice. Characteristics of traditional as well as innovative instruction had to be considered so resulting student work would reflect the ways that students demonstrate learning. Since the standards were written sequentially and hierarchically for K–12 schooling, the sequence and connection to skills and knowledge were essential for each Model Cornerstone Assessment.

In each MCA, teachers will find a narrative description of the intent and summary of content and an estimate of the time required to prepare and administer the assessment. The MCA makes clear that their students need certain prerequisite skills and knowledge before the assessment task is presented. This description is included to guide the music educator in appropriate preparation to enable student success. Included in many of the MCAs are instructional ideas for preparing students for the assessment. The intent was not to define curriculum, but to offer examples that could be used when guiding students through artistic processes.

The assessment tasks in each MCA are presented as an outline, visibly aligning each segment with the appropriate performance standard. Achievement indicators are defined by the performance standards at each grade/strand level. Each part of an assessment task is broken down in detail to guide (a) instructional preparation, (b) classroom environment for the task, and (c) administration protocol and data collection. In the administration of an MCA, teachers can choose to use the content suggested through the pilot stage or adapt the MCA to their school's curricular content. Teachers will maintain difficulty and complexity reflective of the performance standard as appropriate for their students. This is appropriate because the measures used in the MCAs are designed to assess continual development of artistic processes using the varied content across multiple curricula and the various means through which the artistic processes can be experienced. Musical content used in the pilot study was offered only as a model to exemplify various levels of difficulty and complexity, but the music teacher can use it if desired. Classroom teachers have the most informed grasp on the appropriate and culturally relevant content through which students can demonstrate artistic processes. Teachers also know best the contextual factors that influence student achievement. Another consideration left to the teachers is the time allowed for students to complete an assessment task. Students in one setting may need more time to complete the task—or even additional instruction to guide successful achievement, while students in another school setting may not.

The MCAs are a framework into which music educators infuse curriculum and traditional knowledge and skills assessment, and they provide an encompassing indication of how students synthesize, integrate, and apply all they learn into demonstrations of artistic literacy through creating, performing, and responding. Student learning of content, experience, and comfort level with the mode of assessment, and an inquiry-based classroom environment (as defined in the model) are essential for student success. Appropriate development of knowledge and skills is also essential in achieving the expectations of the music standards. Music educators should integrate their own assessments of knowledge, technical proficiencies, and musical skills that additionally evaluate learning beyond the artistic process components.

Provided with each MCA are adaptable and printable assessment materials with scoring rubrics that assist in making evaluative decisions focused on the performance indicators of each process component. Process components are the actions students carry out as they complete each artistic process. The intent of each MCA is to provide research-based assessment frameworks that are specifically focused on the criteria indicated in the performance standards via rubrics that have been confirmed for scoring consistency. The MCAs are created as models to allow for usefulness in a variety of curricular contexts and demographics. The MCAs take into consideration the many opportunities to learn music, which are markedly varied across classrooms, schools, and entire districts in the United States. Adaptability of content allows for teachers in music programs at all levels to assess progress in artistic process without the construction of specifically defined knowledge and skills.

NOTE

1. Kelly Parkes—Virginia Tech, now Teachers College, Columbia University; Frederick Burrack—Kansas State University; Wendy Valerio—University of South Carolina; Ann Clements—Penn State University; Patricia Riley—University

of Vermont; Bret Smith—Central Washington University; Glenn Nierman—University of Nebraska–Lincoln; Al D. Holcombe—Rider University; Carla Maltas—Central Missouri State University; Phillip Payne—Kansas State University; Daniel Johnson—University of North Carolina, Wilmington; Wendy Matthews—Wayne State University; and Denese Odegaard—Fargo Public Schools.

REFERENCES

Colorado Professional Learning Network. (2018). *Assessment resource bank*. Retrieved from http://www.coloradoplc.org/assessment/assessments

Connecticut State Department of Education. (2016). *Arts curricular content areas*. Retrieved from http://www.sde.ct.gov/sde/cwp/view.asp?a=2618&q=320840

McTighe, J., & Wiggins, G. (2004). *Understanding by design: Professional development workbook*. Alexandria, VA: Association for Supervision and Curriculum Development.

National Coalition for Core Arts Standards (NCCAS). (2014). *A conceptual framework for arts learning*. Retrieved from https://nccas.wikispaces.com/Conceptual+Framework

State of Washington Office of Superintendent of Public Instruction. (2017). *OSPI—Developed performance assessment for the arts*. Retrieved from http://www.k12.wa.us/arts/PerformanceAssessments/default.aspx

TWO

The Pilot Study Process

Frederick Burrack and Kelly A. Parkes

The entire development and pilot testing of the Model Cornerstone Assessments (MCAs) required thousands of volunteer hours by teachers and researchers across the United States. The pilot study was designed by researchers for public school teachers to identify the usefulness of the assessments and the integrity of the tasks and measures, and to provide suggestions that would enhance the applicability and effectiveness of the MCAs. As student achievement scores were amassed and examples of student work collected, our study provided evidence of the extent to which the MCAs are reliably administered, whether they authentically reflect student learning and achievement, and the extent to which they can be integrated into current music teaching.

In 2014, the National Association for Music Education (NAfME) put forward a call to all members who wanted to be involved in piloting the new standards and the MCAs in K–12 settings. This open call was sent via e-mail to the NAfME membership and to state music education association (MEA) members through each state's leadership. Members were asked to take a survey, which was used to collect contact information, number of years of teaching, NAfME region in which their school was located, size and socioeconomic status (SES) of their school district, grade levels taught, prior experience in administering externally designed assessments, and the cornerstone assessment they desired to pilot. A second survey was completed as a commitment for the pilot and included foundational questions pertaining to the teachers' students' opportunity to learn, the selected MCA for implementation, their own teacher perceptions of the Model Cornerstone Assessments prior to use, relationship of the selected MCA to their own instructional goals, and teacher confidence to administer the selected MCA. Results from this second survey were used to select the 300 participants for the initial pilot that was representative of NAfME regions, school size, socioeconomic status, and opportunity-to-learn situation.

The fall 2014 pre-pilot study focused on issues associated with instructional planning, instructional experiences, and resulting student achievement associated with the performing MCA in grades 2, 5, 8, and ensembles; clarity and ease of administration of pilot protocol; ways that the MCA was adapted to fit context; and suggestions for improvements to be implemented in spring 2015. During fall 2015, further solicitation for participation continued until there were multiple pilot sites from each region; representations from various SES, school size, and district type demographics; and sufficient administrations of each MCA.

Each pilot site (teacher) agreed to administer the MCA as published in the associated protocols. Although the intent of the finalized MCAs was to allow for curricular integrations and adaptations for opportunity to learn, protocols remained consistent for the pilot study while including designated sections that allowed options for adaptations to confirm consistency across various settings. In addition to completing the pre- and postsurvey questions, the teachers were asked to provide (a) individual student scores for the assessment of each process component, (b) student work for each achievement level of each assessment component, and (c) examples of adaptations made to necessitate successful administration of the MCA. Documents collected from the assessments included video/audio-recorded performance of students, scans (PDFs) of student work such as self-reflections, musical analyses, and notational manuscript, and completed worksheets if submitted electronically. Student scores (obtained from rubrics evaluating musical performances, assignments from in-class work, test scores) were submitted for aggregate data analysis.

In the initial pilot, each teacher provided one anonymous example of student work in the following achievement levels: emerging, approaching standard, meets standard, and exceeds standard. In subsequent pilots, all levels of student works were collected. Student work (rubrics evaluating musical performances, assignments from in-class work, test scores) had all identifying information removed by the K–12 teachers or the pilot researchers before aggregate data analysis. In the aggregate analysis, only teachers remained aware of their students' identities as they uploaded work for analysis. Identifying features (school name, class name, faces) were later removed or blurred from the documents used as illustrative examples.

After all materials were collected, each teacher scored two sets of student work from another unidentified school. Following the first full year of piloting, in addition to the pilot-teacher score and two peer-teacher scores, student work was also scored by the State Education Agency Directors of Arts Education (SEADAE) benchmarking committee, which consisted of high-quality teachers who had not administered the MCA.

These trained external scorers were to identify an unbiased view of student achievement as defined by the MCA assessment measures. This practice was eliminated after the first year of piloting because the scores from the trained external scorers were statistically inconsistent and unreliable, while the pilot teacher and peer scorers demonstrated an extremely high level of consistency. Neither the teachers nor the peer scorers demonstrated any bias in scoring student work. Conclusions were that direct experience with the MCAs in a classroom context is essential for reliable scoring of student work, and the classroom teacher is the best source of scoring student work for the MCA since there was little or no difference between teacher scores and multiple peer scores. In the pilot study, the peer-scorers were teachers from the same grade level who had used the same MCA in their own classrooms. In subsequent pilot administrations, only teacher and peer scoring were used for investigating evidence of reliability.

A result of the first two semesters of piloting, feedback from the participating teachers provided guidance for enhancements and revisions made to the MCAs, rubrics, and/or protocols as appropriate for action research. Revised MCAs were administered in fall 2015, spring 2016, and fall 2016 to affirm that the MCAs were acceptable for and applicable to the needs of schools prior to a national dissemination. During these pilot semesters, all artistic processes for grades 2 and 5 and grade 8 general music, for ensembles, theory/composition, technology, and harmonizing instruments were piloted. All participating schools were asked to submit all student work and scores from one class. Schools and individual teachers were allowed to repeat piloting the same MCA or a different MCA across multiple semesters.

All scores from assessments and student work samples were collected using online technology. Qualitative data was collected through two pre-pilot surveys and one postpilot survey using the Qualtrics survey tool. The postpilot questions focused on instructional intent, observing student response, curricular impact, and adaptations made to the MCAs to fit curriculum. The postpilot survey was also used to identify changes in teacher perception, conceptions of transferability and educational impact, and suggestions for improvements. The pilot surveys and statistical table can be found at https://nafme.org/my-classroom/standards/assessing-student-learning. The findings for each MCA can be found in the publication in their respective chapters.

During summer 2017, all remaining pilot data was analyzed to identify the cognitive domains associated with each process component of the MCAs and interactions across artistic processes using Rasch Measurement (RM), as described in chapter 11.

THE PURPOSE OF THE RESEARCH

The purpose of this research was to test the MCAs such that they would have the highest level of applicability and usefulness possible, align the administration protocol for the MCAs with school music programs in the United States, and collect reliability and validity evidence about the use of MCAs in a variety of school settings to measure student learning and achievement in music. The findings illustrate how Model Cornerstone Assessments can be used in a school music setting and the ways music teachers can assess students in the artistic processes of creating, performing, and responding.

This study provided illustrative examples to guide music teachers as the new standards are implemented. Beyond this project, an extended desire is for this research to garner a deeper understanding of the ways in which musical skills, processes, understandings, and knowledge can be measured using Model Cornerstone Assessments as part of the National Standards for Music Education.

The primary research questions were:

1. To what extent do teachers recognize that the Model Cornerstone Assessments (MCAs) relate to their expectations of student learning at each grade band, grades 2, 5, and 8, and each proficiency level for the ensemble, harmonizing instruments, theory composition, and technology strands?
2. To what extent can the MCAs be administered and scored with consistency across settings?
3. How effectively can the MCAs identify student achievement as intended by the performance standards?
4. How do practicing teachers in various school settings adapt the Model Cornerstone Assessments to usefully coincide with current practice?
5. Are there relationships of learning domains across settings, grade levels, and process components?
6. In what ways do the MCAs modify the current paradigm of school music education and the educational experiences of music students?

There were 161 music teachers involved in the development and revision of the MCAs. Following initial analysis of student work, the MCAs were ready for the final step in the pilot. See table 2.1 for the demographics for music classes reported in this book.

Table 2.1. Pilot Demographics for Model Cornerstone Assessments (MCAs)

MCA	Number of Schools	Region		Type		Socioeconomic Status (SES) Defined as the percentage of students receiving free or reduced-cost lunches	
Grade 2	38 schools	Eastern	13%	Metropolitan Inner-City	10%	<20%	5%
		North Central	11%	Metropolitan Suburban	10%	20–39%	5%
		Northwest	8%	Midsize City	10%	40–59%	28%
		Southern	16%	Small Town	66%	60–79%	10%
		Southwest	44%	Rural	4%	80–100%	52%
		Western	0%				
		Other	8%				
Grade 5	27 schools	Eastern	25%	Metropolitan Inner-City	7%	<20%	7%
		North Central	21%	Metropolitan Suburban	36%	20–39%	15%
		Northwest	14%	Midsize City	18%	40–59%	30%
		Southern	18%	Small Town	25%	60–79%	30%
		Southwest	14%	Rural	14%	80–100%	18%
		Western	4%				
		Other	4%				
Grade 8	2 schools	Eastern	1	Midsize City	2	20–39%	1
	32 students	North Central	1			40–59%	1
Ensemble	57 schools	Eastern	45%	Metropolitan Inner-City	10%	<20%	27%
		North Central	28%	Metropolitan Suburban	18%	20–39%	21%
		Northwest	8%	Midsize City	26%	40–59%	31%
		Southern	4%	Small Town	22%	60–79%	7%
		Southwest	9%	Rural	24%	80–100%	14%
		Western	6%				

(continued)

Table 2.1. *(Continued)*

MCA	Number of Schools	Region		Type		Socioeconomic Status (SES) Defined as the percentage of students receiving free or reduced-cost lunches	
Theory/ Composition	7 schools	Eastern	71%	Metropolitan Inner-City	43%	<20%	43%
		North Central	29%	Metropolitan Suburban		20–39%	14%
		Northwest	0	Midsize City		40–59%	14%
		Southern	0	Rural	43%	60–79%	29%
		Southwest	0	Small Town	14%	80–100%	
		Western	0				
Harmonizing Instruments	6 schools 6 students	Eastern	2	Metropolitan Inner-City	1	<20%	2
		North Central	2	Metropolitan Suburban	2	20–39%	1
		Northwest	0	Midsize City	1	40–59%	2
		Southern	0	Rural	1	60–79%	1
		Southwest	0	Small Town	1	80–100%	0
		Western	2				

The advantage for teachers participating in this research was the opportunity to experience the 2014 Standards and the Model Cornerstone Assessments prior to public dissemination. Their feedback during the pilot redesigned the structure and content of the final products and exemplified how these MCAs would be implemented in schools across the country.

Throughout the pilot study, all teachers were provided summaries of the findings and were encouraged to contact the pilot study's research advisors (RAs) with questions or concerns. Professional development on the curricular integration of the Model Cornerstone Assessments and implementation of the new National Standards for Music Education will be essential for educational impact in the future. Detailed methodology and the findings are presented in the following chapters.

THREE

Grade 2 Model Cornerstone Assessments

Daniel C. Johnson

The purpose of this chapter is to summarize and explain the second-grade creating, performing, and responding Model Cornerstone Assessments (MCAs) in terms of their perceived alignment with student learning, consistency in scoring, standards-based effectiveness, and utility in practice. For these purposes, this chapter contains an examination of pre- and post-test data collected from a group of pilot-testing teachers (fall 2015–spring 2017). By analyzing these data, this chapter presents a synthesis of teacher feedback through content analysis, descriptive statistics, thematic organization, and emergent qualitative themes.

ASSESSING MUSIC LEARNING AMONG SECOND-GRADE LEARNERS

Assessment should be an integral part of every music education program, embedded in the curriculum in a way to further programs goals and learning outcomes (Lehman, 1992). More specifically, assessment in music education is important for several reasons. Systematic and thoughtful assessment practices can provide evidence of successful music learning, guide curricular choices, offer ways to demonstrate musical progress to others, and enhance accountability among both teachers and students (Brophy, 2000). In elementary general music education, assessment and other evaluative measures of student learning may seem subjective and personal. In the absence of targeted knowledge levels and skill proficiencies, how well students learn music in nonperformance settings lacks clear goals and rigor. Instead, successful assessment practices in general music education are based on rubrics, higher-order thinking prompts, and self- and peer-assessments.

In the early elementary grades (K–2), a combination of singing, listening, moving, and playing percussion instruments can lead to a varied and successful music education curriculum. Integrated in these activities is the essential practice of improvising to generate and express musical ideas. By monitoring student engagement and participation, music teachers in these grades can readily practice authentic assessment to measure student success through participation in the musical activities themselves.

At their developmental stage, second-grade learners have these general characteristics: they are diligent, fact-oriented, and focused on rules, and they often avoid taking risks (Wilson, 2010). Typically, they prize accuracy and order to prevent making mistakes. Cognitively, second-grade learners are attracted to activities such as sorting and reviewing, consistent with striving for accuracy and precision in finished work (Wood, 2007). Even though these tendencies do not necessarily apply to all learners at this level, and certainly some maturation during second grade affects student learning and behavior, they inform the following examination of the second-grade creating, performing, and responding MCAs.

During the second-grade year, students often have a heightened focus on words and quickly build their vocabulary (Pruitt, 2000). Even though they work well with sequential directions, second-grade learners readily respond to open-ended tasks without rigid time constraints (Howe, 1993). Also, they have more acute listening skills than in earlier grades. This facet in particular is important for music listening exercises and other aural activities. Musically, children at this stage can perform predictable rhythmic and tonal patterns (Flohr, 1985; Kratus, 1985, 1991). They also have developed skills to imitate aural models expressively, and they have a command of ostinato, meter, and dynamics (Tillman & Swanwick, 1989).

For second-grade learners, creativity is an essential part of music education. At this grade level, the teacher's role is to help students develop their own musical ideas, their understanding of musical concepts, their technical accuracy, and ways to evaluate their own musical skills (Campbell & Scott-Kassner, 2014; Webster, 1990). With a variety of pedagogical methods, music teachers also regularly use singing as a music-making activity. At this stage, students can generally sing in tune for the span of one octave (approximately middle C to the octave above). Assessment of singing includes attention to the accuracy of pitch and rhythm, vocal quality, and musical expression (Demorest, Nichols, & Pfordresher, 2016; Orman, 2002). Another accessible but sometimes overlooked activity at this age is music listening. By listening actively and attentively, students at this age can develop their understanding of multiple musical elements and concepts. Using words, movement, illustrations, or other response modes, teachers can engage students in structured listening activities that can lead to thoughtful, creative, and purposeful musical experiences (Cutietta & Stauffer, 2005; Johnson, 2011, 2013).

Because many general music activities involve covert behaviors that are not readily observable, teachers should develop strategies to elicit overt responses (Campbell & Scott-Kassner, 2014). For example, students can demonstrate attentive music listening skills with movement and written responses. They can also improvise or create musical ideas as a way to demonstrate aural imagination or inner hearing; similarly, students can display aesthetic, musical experiences that evoke feelings with thoughtful discussions or matching illustrations. In other words, assessment in the general music classroom can take many forms. Each of these examples corresponds to assessment strategies in each of the three Grade 2 MCAs: creating, performing, and responding.

THE GRADE 2 MODEL CORNERSTONE ASSESSMENTS

The MCAs are assessment frameworks embedded into example curricular practices. Because the context of each school and classroom is different, music educators should modify and adapt the MCAs to offer the best fit to enhance their own students' learning. The MCAs are not intended to evaluate teachers or to specify the outcomes of a national music curriculum. Instead, they are based on the revised National Standards for Music Education (State Education Agency Directors of Arts Education, 2016) and offer a curricular framework for teachers to use. From a practical perspective, they include a number of assessment strategies, pedagogical resources, and recommendations to monitor and document student learning.

The Grade 2 MCAs provide formative and summative ways to guide and measure second-grade students' achievement as they engage in the artistic processes of creating, performing, and responding to music. Each MCA addresses three Anchor Standards and contains a series of curriculum-embedded assessment tasks. These MCAs are not tests but instead are activities, completed over time, for students to demonstrate qualities of involvement in the artistic processes. Consistent with 21st-century learning (Trilling & Fadel, 2009), the MCAs also encourage collaboration, communication, critical thinking, and creativity. In practical terms, the MCAs include formative and summative assessments, i.e. assessment *for* learning as well as assessment *of* learning. Ideally, the MCAs enhance the development of independent musicianship and lifelong music learning.

During this pilot study, participating teachers' input was critical to evaluate the MCAs themselves. By providing qualitative and quantitative feedback, those music teachers guided the researcher in evaluating how each MCA could be integrated successfully into the context of their existing curricula. Teacher feedback also directly influenced modifications to the content of each MCA. Although the original intent of each MCA was to be one instructional sequence, participating teachers used their best professional judgment to expand the time frame. In addition, student work from these MCAs provided examples to illustrate the level of achievement envisioned by each of the 2014 National Core Music Standards (accessed on the NAfME website in the Standards section: https://nafme.org/my-classroom/standards/mcas).

The Grade 2 Creating MCA

The Grade 2 Creating MCA addresses Anchor Standards 1, 2, and 3. Using the format outlined by Wiggins and McTighe (2005) in their *Understanding by Design* curricular framework, corresponding Enduring Understandings (EU) and Essential Questions (EQ) provide a foundation for understanding each:

1. Generate musical ideas for various purposes and contexts.

   EU: The creative ideas, concepts, and feelings that influence artists' work emerge from a variety of sources.
   EQ: How do musicians generate creative ideas?

2. Select and develop musical ideas for defined purposes and contexts.

   EU: Musicians' creative choices are influenced by their experience, context, and expressive intent.
   EQ: How do musicians make creative decisions?

3. Evaluate and refine selected musical ideas to create musical work(s) that meet appropriate criteria.

   EU: Musicians evaluate and refine their work through openness to new ideas, persistence, and the application of appropriate criteria.
   EQ: How do musicians improve the quality of their creative work?
   EU: Musicians' presentation of creative work is the culmination of a process of creation and communication.
   EQ: When is a creative work ready to share?

In sequence, the four-step process components of this MCA are: imagine, plan and make, evaluate and refine, and present. The first step of creating music is the process of imagining, during which students improvise rhythmic and melodic patterns and then generate musical patterns and ideas in the context of a given tonality. In this MCA, the teacher chants a rhythmic prompt on a neutral syllable (e.g., *ba, ba, ba-ba, ba*). Then, students respond by improvising a rhythmic answer. In this way, students improvise and generate musical ideas with no concern for using specific rhythmic syllables. In the second step, plan and make, students answer thoughtful questions to demonstrate and explain their reasons for selecting the patterns to represent their musical intentions, for example: "How did you use rhythmic patterns, steady beat, or expression to make your answers sound more like a conversation than an echo?" Students then use iconic or standard notation and/or recording technology to combine, sequence, and document personal musical ideas. In the third step, evaluate and refine, students reconsider and review their musical ideas by completing a self-assessment of their improvisations in step 2. In this way, they interpret and apply feedback to revise their rhythmic patterns. In step 4, perform, students share their rhythmic patterns after practicing them individually. With their presentations, the students show expressive intent by sharing a final version in a performance for their teacher or peers.

The Grade 2 Performing MCA

The Grade 2 Performing MCA addresses Anchor Standards 4, 5, and 6, with corresponding EUs and EQs providing a foundation for each:

4. Select varied musical works to present based on interest, knowledge, technical skill, and context.

    EU: Performers' interest in and knowledge of musical works, understanding of their own technical skill, and the context for a performance influence the selection of repertoire.
    EQ: How do performers select repertoire?
    EU: Analyzing creators' context and how they manipulate elements of music provides insight into their intent and informs performance.
    EQ: How does understanding the structure and context of musical works inform performance?
    EU: Performers make interpretive decisions based on their understanding of context and expressive intent.
    EQ: How do performers interpret musical works?

5. Evaluate and refine personal and ensemble performances, individually or in collaboration with others.

    EU: To express their musical ideas, musicians analyze, evaluate, and refine their performance over time through openness to new ideas, persistence, and the application of appropriate criteria.
    EQ: How do musicians improve the quality of their creative work?

6. Perform expressively, with appropriate interpretation and technical accuracy, and in a manner appropriate to the audience and context.

> EU: Musicians judge performance based on criteria that vary across time, place, and cultures.
> EQ: When is a performance judged ready to present?
> EU: The context and how a work is presented influences the audience response.
> EQ: How do context and the way a musical work is presented influence audience response?

In the performing MCA, second-grade students follow a five-step process: selecting musical material; analyzing for musical concepts; interpreting for expressive effect; rehearsing, evaluating, and refining their performances; and presenting a final performance. In the first step, students respond to a selection of songs that the teacher presents. Students demonstrate their knowledge of and personal interest in the musical selections. Next, with or without their teacher's assistance, the students select one song to perform. By performing this music, the students demonstrate knowledge of musical concepts (such as tonality and meter). By reading and performing the selected song, they analyze rhythmic and melodic patterns (in iconic or standard notation). In step 3, the students interpret their own performances as a way to demonstrate their understanding of musically expressive qualities (such as tempo and dynamics). To facilitate this step, the teacher plays a recording of each student's performance, and students complete the singing self-assessment activity while listening to their own recording. Independently, the teacher scores the student's recorded performance using the Singing Performance Scoring Form and compares the accuracy of student's response with teacher's score using the Accuracy Scoring Guide. In step 4, the teacher shares his or her feedback with the student and provides opportunities for him or her to listen to the recorded performance. Based on this feedback and by practicing for another performance, the students rehearse, evaluate, and refine their performance skills. In the final step, each student performs again to address the goals of performing for a specific purpose, with musical expression and technical accuracy. The teacher records the final performance in class and then scores each performance using the Singing Performance Scoring Form.

The Grade 2 Responding MCA

As described by the corresponding EUs and EQs, the second-grade Responding MCA addresses Anchor Standards 7, 8, and 9:

7. Perceive and analyze artistic work.

   EU: Individuals' selections of songs are influenced by prior experiences with similar music, understandings of musical elements, and interests.
   EQ: Why do you like the music you chose?

8. Interpret intent and meaning in artistic work.

   EU: Response to music is informed by understanding musical elements and the cultural and historical contexts of elements of music.
   EQ: How does understanding the story and musical elements used inform your response?

9. Apply criteria to evaluate artistic work.

   EU: The personal evaluation of the musical selection and performances is informed by analysis, interpretation, and established criteria.
   EQ: How do we judge the quality of the musical work and performance?

The Grade 2 responding MCA consists of a four-step process: selecting personal responses to a musical experience, analyzing music in terms of specific musical concepts, interpreting music with respect to expressive intent, and evaluating contrasting musical performances. In the first step, the teacher instructs the students to listen to a traditional version of a musical selection (e.g., Peer Gynt's "In the Hall of the Mountain King"). In response, students complete the corresponding call chart and share reactions with other students, focusing on the elements of music. In the second step, students analyze the music and use locomotor or non-locomotor movements to show their understanding of tempo changes. Then, they verbally explain how their movements reflect their listening experience. In step 3, the students demonstrate their knowledge of musical concepts used to tell the story by explaining the composer's or performer's expressive intent. They interpret musical elements (especially tempo) by again responding with movement to three different arrangements or interpretations of the same musical selection. Finally, in step 4, students consider the specific purposes of the musical selection and evaluate each version of the music by applying personal and expressive preferences. In either written or verbal format, they explain which version they liked best, and why.

After designing the above MCAs, the researcher aimed to answer the following four research questions to evaluate the appropriateness, scoring consistency, effectiveness, and practicality of the MCAs:

1. To what extent do teachers recognize that the MCAs relate to their expectations of student learning?
2. To what extent can the MCAs be administered and scored with consistency across settings?
3. How effectively can the MCAs identify student achievement as intended by standards?
4. How do practicing teachers in various school settings usefully adapt the MCAs to coincide with current practice?

To assist the researcher in addressing these questions, a group of music teachers volunteered to pilot-test one or more of these MCAs. Findings and an analysis of their input, together with a discussion of the implications, follow in the next section of this chapter.

PARTICIPANTS

Thirty-eight (38) music educators served as pilot-testing teachers for this study. While some teachers completed one of the three MCAs, several teachers reported data for multiple MCAs. Most of the teachers instructed the class(es) for their MCAs either once or twice a week (78%), while the others taught their students either three or five times a week. Most teachers (57%) taught class periods of between 20 and 40 minutes, while the remainder had class sessions lasting 40 to 60 minutes. Geographically, the largest group of teachers (44%) represented the southwestern United States, with other groups relatively evenly distributed through the country. Most of the schools represented in this study (52%) had low socioeconomic status, defined as 80–100% of students qualifying for free or reduced-cost lunch. More than a quarter of the schools (28%) had 40–59% of their students on free or reduced lunch. Most school districts were in small towns (66%); most of the remaining districts consisted of metropolitan inner-city, suburban, and mid-sized cities. Finally, most of the teachers (63%) had 11–30 years of teaching experience, while the remaining teachers had less teaching experience. Table 3.1 displays more details about each of these demographics.

Table 3.1.   **Demographic Information for Model Cornerstone Assessments**

Thirty-eight (38) Classrooms		All Grade 2 MCAs
Number of class meetings	1	39.1%
per week	2	39.1%
	3	17.4%
	4	0
	5	4.3%
Number of Minutes per class	20–40	56.5%
period	40–60	34.8%
Region	Eastern	13%
	North Central	11%
	Northwest	8%
	Southern	16%
	Southwest	44%
	Other	8%
Socioeconomic Status (SES)	Less than 20%	5%
Defined as the percentage	20–39%	5%
of students receiving free	40–59%	28%
or reduced-cost lunches	60–79%	10%
	80–100%	52%
District Type	Metropolitan Inner-City	10%
	Metropolitan Suburban	10%
	Midsize City	10%
	Rural	4%
	Small Town	66%
Years of Teaching Experience	1–10	37%
	11–30	63%

FINDINGS ACROSS ALL MCAs

The following section highlights the findings from the Grade 2 MCA pilot tests. It summarizes how the participating teachers responded to an on-line survey questionnaire about each MCA. It also includes their qualitative comments to further enrich these findings.

Before beginning the pilot tests in their classrooms, teachers reported their perspectives on the MCAs. Considering all the MCAs, 83% of participating teachers said that they were clearly confident or mostly confident in preparing their students to do well, 75% projected that the MCAs would clearly contribute or mostly contribute to their music curriculum, and 79% expected that the MCAs would clearly or mostly improve student learning. See Table 3.2 for specific response scores.

Table 3.2. Pre-pilot Responses to Model Cornerstone Assessment (MCA) Survey Items

Survey Item	Clearly Describes My Feelings	Mostly Describes My Feelings	Somewhat Describes My Feelings	Mostly Does Not Describe My Feelings
Confident in my ability to prepare students for this MCA.	45.8%	37.5%	12.5%	4.2%
MCA will contribute to the curriculum.	58.3%	16.7%	20.8%	4.2%
MCA will improve student learning.	41.7%	37.5%	20.8%	0%

Following the pilot-testing period, most participating teachers strongly agreed that the MCAs integrated into their instruction, that the MCAs had a positive influence on their teaching, and that they would use or adapt the assessment tasks in the future. A minority of teachers either disagreed or strongly disagreed with these statements. For specific response rates, see Table 3.3.

Teachers' qualitative comments support these quantitative data. For example, one teacher observed, "I will have greater rigor in my teaching through the following of this task." Another teacher complimented the format of the MCAs by noting, "[The MCAs are] so well-structured, it is easy for students to succeed." Although a third teacher noted that the content did not easily align with the expectations of the school curriculum, a fourth teacher recognized how her curriculum could be enhanced and wrote, "I realized while scoring the student work that I am not encouraging expressive qualities in their singing clearly enough."

As to the impact the MCAs had on teaching, one teacher observed, "This has helped me in [providing] measurable data for my school." Finally, as a description of how these MCAs may influence future instruction, one teacher reported,

> I feel like I am getting solid professional development for my own teaching through piloting the MCAs. I really have enjoyed seeing another way to

Table 3.3 Postpilot Responses to MCA Survey

Survey Item	Strongly Agree	Agree	Don't Know	Disagree	Strongly Disagree
Integrated MCA into my instruction.	55.6%	33.3%	0%	5.6%	5.6%
Had a positive influence on my teaching.	66.7%	5.6%	11.1%	11.1%	5.6%
Will use or adapt assessment tasks in the future.	55.6%	22.2%	11.1%	5.6%	5.6%

assess learning and have already implemented these assessments in other ways in my teaching while I learn to integrate the new standards.

Following the pilot tests, most teachers reported that they were able to integrate the assessment tasks into their instruction. Most teachers also indicated that the MCAs reflected standards-based expectations, included appropriate scoring measures, and offered a good fit to their teaching plans. Because a third of teachers reported that they needed to modify the MCAs during the pilot testing, minor adjustments to some instructional sequences and some worksheet revisions are probably in order to enhance instructional efficiency. Furthermore, a large majority of teachers agreed or strongly agreed that the MCAs provided clear and concise instructional sequences (88.6%) and that the MCA objectives were clear and measurable (94.4%). See Table 3.4 for specific response scores.

When asked, teachers commented that, "the MCA layout of the process was clear . . . just not always exciting for the kids." Other comments noted that "a paragraph or two explaining the skills needed should be added to assessments," and a timeline guide to clarify "how to proceed, how long to spend on which portion of the tasks, and how to encourage my students' writing." Another teacher described her appreciation and plan for incorporating a portion of the MCA in her regular teaching:

> I loved the idea of text evidence form the lyrics allowing us to connect and incorporate writing/literacy strategies. I intend to use portions of the [Model] Cornerstone Assessment throughout the year. My plan is to: (1) have them listen to pieces of music and identify music elements during the course of

Table 3.4. Integration and Modifications Survey Responses about the MCAs

Survey Item	Strongly Agree	Agree	Don't Know	Disagree	Strongly Disagree
I have the ability to integrate the assessment tasks into instruction.	41.7%	45.8%	4.2%	4.2%	4.2%
Need to modify the MCA.	8.3%	33.3%	12.5%	33.3%	12.5%
MCA reflects expectations of the 2014 National Standards.	45.8%	45.8%	4.2%	0%	4.2%
Scoring measures are appropriate.	33.3%	54.2%	0%	8.3%	4.2%
MCA fits into my teaching plans.	41.7%	41.7%	8.3%	4.2%	4.2%
MCA clearly and concisely conveys instructional sequence.	33.3%	53.3%	0%	13.3%	0%
Objectives were clear and measurable.	38.9%	55.6%	0%	0%	5.6%

the year using a similar checklist form the responding assessment; (2) have exit slips explaining the composer's purpose/intent using the elements; (3) employ exit slips throughout the year asking why they liked/disliked a piece . . . citing text evidence/historical content/music elements; and (4) use [Model] Cornerstone Assessment at the middle or end of the year.

Participating teachers completed one or more of the MCAs with an overall positive impression of their scope, design, and potential for improving instruction. The teachers rated each MCA in four areas: appropriateness, curriculum, general characteristics, and utility. The following sections describe each MCA independently and list some of their strengths and weaknesses in more detail.

Findings: Creating MCA

Participating teachers rated the creating MCA highly on every question in the post-pilot survey. They either agreed or strongly agreed with statements that supported the Creating MCA's age-appropriateness, curricular value, overall positive characteristics, and utility. Teachers rated this MCA as highly appropriate for their students, indicating that it clearly reflected what the students should learn and aligned with practical teaching priorities. As to the curriculum, this MCA addressed student needs, included a diversity of learners, informed instructional decisions, and provided useful professional development.

Nearly half the responding teachers indicated that they needed to modify instructional procedures for this MCA in some way, such as organizing groups of students to record during different class periods. With this assignment, the other students could simultaneously engage in the movement activities. For this and other MCAs, it is important to remember that adjustments and updates are certainly necessary to offer students the best fit given their school context and to accommodate prior knowledge.

Most teachers described the Creating MCA as developmentally appropriate, free from bias, and appropriately scored. They also indicated that this MCA clearly conveyed and aligned with instructional objectives, reflected the standards, provided for learning tasks, and fit with their teaching plans. See Tables 3.5 and 3.6 for specific response scores and ratings.

Findings: Performing MCA

Similar to the teachers in the Creating MCA, teachers rated the Performing MCA highly on the post-pilot survey. They either agreed or strongly agreed with statements that demonstrated the Performing MCA's curricular value, overall positive characteristics, and utility. Most teachers indicated that they could successfully prepare their students for this MCA, which

Table 3.5. Grade 2 Creating MCA—Survey Responses about Appropriateness

Survey Item	Clearly Describes My Feelings	Mostly Describes My Feelings	Somewhat Describes My Feelings	Mostly Does Not Describe My Feelings	No Response
Accurately measures intended student learning.	4.8%	33.3%	14.3%	4.8%	42.9%
Reflects what students should learn.	23.8%	14.3%	19%	0%	42.9%
It is possible to successfully prepare my students.	42.9%	23.8%	23.8%	9.5%	0%

Table 3.6. Grade 2 Creating MCA—Survey Responses about Curriculum, Characteristics, and Utility

Survey Item	Strongly Agree	Agree	Don't Know	Disagree	Strongly Disagree
Curriculum					
Addresses varied student needs.	21.1%	63.2%	0%	15.8%	0%
Allows for inclusion of all learners.	21.1%	68.4%	0%	5.3%	5.3%
Informs instructional decisions.	42.1%	47.4%	10.5%	0%	0%
Useful as professional development.	52.6%	36.8%	0%	10.5%	0%
Characteristics					
Developmentally appropriate.	42.9%	42.9%	0%	14.3%	0%
Free of bias.	31.6%	52.6%	15.8%	0%	0%
Scoring rubrics were appropriate.	38.1%	47.6%	4.8%	9.5%	0%
Clearly and concisely conveys instruction.	31.6%	52.6%	0%	15.8%	0%
Objectives were clear and measurable.	52.4%	42.9%	0%	0%	4.8%
Able to integrate tasks.	44.4%	44.4%	5.6%	0%	5.6%
Need to modify MCAs.	11.1%	38.9%	16.7%	16.7%	16.7%
Reflects standards.	38.9%	50%	5.6%	0%	5.6%
Scoring measures are appropriate.	33.3%	50%	0%	11.1%	5.6%
Will fit into my teaching plans.	38.9%	44.4%	11.1%	0%	5.6%
Utility					
Able to integrate with my instruction.	57.1%	33.3%	0%	4.8%	4.8%
Has a positive influence on my teaching.	61.9%	14.3%	9.5%	9.5%	4.8%
Will use/adapt in the future.	66.7%	9.5%	9.5%	9.5%	4.8%

most of them rated as accurately measuring student learning and reflecting what students should learn. From a curricular perspective, most teachers reported that the Performing MCA addressed a variety of student needs, included all learners, informed instructional decisions, and was useful as professional development. Similarly, most teachers indicated that this MCA was free from bias, was developmentally appropriate, and reflected pedagogical standards.

Compared with teacher responses to the Creating MCA, fewer teachers reported that they would need to modify the Performing MCA in some way. Most teachers rated the Performing MCA as having appropriate scoring rubrics and measures and clear and measurable objectives. In addition, most teachers indicated that this MCA fit with their teaching plans, clearly conveyed instructional goals, and had tasks they could easily integrate with their instruction. Most teachers reported that the Performing MCA had a positive influence on their teaching and that they would adopt it in the future. See Tables 3.7 and 3.8 for specific response scores and ratings.

Findings: Responding MCA

As with the creating and performing MCAs, participating teachers rated the responding MCA highly on every question in the postpilot survey. As to age-appropriateness, curricular value, overall positive characteristics, and utility, teachers either agreed or strongly agreed with the given statements. Most teachers indicated that the responding MCA ac-

Table 3.7. Grade 2 Performing MCA—Survey Responses about Appropriateness

Survey Item	Clearly Describes My Feelings	Mostly Describes My Feelings	Somewhat Describes My Feelings	Mostly Does Not Describe My Feelings	No Response
Accurately measures intended student learning.	5.9%	35.3%	11.8%	5.9%	41.1%
Reflects what students should learn.	35.3%	0%	23.5%	0%	41.2%
It is possible to successfully prepare my students.	41.2%	23.5%	29.4%	5.9%	0%

Table 3.8. Grade 2 Performing MCA—Survey Responses about Curriculum, Characteristics, and Utility

Survey Item	Strongly Agree	Agree	Don't Know	Disagree	Strongly Disagree
Curriculum					
Addresses varied student needs.	25%	50%	0%	25%	0%
Allows for inclusion of all learners.	31.3%	62.5%	0%	6.3%	0%
Informs instructional decisions.	50%	37.5%	12.5%	0%	0%
Useful as professional development.	68.8%	18.8%	0%	12.5%	0%
Characteristics					
Developmentally appropriate.	41.2%	52.9%	0%	5.9%	0%
Free of bias.	31.3%	50%	12.5%	6.3%	0%
Scoring rubrics were appropriate.	47.1%	41.2%	0%	11.8%	0%
Clearly and concisely conveys instruction.	37.5%	56.3%	0%	6.3%	0%
Objectives were clear and measurable.	52.9%	41.2%	0%	0%	5.9%
Able to integrate tasks.	40%	40%	6.7%	6.7%	6.7%
Need to modify MCAs.	6.7%	26.7%	20%	26.7%	20%
Reflects standards.	40%	46.7%	6.7%	0%	6.7%
Scoring measures are appropriate.	33.3%	60%	0%	0%	6.7%
Will fit into my teaching plans.	26.7%	53.3%	13.3%	0%	6.7%
Utility					
Able to integrate with my instruction.	52.9%	41.2%	0%	0%	5.9%
Has a positive influence on my teaching.	64.7%	11.8%	11.8%	5.9%	5.9%
Will use/adapt in the future.	70.6%	5.9%	11.8%	5.9%	5.9%

curately measured intended student learning and reflected what students should learn. Although slightly fewer teachers were as confident about preparing their students for the responding tasks, most teachers reported that this MCA addressed varied student needs, included all learners, and informed their instructional decisions. In addition to indicating that it was useful as professional development, most teachers indicated that the Responding MCA was developmentally appropriate, free from bias, and reflected pedagogical standards. Also, most teachers rated this MCA as

Table 3.9. Grade 2 Responding MCA—Survey Responses about Appropriateness

Survey Item	Clearly Describes My Feelings	Mostly Describes My Feelings	Somewhat Describes My Feelings	Mostly Does Not Describe My Feelings	No Response
Accurately measures intended student learning.	10.5%	42.1%	10.5%	5.3%	31.6%
Reflects what students should learn.	31.6%	21.1%	10.5%	5.3%	31.6%
It is possible to successfully prepare my students.	31.6%	26.3%	36.8%	5.3%	0%

having clear and measurable objectives that conveyed instructional goals and included appropriate scoring measures.

Demonstrating another parallel with the Creating MCA, almost half of the teachers indicated that they needed to modify the Responding MCA in some way, such as making small adjustments to the worksheets and organizational sequence to enhance their practicality for classroom use. Especially given the range of response activities and variety in students' prior knowledge, adjustments are certainly understandable in order to adapt assessments to fit individual school contexts. Because the MCAs are frameworks into which teachers integrate their chosen curricular content, some contextual modifications are both appropriate and expected to provide the most accurate assessment of student learning. Most teachers, however, rated the Responding MCA as consistent with their teaching plans, including tasks they could integrate into their instruction. Overall, most teachers reported that this MCA had a positive influence on their teaching, and that they would adopt it for future classroom use. See Tables 3.9 and 3.10 for the specific response scores and ratings.

TEACHER FEEDBACK

Qualitative feedback from teachers included answers to open-ended survey questions and ongoing comments made during the pilot-testing phase. By asking for clarification, sharing their insights, and reporting developments, teachers provided in-process perspectives on their work

Table 3.10. Grade 2 Responding MCA—Survey Responses about Curriculum, Characteristics, and Utility

Survey Item	Strongly Agree	Agree	Don't Know	Disagree	Strongly Disagree
Curriculum					
Addresses varied student needs.	29.4%	47.1%	0%	23.5%	0%
Allows for inclusion of all learners.	29.4%	70.6%	0%	0%	0%
Informs instructional decisions.	58.8%	23.5%	11.8%	5.9%	0%
Useful as professional development.	58.8%	29.4%	0%	11.8%	0%
Characteristics					
Developmentally appropriate.	42.1%	52.6%	0%	5.3%	0%
Free of bias.	23.5%	52.9%	17.6%	5.9%	0%
Clearly and concisely conveys instruction.	35.3%	58.8%	0%	5.9%	0%
Objectives were clear and measurable.	52.6%	47.4%	0%	0%	0%
Ability to integrate tasks.	37.5%	56.3%	6.2%	0%	0%
Need to modify MCAs.	6.3%	37.5%	12.5%	31.3%	12.5%
Reflects standards.	37.5%	56.3%	6.3%	0%	0%
Scoring measures are appropriate.	37.5%	62.5%	0%	0%	0%
Will fit into my teaching plans.	43.8%	37.5%	12.5%	6.3%	0%
Utility					
Able to integrate with my instruction.	57.9%	42.1%	0%	0%	0%
Has a positive influence on my teaching.	68.4%	10.5%	10.5%	10.5%	0%
Will use/adapt in the future.	57.9%	21.1%	10.5%	10.5%	0%

with these MCAs. From these data, three themes emerged: pedagogical insights, practical challenges, and conflicting standards.

Pedagogical Insights

In addition to reporting that they were surprised about how well their students performed, some teachers reported that students gained a sense of self-confidence and responsibility through their work with the MCAs. For example, students took the process more seriously and spent more time on-task than their teachers expected. This theme is consistent with the way learners at this age tend to strive for accuracy and try to avoid making mistakes (Wood, 2007). Other teachers reported that they began to reconsider how they scored student work. One teacher wrote,

> The expressive quality category really made me think about how I teach. Beyond singing a lullaby quietly or a dance song a little faster, how much am I encouraging this important part of our curriculum? In an effort to accurately teach a song, I make very few variations while I present it and, therefore, often get near exact copies of my rendition of the song. I look forward to working on this to promote more expressiveness.

A third insight addressed the value of creativity in music education. After using the Creating MCA, one teacher commented, "One of the areas we miss out on most in music education is the pure joy a student emotes when creating. From a simple rhythmic phrase to a full solo in jazz band, when they create, students own music." This observation is consistent with improvisation and creativity being weaker areas in American music education (Johnson & Fautley, 2017).

Practical Challenges

Several teachers noted that the time required to administer the MCAs and score student work was a burden, often exceeding the allotted instructional time. Similarly, other teachers commented that entering student data into an online database, for the purposes of the pilot testing, was cumbersome and sometimes overwhelming. For those teachers, music classes were only 30 minutes long. Finally, some teachers found that there was an overemphasis on student writing tasks, a challenge that may indicate the need for a more balanced approach to demonstrating student learning.

Conflicting Standards

Some teachers expressed confusion about conflicting expectations from different sets of standards. For example, some state-level standards did not align with the MCA Anchor Standards. Other systems used by district-level administrators include the Student Learning Outcome method and the Danielson Framework (2011). This theme related to an overarching lack of familiarity most music teachers have with the underlying framework for the 2014 National Standards for Music Education, *Understanding by Design* (Wiggins & McTighe, 2005). As described in a recent study, most music educators are unfamiliar with this framework and could benefit from targeted professional development about the foundation of the standards revision (Johnson, Peterson, Spears, & Vest, 2017).

DISCUSSION

The purpose of this chapter on the Grade 2 MCAs was to evaluate the appropriateness, scoring consistency, effectiveness, and practicality of the MCAs. In summary, the pilot tests offered strong support for the success of each facet, with implications reaching far into the future for both teachers and students. The synopsis below addresses these topics in four corresponding research questions, based on the data and content analysis presented in this chapter.

Research Questions

1. To what extent do teachers recognize that the MCAs relate to their expectations of student learning?

Before beginning the pilot tests, most participating teachers (79%) indicated that they believed the Grade 2 MCAs would improve student learning. Following the pilot administration of the MCAs, the researcher asked the same teachers if MCA scores accurately measured what they perceived as typical student learning in their classroom. Most teachers agreed for each MCA: creating 52%, performing 53%, and responding 63%. It is difficult to know whether the teaching and learning experiences, as detailed in each MCA, reflected what the teachers were defining as "learning" prior to the pilot tests. Given that slightly more than half the teachers rated the MCAs as accurate measures of student learning, perhaps there were components of learning that extended beyond what the MCAs could address. Instead, teachers should consider the MCAs as one part of a complete and varied assessment process. It is important to recognize that the MCAs are not designed to be distinct measures for all student "learning" in music. Instead, they provide indicators of students' engagement with the three artistic processes, while the results inform teachers' instructional decisions guiding curricular adjustments.

2. To what extent can the MCAs be administered and scored with consistency across settings?

Statistical analyses indicated that teachers' scores have a high degree of consistency, expressed by a statistically significant reliability of separation measure. Without introducing statistical complications beyond the scope of this chapter, it is sufficient to state that the Grade 2 MCAs provided internally consistent results. Additional statistical analyses provided the researcher with a high level of confidence when interpreting the results. Those markers indicated that these data had a high degree of predictability, and that the teachers consistently applied similar standards when scoring student work. Therefore, general music teachers can use the MCA tasks and rubrics to assess their own students consistently.

3. How effectively can the MCAs identify student achievement as intended by the standards?

Given that more than 90% of teachers agreed or strongly agreed that the Grade 2 MCAs reflect expectations of the standards, these MCAs clearly demonstrated effective ways to address the corresponding standards. One teacher wrote that these MCAs provided ways to meet the 2014 National Standards for Music Education. In that sense, the MCAs provided integrated professional development and practical guidance for in-service teachers.

4. How do practicing teachers in various school settings usefully adapt the MCAs to coincide with current practice?

Following the pilot tests, 78% of participating teachers indicated that they would adapt one or more of the MCAs in the future. This percentage was nearly equal for all three Grade 2 MCAs. Consistent with this high degree of satisfaction about the MCAs themselves, multiple teachers indicated that the MCAs had a high degree of curricular relevance and reinforced their existing teaching practices. In related comments, teachers recognized the MCAs as addressing their need to provide "measurable data" on specific knowledge and skills as evidence of student learning. It was clear that the majority of teachers did not consider the MCAs as additional "busy work."

Enhancing Assessment Practices

The MCAs are not stand-alone assessment strategies; instead, they are designed to augment the regular music curriculum. As such, they enhance and add musically rigorous assessment practices to existing curricula. By articulating with established pedagogy, the MCAs also respect teachers' professionalism, as demonstrated by this exploration of their input and feedback. To that end, the MCAs are not static evaluations; they are flexible and responsive to teachers' needs and students' backgrounds. As documented in this chapter, the teachers who pilot-tested the Grade 2 MCAs offered clear evidence for having met each of these goals, along with ideas for constructive modifications. Following this pilot-testing project, MCA organizers plan to incorporate teachers' suggestions and add additional grade levels.

Fundamentally, the MCAs represent a paradigm shift in music education assessment. Instead of evaluating end-of-term performances or giving end-of-grade tests, the MCAs embrace the creating, performing, and responding processes that lead to meaningful demonstrations of performance skills and musical knowledge. The MCA design accomplishes this by examining musical practices authentically, with the invaluable and essential participation of music teachers and their students.

REFERENCES

Brophy, T. S. (2000). *Assessing the developing child musician: A guide for general music teachers.* Chicago, IL: GIA Publications.

Campbell, P. S., & Scott-Kassner, C. (2014). *Music in childhood.* Stamford, CT: Schirmer.

Cutietta, R., & Stauffer, S. L. (2005). Listening reconsidered. In D. Elliot (Ed.), *Praxial music education: Reflections and dialogues* (pp. 123–142). New York: Oxford University Press.

Danielson, C. (2011). *Enhancing professional practice: A framework for teaching.* Alexandria, VA: Association for Supervision and Curriculum Development.

Demorest, S., Nichols, B., & Pfordresher, P. Q. (2016). The effect of focused instruction on young children's singing accuracy. *Psychology of Music.* doi:10.1177/0305735617713120

Flohr, J. (1985). Young children's improvisations: Emerging creative thought. *Creative Child & Adult Quarterly, 10,* 79–85.

Howe, F. C. (1993). The child in the elementary school. *Child Study Journal, 23*(4), 227–362.

Johnson, D. C. (2011). The effect of critical thinking instruction on verbal descriptions of music. *Journal of Research in Music Education 59*(3), 257–272.

Johnson, D. C. (2013). Creating meaningful music listening experiences with active music-making. *Musicworks, Journal of the Australian National Council of Orff Schulwerk, 18*(1), 49–56.

Johnson, D. C., & Fautley, M. (2017). Assessment of whole-class instrumental music learning in England and the United States of America: an international comparative study. *Education International Journal of Primary, Elementary and Early Years Education, 45*(6), 1–9.

Johnson, D. C., Peterson, A., Spears, A., & Vest, J. (2017). *Investigating "Understanding by Design" in the National Music Education Standards: Perspectives and Practices of Music Teachers and Music Teacher Educators.* Visions of Research in Music Education, 30. Retrieved from http://www.rider.edu/~vrme

Kratus, J. (1985). The use of melodic and rhythmic motives in the original songs of children aged 5 to 13. *Contributions to Music Education, 12,* 1–8.

Kratus, J. (1991). Growing with improvisation. *Music Educators Journal, 78*(4), 36–40.

Lehman, P. R. (1992). Curriculum and program evaluation. In R. Colwell (Ed.), *Handbook of research on music teaching and learning* (pp. 281–294). New York: Schirmer.

Orman, E. K. (2002). Comparison of the national standards for music education and elementary music specialists' use of class time. *Journal of Research in Music Education, 50*(2), 155–164.

Pruitt, D. (2000). *Your child: Emotional, behavioral, and cognitive development from birth through preadolescence.* New York: HarperCollins.

State Education Agency Directors of Arts Education. (2016). *National core arts standards.* Retrieved from http://nationalartsstandards.org/

Tillman, J., & Swanick, K. (1989). Towards a model of development of children's musical creativity. *Canadian Music Educator, 30*(2), 169–174.

Trilling, B., & Fadel, C. (2009). *21st century skills: Learning for life in our times.* Hoboken, NJ: John Wiley & Sons.

Webster, P. R. (1990). Creativity as creative thinking. *Music Educators Journal, 76*(9), 22–28.

Wiggins, G. P., & McTighe, J. (2005). *Understanding by design.* Alexandria, VA: Association for Supervision and Curriculum Development.

Wilson, M. B. (2010). *What every 2nd grade teacher needs to know about setting up and running a classroom.* Turners Falls, MA: Center for Responsive Schools.

Wood, C. (2007). *Yardsticks: Children in the classroom ages 4–14.* (3rd ed.). Turners Falls, MA: Center for Responsive Schools.

FOUR

Grade 5 Model Cornerstone Assessments

Denese Odegaard, Michael J. Ruybalid, and Mary Kate Newell

LEARNING FOR A FIFTH-GRADE STUDENT

How do students in fifth grade, typically 10- and 11-year-olds, develop their musical skills? What skills can a general music student be expected to achieve by the end of their fifth-grade year? Let's first examine the developmental milestones of typical fifth graders.

Academically, fifth-grade students face more challenges than they had earlier experienced: developing abstract thinking skills, solving increasingly elaborate problems in math and other content areas, and reading complex material, as well as researching and organizing their writing into lengthier essays (Great Schools Staff, 2016). *Socially*, fifth-grade students are increasingly talkative and interested in spending time with friends. Being accepted by a peer group and gaining gradually more independence from their family are milestones of this age group. *Emotionally*, fifth-grade students begin to develop the ability to see others' point of view or argue both sides of an issue. *Physically*, their bodies change rapidly. Some experience growth spurts, increased appetite, and fatigue (Anderson, 2011). All these characteristics are important to consider when teaching fifth-grade general music.

Music is learned through listening, creating, and performing it. Fifth-grade general music instruction continues skill development from previous elementary grade levels. Because this varies from one school district to another, we examined some curricula and noticed common expectations in terms of fifth-grade musical skills. Students in fifth grade continue to develop musical concepts and skills such as singing, playing instruments, reading musical notation, listening to a variety of music, and composing and improvising short segments of music. At this age, they are working on becoming accurate and consistent musicians while coordinating movement and dance to music. Fifth-grade students play instruments such as recorders and Orff instruments, and learn to read rhythmic, melodic, and harmonic notation with increasing sophistication. With guidance, fifth-grade students listen to a variety of music from different periods of history and cultures, analyze elements of music, and form defensible opinions about their own musical preferences. They can identify musical symbols (e.g., crescendo and diminuendo), compose and improvise short melodies and rhythms such as through call-and-response, participate and remember the sequences of complex dances, and understand more theoretical concepts such as *interlude* and *coda* (Garner & Massaro, 2011).

ASSESSING LEARNING IN GRADE 5

To determine whether high levels of learning have occurred, an extensive assessment program that charts progress while facilitating learning in the areas of facts, skills, understandings, self-esteem, metacognition, and interest in continuing to learn is necessary (Brophy, 2007). In reference to assessment of learning, Colwell (2002) stated, "Assessment has always been a part of teaching and learning" (p. 1128). What follows is a brief overview of past scholarship that discusses how to assess children's musical performances, their musical creativity, and how they respond to music.

An article in the *Music Educators Journal* (Wesolowski, 2012) affirms that when assessing music performance, objective measures such as well-designed rubrics are useful and beneficial. Wesolowski stated that rubrics provide a formative method of assessing student musical performance that can contribute to music educators' modification and improvement of their own instruction based on predetermined criteria of quality performance. Rubrics can be a valuable tool to aid music educators in identifying levels of student learning and achievement and in improving classroom instruction. Indeed, many studies have attempted to ascertain the effectiveness of rubrics to measure student musical performances, including performances before college juries (Ciorba & Smith, 2009) and in high school band, orchestral, and choral performance festivals (Latimer, Bergee, & Cohen, 2010). McQuarrie and Sherwin (2013) examined 10 years (1999–2009) of music teacher literature in two music teacher practitioner journals, *Teaching Music* and the *Music Educators Journal*, and found that the use of rubrics was one of the most commonly mentioned assessment strategies in the music teacher literature. McQuarrie and Sherwin also examined what assessment practices current music educators use in their classrooms. They found that music teacher practitioners do not commonly use formal assessment strategies, including rubrics, as frequently as more informal assessment strategies such as grading effort or behavior. These findings reveal a potential disconnect between teacher practices regarding assessment and the content of the literature in music teacher practitioner journals. Furthermore, it may signal a greater need for assessment strategies that are more formal and provide more reliable data on students' musical progress in the music classroom, including the assessment of music performances.

Webster and Hickey (1995) examined the use of ratings scales with fifth- and sixth-grade children's creating of musical compositions, specifically related to which type of ratings scale had greater interrater reliability. Two separate ratings forms were used, one implicit (open-ended and purposefully vague) and the other explicit with lengthier explanations of what was to be evaluated. The researchers reported that the implicit scale had greater interrater reliability and was preferred by the scorers. Hickey (2001) tested the reliability of a more subjective method of assessing the creativity of fourth- and fifth-grade students' musical compositions. She used a *consensual assessment* technique originally devised by Amabile (1983, 1996). Hickey also sought to ascertain which groups of people were best suited to evaluate students' musical compositions. These groups included different groups of music teachers (including a group of general/ choral music teachers), as well as composers, college theory professors, seventh-grade children, and second-grade children. Results of the study revealed that the group of general/choral music teachers were the most reliable in their scoring of the compositions, while the composers were the least reliable.

Madsen (2011) discussed the importance of using directed listening techniques when asking music students to respond to music. By giving students something specific to listen for (e.g., a certain motif or specific musical element), overall attentive response to the music being listened to can increase. Results of a study by Paul (2003) suggested that while purposefully listening to music, participants relate to memories of happy and sad events in their lives. It is reasonable to assume that children in the upper-elementary grades can have knowledgeable and affective responses to music through directed listening activities, such as comparing several versions of a piece of music and evaluating the quality of performances based on certain criteria. Researchers (e.g., Weikart, 2006; Russell & Reese, 2015) developed rubrics that can be used to assess students' use of movement in the music classroom, including students' competence in expressing the beat of music (Weikart) and in their competence in more complex movements such as when responding physically to music (Russell & Reese). In both cases, the authors describe how the results of these formal assessments can be used to tailor classroom instruction, specifically in the areas of responding to music through movement.

GRADE 5 MCA FOR CREATING

One of the ways students can experience music in a unique way is through the process of creating music. The artistic process of creating addresses Anchor Standards 1, 2, and 3, which address the process components of imagine, plan and make, evaluate and refine, and present. An experience of creative musical expression can occur through the creation of a simple rhythmic phrase to a fully improvised or created composition.

The first portion of the creating music MCA is the process component of imagine, under Anchor Standard 1: generate and conceptualize artistic ideas and work. This is assessing students using their musical imagination, which is often considered *musical play* to a fifth-grade student. This task begins with the students responding to a phrase performed by the teacher. Using the call and response strategy, students improvise a musical response to the teacher's prompt; in other words, a musical answer to a musical question. This is to prepare students to independently create their own musical phrases. Another option that would fulfill the process component of imagine is having students improvise a different ending to a song or improvise sounds to reflect the plot of a story. Other options that fit into the imagine process component are accompaniments to simple melodies being improvised by changing rhythms, or by creating an ostinato. The MCAs are designed for students to demonstrate artistic process components in a variety of ways and for the teacher to assess their work using the common scoring device (rubric). An important component of this MCA is to observe students exploring how they manipulate musical elements to elicit a variety of musical ideas. In addition to observing and scoring the imagining portion of this MCA, student experiences can be captured on audio or video recordings for the student to replay and decide which ones will be used in the composition. Students may need to have a recorded representation of their musical ideas to remember and use in the next component of the MCA.

The next segment of the MCA focuses on Anchor Standard 2: organizing and developing artistic ideas and work. Using standard or iconic notation, students organize their imagined musical ideas and develop an expressive flow that transitions from one musical idea to another. Students demonstrate expressive intent through the organization of their musical ideas, explanation of their choices, and manipulation of musical elements in their improvisation, arrangement, or composition.

The MCA leads students through Anchor Standard 3: musicians evaluate and refine their work through openness to new ideas, persistence, and the application of appropriate criteria. Similar to the performing MCA, students gather feedback from a teacher or peers and determine what components of this feedback they want to use in their final work. Because the standard suggests that evaluations are based on both teacher-provided and collaboratively developed criteria that reflect the standards, students select and explain their rationale for specific criteria that will determine when is a work ready to present. The second part of Anchor Standard 3 states that a musician's presentation of creative work is the culmination of a process of creation and communication. The MCA concludes with students presenting the final version of personal created music to others to demonstrate craftsmanship and explain connections to expressive intent.

GRADE 5 MCA FOR PERFORMING

The Grade 5 Model Cornerstone Performance Assessment addresses Anchor Standards 4, 5, and 6, which are divided into five process components: select; analyze; interpret; rehearse, evaluate, and refine; and present.

Anchor Standard 4 focuses on students' learning to select, analyze, and interpret a musical work to prepare for performance. This standard addresses recognition that the context of a performance will influence the selection of repertoire, the performers' interest in and knowledge of musical works, and the extent that students understand their own technical and musical skills. Since student engagement may be increased if students have an interest in the selection used for performance, the first process component, selecting, asks students to choose a piece for performance from a specified group of pieces studied in class (vocal, mallet, or recorder). Although the music teacher is to select the pieces for this MCA from the current curriculum, the pieces used in the pilot are provided as examples. Following the students' selections of their preferred piece to prepare for performance, they explain their choices based on their personal interest in the particular piece, knowledge of the musical content in the piece, understanding of the intended context for performance, and relationship of the piece to their current technical skills. This task can be experienced prior to the assessment at various points in the elementary coursework after students learn to perform a variety of pieces for singing, mallet, or recorder.

The second part of Anchor Standard 4 assesses students' analysis of how the elements of music in the piece were manipulated to provide insight into the expressive intent of the piece and to inform preparation for performance. The process components of interpreting and analyzing are addressed and assessed under this standard. By learning the structure of music or how musical elements are used to make different kinds of music, students are able to see patterns or recognize previously learned compositional techniques that can make their practice and performance more meaningful. Students are then able to independently make interpretive decisions prior to performance.

Anchor Standard 5 assesses an important step in preparing repertoire for performance as the student develops and refines performance techniques. Students express their musical ideas, analyze, evaluate, and refine their performance over time through openness to new ideas, persistence, and the application of appropriate criteria. In the process component rehearse, evaluate, and refine, students self-assess their current progress, receive feedback from the teacher, and have peers offer statements on what has been performed well and ideas to improve the performance. The feedback from peers may or may not be useful; students will independently determine the extent to which they will incorporate the comments as the context preparing for performance.

The final product is presented after analyzing the music, determining the composer's intent, and seeking out feedback on how to improve the performance. In Anchor Standard 6, students and the teacher assess the final performance based on defined criteria.

Music teachers may find the process of the MCA familiar since it is a common preparation sequence for performance. The components of this MCA that teachers may not be as familiar with are selecting, evaluating, and refining, since music teachers often select the repertoire for performance and tell the students on which components to concentrate in rehearsal. As suggested by the process in this MCA, there is great value in having students learn to appropriately select repertoire, analyze compositional constructs, and self-assess and receive feedback from peers. Teachers may be quick to tell students how to fix a performance issue, but this assessment requires students to discover the answers for themselves. Student engagement in musical performance increases when they are taught to be self-directed, to give and receive feedback, and to refine performance.

GRADE 5 MCA FOR RESPONDING

The responding MCA addresses Anchor Standards 7, 8, and 9, which include the process components of select, analyze, interpret, and evaluate. Although these processes are experienced in the other MCAs, the intellectual processes are in some ways unique to each artistic experience. All three artistic processes strengthen a student's ability to interact with music in an expressive and meaningful manner.

This MCA begins with the teacher presenting lyrics to a cultural/historical piece associated with the curriculum for students to interpret how the message of the song connects to historical/cultural/ethnic constructs already learned by the students. Students analyze the use of musical elements in three different versions of this piece. The pilot study used the song "Simple Gifts" with its connection to Shaker history and the current Shaker culture; however, any song that is culturally relevant to the students is appropriate and should be used. This portion of the MCA addresses Anchor Standard 8: interpret intent and meaning of an artistic work. It is designed to allow students to recognize how composers and performers manipulate elements and structures of music to explore and project expressive intent. Students are asked to respond to a series of questions that requires critical listening and transfer of prior knowledge. When taught how to apply understandings through aural analysis, students begin to listen to music critically, begin to recognize structure, patterns, and musical elements, and begin to carry these over to performing and creating.

Students are then charged with evaluating the appropriateness of the three recorded performances in relation to the context in which they are being performed as well as whether the expressive qualities of the performances match the intended message of the musical work. This addresses Anchor Standard 9: apply criteria to evaluate a musical work, which suggests personal evaluation of musical work(s) and performance(s). Students are required to be informed by analysis, interpretation, and established criteria. In the MCA, students explain the conceived appropriateness of the pieces to the context by citing examples of musical elements manipulated by the composer and/or performer.

The MCA concludes by addressing Anchor Standard 7: perceive and analyze artistic works. This standard is founded on individuals making selections of musical works and being influenced by their interests, experiences, understandings, and purposes. It is important that students be asked their opinions of music and share their experiences with the music being studied. The process component select is implemented at the end of the MCA for students to select which of several versions they preferred over the others. After analyzing, interpreting, and evaluating several musical works, a student is able to select one of them to show personal choice, citing evidence from the elements of music. With an ever-changing student demographic, what appeals to one student may not appeal to another. Social, cultural, and historical context plays a large part in students' preferences, and all of these factors must be intentionally incorporated into the educational development of responding to music.

HOW THE MCAs WERE PILOTED

Methodology

The purpose of this section is to examine pre- and postsurvey data, namely, educator feedback and responses to piloting the fifth-grade

Model Cornerstone Assessments for create, perform, and respond through content analysis, descriptive statistical analysis, thematic organization, and inductive/deductive analysis. Twenty-eight fifth-grade music educators and their classes in various regions of the United States piloted the Model Cornerstone Assessments in their respective schools: western (1), southwest (4), southern (5), northwest (4), north central (6), eastern (7), and other (1). After one educator dropped out because of time demands, 27 completed the entire MCA pilot across five semesters (fall 2014, spring 2015, fall 2015, spring 2016, fall 2016). The distribution of participants across school district types was as follows: metropolitan inner-city (2), metropolitan suburban (10), mid-size city (5), small town (7), and rural (4). Educators assessed their students during scheduled class time, which varied from one to three days per week for general music, and anywhere from 20 minutes to 60 minutes instruction time per class period. It is important to note the differences here with respect to students having greater and lesser access and opportunities to learn music.

Teachers were given the MCAs and asked for feedback in a prepilot survey. Teachers used the MCAs in their classrooms for an entire semester. Some teachers used them for more than one semester and moved from the perform MCA one semester to the create MCA the next. Teachers submitted student work and scored it for the purposes of the pilot methodology and also completed a postpilot survey. Teachers also shared student responses about the MCAs with the researchers.

Findings for Each of the Artistic Processes

In the following section, teacher postpilot survey responses are highlighted including richly descriptive teacher comments for the Grade 5 MCA. Teacher survey responses indicated a strong appreciation for multiple facets of the pilot study. The pilot demonstrated that the Model Cornerstone Assessments fit into the instructional sequence of a classroom setting:

- 79% of teachers agreed or strongly agreed that they were able to integrate the MCAs into their instruction.
- 87.8% agreed or strongly agreed that the MCAs already fit into current teaching plans.
- 84.2% of teachers strongly agreed or agreed that they will use or adapt this assessment task for future lessons.
- 94% of teachers agreed or strongly agreed that the MCA reflects the expectations of the performance standards.

The act of participating in this study informed teachers and their instructional practices as a means of professional development. For example, some teachers considered alternate and new ways of assessment, such as student-to-student feedback, because of its use in these MCAs. In postpilot survey responses, teachers agreed/strongly agreed (73.7%) that participating in the MCAs had a positive influence on their teaching and assessment. One teacher stated, "After using these assessments, I came to realize that my students can accomplish more than I had considered, and to deeper levels of understanding."

The most disparate grouping of responses from fifth-grade teachers was on the postpilot curricular questions about whether the MCAs allowed for the inclusion of students with special needs (21.4% strongly agreed, 28.6% agreed, 28.6% disagreed, 21.4% strongly disagreed) and "allows for inclusion for all learners" (15% strongly agreed, 50% agreed, 10% don't know, 25% disagreed). It is important to recognize that the differentiation strategies had not been added at the time of the MCA pilot study, but are now included in the public final versions. Because the pilot study defined the content used and means of student responses, these differentiation strategies were difficult to collect within student work and have peer-scored. Since the MCAs are intended to be teacher-scored, allowing for differentiation of student learning demonstrations will be possible and is strongly encouraged.

Most fifth-grade music teachers recognized that the MCAs related to their own expectations of student learning, with the majority of teachers (90.9%) agreeing/strongly agreeing that the scoring assessment measures are age appropriate. This is an important finding from the study; it suggests that teachers across a variety of classroom contexts consider the MCAs relevant to music learning in their setting. Related to this finding, most teachers' comments focused on the time it took to prepare their students for the tasks. Many teachers found preparation a challenge when addressing the MCAs as an additive to the curriculum. Even when the instruction was appropriate for the developmental levels of their students, teachers found it essential to enrich their instruction with additional preparation for students prior to the administration of the assessment. Findings from the pilot study reinforce the concept that instruction must be designed so that students have sufficient opportunities to experience each component of the artistic processes through the planned curriculum. Such planning will alleviate some challenges experienced in the pilot study when teachers did not have the opportunity to integrate the MCAs throughout their instructional sequence. One respondent stated, "I have programs that are pre-scheduled [in my curriculum], so [fitting them in] at a specific time of year may be difficult." Another point of discussion from teachers was about the amount of time it took to administer the assessments. Planning and integrating the MCAs into and throughout instruction are needed; this will help contribute to essential learning.

A high percentage (89.4%) of teachers considered the objectives of the MCA to be clear and concise, measurable, and linked to performance standards. Of teachers who disagreed (28.6%), some requested more specificity in the tasks or rubrics. It was suggested that students composing at this age need additional parameters. "Several adjustments had to be made to the MCA for my class. First, I had to set restrictions for the creation of a song for my students that were not clearly described within the rubric" (response to postpilot survey, mid-size city comment). This is an important issue because composers at any stage of development use parameters to guide creativity. These MCAs do not define teachers' curricula but design a framework into which teachers insert their curricular expectations. Each teacher chooses the parameters and includes those in the designed task. The same is to be said about students' prior knowledge and skills that come from former instruction. It is expected that the teacher will add these into the task and, if necessary, add them into the scoring device used to measure learning. The rubrics are designed around the standards defined with each process component. Content, knowledge components, and associated skills are defined in teachers' curricula and added appropriately by the teacher. Even with this openness for content in the design of the MCAs, when participating teachers were asked if they had to make modifications to the MCAs, a majority of respondents felt that modifications were not necessary. Only 33.1% of the participants stated that modifications would be necessary, with an additional 18.5% of the participants answering that they did not know if modifications needed to be made to fit district curriculum.

Participating teachers were given the opportunity to provide comments regarding the need for changes to the MCAs. The narrative responses revealed some interesting thoughts regarding possible modifications to the MCAs, many of which discussed how modifications were needed to help meet specific needs in their classrooms. Below are a few teacher comments about creating, performing, and responding.

About creating: "Using this MCA helped me reflect on the rubrics that I currently use in my own class. I have improved my own rubrics to be more student friendly." "The creating assessment has more possibilities for inclusion than responding does. I don't know how to modify the responding unit."

About performing: "I love the idea of getting my kids thinking about the quality of their performances." "I think it was positive for the students to perform in front of each other during class. I didn't have time during their regular class to record them, so I recorded them outside of their music class, and they were alone with me and the recorder in a room adjacent to their classroom. They were a little intimidated by the recorder and not being in front of their peers."

About responding: "The responding MCA is thorough, includes necessary background information, audio examples, and has multiple response areas. My concern is how text heavy it is. I am interested to know what accommodations might be provided to support students with IEPs [Individualized Education Programs] and English Language Learners."

"The whole process is good, but so much writing in the music classroom. My students are used to playing, singing, creating/composing, writing on the staff, listening and moving and when there is writing it is short and simple so that I know they are getting what they should be learning. Sometimes I use Plickers or iPads to assess. I am making adjustments, but I don't think they need this much writing in fifth-grade music or they may not continue in music when they arrive in M.S. or H.S." and "My fifth-grade students don't want to be doing this much writing in music. They want to be playing instruments and working on composing and assessments on creating."

ADMINISTERING MCAs

A common misconception about assessment in schools is that assessment is something done to students rather than done with students, allowing for student input (Raiber & Teachout, 2014). When assessment is done to students, it is often detached from the actual teaching and learning that has occurred in the classroom. Fautley (2010) states that this kind of detached assessment of student performance is commonly completed by a third party who has had little or no contact with the research participants before or after the data collection is completed. Within the MCAs, students have input into their learning, and their reactions to the learning process inform the teacher's decisions as the MCAs are being implemented. Furthermore, the teacher is the administrator of the assessment. Unlike when assessment is administered by a detached third party, the teacher can provide formative feedback to students during the assessment process to help ensure that the assessment is connected to the classroom curriculum. This is an essential component of the MCAs. Within the MCAs, teacher input was sought regarding any modifications that may be needed as they were being developed and redeveloped. Among the teachers who piloted the Grade 5 MCAs, some stated that they had students in their classrooms who had difficulties articulating their own thoughts through writing. Other teachers stated that they had to consider how best to assess English language learners. Some teachers took the liberty of creating Smart Board lesson plans to present the information to their students. Feedback and ideas from the pilot study teachers have been added to the final versions of the MCAs. Teachers are encouraged to make appropriate decisions based on the needs of their students. The task is designed with sufficient flexibility for curriculum content and learning needs, while the rubric measures have been shown to reliably assess the criteria of the performance standards with the variable content.

FINDINGS OF VALIDITY AND RELIABILITY

The Grade 5 performing and responding MCAs demonstrated overall strong construct validity as demonstrated by the reasonable parameter separation for each of the considered parameters. The parameters considered were (a) student work, (b) scorers, (c) scoring type, and (d) criteria. Reasonable parameter separation indicates that one set of parameters (the performance achievement of student work, for example) can be estimated without any interference from any of the other parameters (the severity of the raters or difficulties of the criteria, for example). For the performing MCA, results indicated that the rank-ordering of criteria by difficulty (from most difficult to least difficult) was (1) expressive quality, (2) accuracy, (3) technical ability, (4) quality of interpretation, (5) appropriateness, (6) context, (7) considerations of personal performance, (8) analyze, (9) consideration of feedback, (10) performance decorum, (11) consideration of teacher-provided criteria and peer feedback, and (12) personal interest. Results for the responding MCA indicated that the rank-ordering of criteria by difficulty (from most difficult to least difficult) was (1) selecting best representation Question 2, (2) reflection Question 2, (3) interpreting qualities Question 3, (4) connections Question 4, and (5) interpreting qualities Question 1. All criteria were found to be appropriate and meaningful in their overall functioning within the context of measuring the *perform* and *respond* construct for fifth grade.

DISCUSSION

The Model Cornerstone Assessments provide assessments that can be embedded in curriculum and that measure fifth-grade music learning in reliable and valid ways. Main themes emerged from fifth-grade educator responses: time as a challenge, assessment as a positive experience, a call for more inclusive assessments for learners with special needs, and changing teaching practice.

Time as a Challenge

Several teachers mentioned that this pilot study participation was time-consuming and a challenge to balance with other duties, including concerts, field trips, and so on. Instruction time and frequency of class meetings allowed for teachers to better complete the requirements of the pilot study. Despite the amount of time the assessments took to complete, teachers remarked that the students welcomed the assessments positively and participated with enthusiasm.

Adaptable and Inclusive Assessments

Teachers adapted and modified how they collected the assessment portion of the Model Cornerstone Assessments to best serve their school population, environment, and teaching schedule. Teachers of students with special needs commented about modifying tasks and assessments to better meet the needs of students. Modifications and presentations of assessments for a specific group of learners should be investigated in future research.

Changing Practice

Teachers commented that the MCAs required a shift in teaching perspective and a requirement that their students think in a different way—using creativity and higher-order thinking skills. Through this pilot study participation, some teachers realized that they were not holding their students to high enough learning expectations. This project made those teachers realize that their students were capable of much more. While some teachers mentioned expecting more of their students, others mentioned that what was expected from the MCAs were common practices at their schools. So, the MCAs benefited many of the teachers who participated in the study by helping them reflect on their teaching practice and making changes to their classroom practices. Teachers reported that students enjoyed the opportunities to create their own songs and compositions, record and revise these creations, and provide feedback for peer work.

The grade 5 MCAs' pilot study data has provided valuable information on how the MCAs could be used to best assess student learning in elementary general music. Taking these findings into consideration, more inquiry would benefit educators on how to best teach and evaluate the three artistic processes of create, perform, and respond.

REFERENCES

Amabile, T. M. (1983). *The social psychology of creativity.* New York: Springer-Verlag.
Amabile, T. M. (1996). *Creativity in context.* Boulder, CO: Westview Press.
Anderson, M. (2011). *What every 5th grade teacher needs to know about setting up and running a classroom.* Turner Falls, MA: Northeast Foundation for Children.

Brophy, T. (2007). *Assessment in music education, integrating curriculum, theory, and practice*. Proceedings of the 2007 Florida Symposium on Assessment in Music Education. Chicago, IL: GIA Publications.

Ciorba, C. R., & Smith, N. Y. (2009). Measurement of instrumental and vocal undergraduate performance juries using a multidimensional assessment rubric. *Journal of Research in Music Education, 57*(1), 5–15. doi:10.1177/0022429409333405

Colwell, R. (2002). Assessment's potential in music education. In R. Colwell & C. Richardson (Eds.), *The new handbook for research in music teaching and learning* (pp. 1128–1158). New York: Oxford University Press.

Fautley, M. (2010). *Assessment in music education*. Oxford, UK: Oxford University Press.

Garner, B., & Massaro, K. (2011). *Curriculum guide: Fifth grade general music*. Hicksville, NY: Hicksville USFD.

Great Schools Staff. (2016, June 13). Kindergarten through fifth grade: What your child should know. Retrieved from https://www.greatschools.org/gk/articles/k-5-benchmarks/

Hickey, M. (2001). An application of Amabile's Consensual Assessment Technique for rating the creativity of children's musical compositions. *Journal of Research in Music Education, 49*(3), 234–244. doi:10.2307/3345709

Latimer, M. E., Jr., Bergee, M. J., & Cohen, M. L. (2010). Reliability and perceived pedagogical utility of a weighted music performance assessment rubric. *Journal of Research in Music Education, 58*(2), 168–183. doi:10.1177/0022429410369836

Madsen, C. K. (2011). From research to the general music classroom. *Music Educators Journal, 98*(2), 78–82. doi:10.1177/0027432111424777

McQuarrie, S. H., & Sherwin, R. G. (2013). Assessment in music education: Relationships between classroom practice and professional publication topics. *Research and Issues in Music Education, 11*(1), 15. Retrieved from https://ir.stthomas.edu/cgi/viewcontent.cgi?article=1010&context=rime

Paul, P. M. (2003). *An exploratory study of children's emotional responsiveness to music as measured by the Continuous Response Digital Interface* (PhD dissertation). Retrieved from ProQuest Dissertations and Theses database. (UMI No. 3109304)

Raiber, M., & Teachout, D. (2014). *The journey from music student to teacher: A professional approach*. New York: Routledge.

Russell, H. A., & Reese, J. (2015). Movement for musical development: Curriculum and assessment. In C. Conway (Ed.), *Musicianship-focused curriculum and assessment* (pp. 131–156). Chicago, IL: GIA Publications.

Webster, P., & Hickey, M. (1995). Rating scales and their use in assessing children's musical compositions. *The Quarterly, 6*, 28–44. Retrieved from http://www-usr.rider.edu/~vrme/

Weikart, P. S. (2006). *Teaching movement and dance: A sequential approach*. Ypsilanti, MI: High Scope.

Wesolowski, B. (2012). Understanding and developing rubrics for music performance assessment. *Music Educators Journal, 98*(3), 36–42. doi:10.1177/0027432111432524

FIVE

Grade 8 Model Cornerstone Assessments

Ann Clements, Katherine Willow, and Kristina R. Weimer

MUSIC IN THE MIDDLE: A CASE STUDY OF GRADE 8 GENERAL MUSIC MCAs

For many students, middle school represents the beginning of one of the largest and most abrupt developmental periods they will face in their entire life. It is a time of physical, emotional, intellectual, and social growth. This time of evolution and change can provide fertile ground for students to contribute in positive and meaningful ways in the music classroom. Despite challenges associated with maturation, middle school general music classes, done well, can not only assist students in expanding their musical skills and interests, but can enhance the formation of identity, navigation of physical changes (such as voice change), and positive social engagement with others (Sweet, 2016, p. 26). Middle school students are developing cognitively, allowing them to "sharpen their ability to think abstractly and draw conclusions from given information" (p. 34). Additionally, there are advances in concrete reasoning, language, and logic.

The continuously growing musical sophistication of middle school students allows music teachers an opportunity to plan and assess activities at a new and advanced level that simply was not possible previously. The growth experienced at this time is dramatic and expansive, with the abilities of sixth-grade students differing greatly from that of eighth-grade students.

The Model Cornerstone Assessments (MCAs) for general music at the eighth-grade level are designed to provide a framework task to be integrated with a school's curriculum, aligning with the Grade 8 Core Arts Standards. This framework is designed to guide planning, implementation, and assessment of student learning. The grade 8 MCAs are presented as flexible models to account for diverse school curricula and student populations. Specific attention was paid to the following teaching and learning attributes.

1. *Student choice and differentiated instruction:* Individual students have the ability to make choices about what they want to focus on and how they will complete various aspects of the assessments. Teachers are given flexibility to adapt and alter the assessments to meet the different learning styles of the students with whom they work.
2. *Higher-order thinking skills:* The assessments require the ability to apply complex concepts to answer questions, solve problems, create and compose, and interpret music.
3. *Cooperative learning and self- and peer-assessment:* The assessments frequently necessitate students working together to complete tasks. Each student in the group is responsible for learning specific information and applying that information to group work. Students are asked to assess their own work and that of their peers in constructive ways intended to enhance metacognitive skills and their understanding of musical knowledge.
4. *Instructional scaffolding:* Each MCA is broken down into levels arranged by anchor standards. These standards are sequential and provide a framework for scaffolding within the assessments.
5. *Student progress monitoring and feedback:* The anchor standard within each MCA is associated with its own rubric, allowing for frequent monitoring of student progress and providing the teacher opportunities to share feedback with the students throughout the process.

DESCRIPTIONS OF THE GRADE 8 MODEL CORNERSTONE ASSESSMENTS

The Creating Model Cornerstone Assessment

The MCA for creating provides music teachers with assessment measures that can be used in their eighth-grade classrooms. This is accomplished through students composing a short piece of music that conveys the expressive intent of a given video or scenario. The task is to be embedded within curricular activities, ensuring that the assessment serves as a way to synthesize disparate skills and content elements. Students apply these by engaging in practices authentic to both amateur and professional composers. A hallmark of the grade 8 MCA for creating is its dynamic nature, meaning the assessment is not the end point of learning, but instead is a call to engage in creative process components. Students receive teacher and peer feedback to guide their creative work, reflecting upon the feedback to revise their work to better achieve the intended outcome.

The MCA for creating consists of four assessment tasks. These tasks can be administered within one instructional sequence or unit, or they may be spread out by component parts of the MCA across multiple units or projects to meet the needs of teachers' particular students and/or curricular structure.

Process Component 1: Imagine—Generate musical ideas for various purposes and contexts.

The student makes informed musical choices regarding their expressive intent and what musical ideas they feel will best convey their expressive intent (performance standard MU:Cr2.1.8a). The assessment task reveals the intended learning by reflecting the student's ability to demonstrate insightful sensitivity in clearly describing the expressive intent of each section of their film/scenario and accompanying musical work.

Process Component 2: Plan and Make—Select and develop musical ideas for defined purposes and contexts.

The student composes or improvises with sound in order to bring these musical ideas to fruition (performance standards MU:Cr1.1.8a and MU:Cr2.1.8b). The assessment task reveals the intended learning by reflecting the student's ability to apply these musical ideas to convey the expressive intent, effectively organizing these ideas using a variety of compositional techniques to realize the expressive intent.

Process Component 3: Evaluate and Refine—Evaluate and refine selected musical ideas to create musical work(s) that meets appropriate criteria.

The student assesses the work of a peer, provides suggestions to enhance the peer's piece, and receives teacher and peer feedback about his or her own piece. The student uses teacher and peer feedback to reengage in the composition process, revising his or her approach and the resultant musical composition (performance standards MU:Cr3.1.8a and MU:Cr3.a.8b). The assessment task reveals the intended learning by reflecting the student's ability to generate new ideas based on synthesized feedback in order to improve the composition; to describe his or her compositional techniques, style, and form in detail; and to articulate the reasons for refining his or her musical ideas to convey expressive intent.

Process Component 4: Present/Perform—Share creative musical work that conveys intent, demonstrates craftsmanship, and exhibits originality.

The student presents his or her work. The presentation consists of the performance of the composition and a verbal explanation of the expressive intent (performance standard MU:Cr3.2.8a). The assessment task reveals the intended learning by reflecting the student's ability to execute his or her expressive intent in emotionally effective ways throughout the composition and to use appropriate composition techniques—including unity/variety, tension/release, and balance—in sophisticated ways to create an effective beginning, middle, and end.

The grade 8 MCA in creating is neither an exhaustive assessment of every key concept an eighth-grade student should understand, nor is it the only means of meaningful assessment in which a teacher can engage his or her music class in order for students to demonstrate and further grow in their understanding of these concepts. Nonetheless, the MCA serves as an effective instrument that music educators may elect to use—either in its current form or after personalizing it for use with their unique group of learners. The creating MCA stands as a strong model for authentic assessment because it engages students in real-world processes. It engages students in a collaborative feedback loop through which they learn how to realize, musically, their intended outcomes. The process allows for augmentation of learning through opportunities to revise their approach, promotes metacognition by engaging students as self-assessors, allows for a culminating product greater than its component parts, and aids teachers in determining whether instruction is well aligned with the standards/learning outcomes.

The Performing Model Cornerstone Assessment

The performing MCA allows students to demonstrate their ability to select, analyze, interpret, rehearse, evaluate, refine, and present music for a musical setting. The MCA for performing consists of three assessment strategies. Each assessment strategy requires prerequisite skills and knowledge, teacher preparation, assessment environment setup, and the assessment itself.

Process Components: Select and Analyze—Select varied musical works to present based on interest, knowledge, technical skill, and context. Analyze the structure and context of varied musical works and their implications for performance.
This task requires students to apply personally-developed criteria for selecting music of contrasting styles for a program with a specific purpose and/or context and explain expressive qualities, technical challenges, and reasons for choices (MU:Pr4.1.8a). When analyzing selected music, students sight-read in treble or bass clef simple rhythmic, melodic, and/or harmonic notation (MU:Pr4.2.8a); compare the structure of contrasting pieces of music selected for performance, explaining how the elements of music are used in each (MU:Pr4.2.8b); and identity how cultural and

historical context influences performance and results in different musical effects (MU:Pr4.2.8c).

Process Component: Interpret—Develop personal interpretations that consider creator's intent; Rehearse, Evaluate, Refine—Evaluate and refine personal and ensemble performances, individually and in collaboration with others.

Students identify and apply personally-developed criteria (such as demonstrating correct interpretation of notation, technical skill of performer, originality, emotional impact, variety, and interest) to rehearse, refine, and determine when the music is ready to perform (MU:Pr5.1.8a). The second assessment strategy asks students to choose one of the pieces to prepare for performance and to rehearse the piece using the practice/ rehearsal log. Students perform contrasting pieces of music, demonstrating and explaining how the music's intent is conveyed by their interpretations of the elements of music and expressive qualities such as dynamics, tempo, timbre, articulation/style, and phrasing (MU:Pr4.3.8a).

Process Component: Present—Perform expressively, with appropriate interpretation and technical accuracy, and in a manner appropriate to the audience and context.

Students perform their selected piece with technical accuracy, stylistic expression, and culturally authentic practices in music to convey the creator's intent (MU:Pr6.1.8a). Each teacher can determine the length of time required to complete the assessment.

The Responding Model Cornerstone Assessment

The MCA for responding is based on comparing and contrasting musical styles, genres, time periods, and composers/performers intentions. It also maintains a focus on the elements of music and expressing programming. Similar to the two other MCAs, responding serves to combine disparate skills in order to deepen and expand learning.

An important quality of the grade 8 MCA for responding is the large amount of student choice that is encouraged within the measurement. The students will hear multiple paired playlists as a class, yet they individually select which songs in the paired playlist on which they would like to focus on. This student-centered approach allows for greater student autonomy and agency and provides the teacher with insight into individual students' preferences and interests.

The MCA for responding consists of four process components. The assessment task is intended to be administered within one instructional sequence or unit, although there is flexibility to expand the sequence over a longer period if students maintain access to the paired playlists they have individually selected.

Process Component: Select and Analyze—Choose music appropriate for a specific purpose or context. Analyze how the structure and context of varied musical works inform the response.

First, the teacher guides the students in selecting a pair of playlists from the accompanying paired playlist list (MU:Re7.1.8.a). Each paired playlist consists of songs of similar genres, time periods, or similarly composed intentions using the select worksheet. The two playlists (Playlist A and Playlist B) have been paired intentionally to maximize students' ability to think deeply about similarities and differences within and across the groupings. The comparisons focus on both elements and expressive qualities of music (MU:Re7.2.a) and programming, genre, cultures, and historical periods (MU:Re7.2.8b). The analysis of musical qualities is explored through the analyze worksheet.

Process Component: Interpret—Support interpretations of musical works that reflect creators/performers/expressive intent.

After students have selected and analyzed the musical materials, they are asked to provide personal interpretations of the contrasting playlist and explain how creators and performers used musical elements, expressive qualities, genre, and culture to convey intent.

Process Component: Evaluate—Support evaluations of musical works and performances based on analysis and interpretation, and establish criteria.

The teacher then guides students in developing criteria to evaluate musical works on both playlists by using the evaluate worksheet. All student work is assessed using rubrics with defined criteria for achievement at the eighth-grade level.

The MCA in responding is comprehensive in scope, yet easy to initiate in music classrooms. Although teachers may use music from their curriculum, recorded music used in the pilot study for the paired playlist comparison is provided from the Smithsonian Folkways Recordings archive and consists of authentic, high-quality works. Accompanying content is provided for every step of the assessment through worksheets. If teachers choose to use the music and cultural content that accompanies the paired playlists, there is no need for music teachers to hunt and search for materials. However, there are multiple paired playlists from which to choose so that teachers and their students can select topic areas that are of most interest and that fit best within the present curriculum. This MCA intends to stimulate both individual thought and application of previous knowledge and to foster class-wide discussion, which requires students to formulate unique and rational points of view while at the same time requiring that students listen to the opinions of others.

CONFIRMING THE QUALITY OF THE MCAs

The grade 8 general music MCAs were pilot-tested nationally to a small number of participating schools. The small number of participants was due to the relatively small number of eighth-grade general music classes offered across the United States and the fact that teachers in many of the schools that do offer eighth-grade general music classes primarily self-identify as performance ensemble directors (who also teach general music). In the latter settings, these teachers frequently elected to pilot-test the ensemble MCAs and not general music MCAs.

Due to the small number of participants, it was deemed more meaningful to explore a single MCA (creating) using a narrative research approach. Narrative research is often a reflective process that relies on the written or spoken words or visual representation of individuals. For this study, the focus is on integrating the creating MCA in an eighth-grade general music setting. In addition to the narrative study, scoring data were analyzed statistically, and the grade 8 creating MCA demonstrated overall strong construct validity as demonstrated by the reasonable parameter separation for each of the considered parameters. As to consistency of scoring, reasonable parameter separation indicates that one set of parameters (the performance achievement of student work, for example) can be estimated without any interference from any of the other parameters (the severity of the raters or difficulties of the criteria, for example). As a result, one can directly and meaningfully interpret the characteristics of each parameter as unique. Results indicated that the rank-ordering of criteria by difficulty (from most difficult to least difficult) was: (1) Applying Criteria, (2) Rationale for Refinement, (3) Evaluation, (4) Music Ideas, (5) Expressive Intent from the Imagine Plan and Make Worksheet, (6) Effective Crafting, (7) Expressive Intent from the Composition Scoring Device, and (8) Craftsmanship. All criteria were found to be appropriate and meaningful in their overall functioning within the context of measuring the *creating* construct for eighth grade.

Support for reliability and validity of the assessment measure will be presented through self-reflection of the participating teacher and through the observations, interviews, and reflective setting. These findings are not intended to be generalizable but may be transferable in similar settings.

Participants

Thirty-two students from two different general music classes participated in the study for the grade 8 MCA in creating. The participants were eighth graders enrolled in a nonelective general music program at an all-boys college preparatory school in the midwestern United States. All participants were males between the ages of 12 and 14. The school serves 870 students from a range of socioeconomic backgrounds, offering 36% of its students need-based financial aid. At the time of the study, the majority of the student population was of Caucasian descent, yet the school also had students who were Latino/Hispanic, Middle Eastern, African American, Asian, or of a number of multiracial heritages. Each of these groups was represented among the study's participants. At the time of the study, none of the school's population were classified as English Language Learners, and the school was well resourced. Each student had parental permission to participate in the study. The study consisted of completion of the grade 8 MCA in creating. The music teacher had 12 years of classroom teaching experience at the time of the study. Student work was selected from diverse scoring levels on various aspects of the assessment. The following material data were collected: (1) *Imagine, Plan, and Make* student worksheet, (2) *Imagine, Plan, and Make* teacher scoring device, (3) recording of the first draft of the student composition, (4) *Evaluate to Refine* student worksheet, (5) *Evaluate to Refine* teacher scoring device, (6) recording of the final draft of the composition, and (7) *Composition* teacher scoring device. The following is a narrative representation of teacher perceptions of administering the creating MCA in an eighth-grade classroom.

The Teacher's Perspective on Completing the Creating MCA

The eighth-grade MCA in creating effectively aided me, a sixth- through eighth-grade general music teacher, in identifying student achievement as it pertained to the [Music] Standards. The Imagine, Plan, and Make worksheet prompted my students to describe not only what they intended to express, but also in what ways they planned to utilize various musical elements to convey this intent in each of their piece's three sections. Even when a student was unable to execute these musical ideas in their composition, I was able to recognize the student's thought process and intended approach through their written work. This demonstrated, at times, understanding of key concepts in the absence of effective implementation in performance.

Concurrently, the composition drafts reflected each student's ability (or inability) to apply these concepts utilizing a variety of compositional techniques. By engaging each student in a process of revision based on peer and teacher feedback, the Evaluate to Refine step aided me in identifying each student's ability (or inability) to generate new ideas in order to improve their composition and to articulate the reasoning behind their musical choices.

The scoring devices/rubrics used to assess student achievement in each of these areas broke down each assessed skill, clarifying varying levels of achievement for each in ways that made it easy to identify mastery and/or areas of challenge for each student. For example, when scoring a student's Evaluate to Refine worksheet, I was prompted to assess "applying criteria," "evaluation," and "rationale for refinement" independently of one another, and each contained specified levels of "emerging," "approaches," "meets," and "exceeds." In addition to serving as an effective summative assessment for the project in question, the MCA also serves as a useful formative assessment by identifying areas of need for each student for me to address in the curriculum moving forward.

The Students' Perspectives on Completing the Creating MCA

Student reflections were solicited by the participating teacher and are presented below as a first-person account. Each section begins with a quotation for the student who was interviewed, then is followed by the teacher's perspectives regarding that student's engagement with the creating MCA.

The most meaningful part of the project is the progress/improvement I made from beginning to end. I improved a lot.

—Kevin

To an outside observer, Kevin might not appear to be a *success story* for the MCA in creating. On his *Imagine, Plan, and Make* scoring device, he qualified as "Level 1/Emerging" in the "expressive intent" category and "Level 2/Approaches" in the "music ideas" and "effective crafting of musical ideas into initial draft" categories. Kevin's first draft did not meet the grade-level standard in any category.

Even after receiving feedback from his peers and from the teacher, Kevin's performance on the *Evaluate to Refine* rubric elicited a "Level 1/Emerging" score in the "evaluation" category and "Level 2/Approaches" scores in the "applying criteria" and "rationale for refinement" categories. On the *Composition* scoring device, Kevin scored at "Level 3/Meets" in the "expressive intent" category and "Level 2/Approaches" in the "craftsmanship" category.

Kevin may not have earned the highest achievement scores, but his post-project reflection indicates that the MCA, nonetheless, allowed him an opportunity for meaningful musical engagement. He wrote, "We made a soundtrack using different themes and skills we have learned about throughout the year. We used elements like pitch, harmony, melody, tempo, contrast, and variation." Kevin was able to take concepts learned in class, apply them via the MCA, receive feedback from his peers and from me regarding his execution of those concepts, think critically about how to revise his approach, and try again. At the end of the project, Kevin reflected, "This project made me feel more capable to create based on the progress I made from beginning to end and all the things I learned about the different parts of music." This is one of those situations in which the achievement scores matter much less to me than the anecdotal evidence: Kevin applied what he learned and—through the assessment process— gained an enhanced understanding of the concepts covered in class, subsequently feeling more capable of applying these processes in the future.

As Walker (1997) pointed out, a successful authentic assessment is not the end point of learning, but rather a springboard for future learning. Moreover, it is important to remember that the MCA is, by definition, an assessment tool. Kevin's teacher gained valuable insight into his areas of challenge throughout this process and thus was able to better create personalized interventions later in the year to his needs. By that measure, the MCA was a success.

> *The project surprised me, because I didn't think I would do well.*
>
> —Sean

Sean did well on the MCA overall. His work qualified as "Level 3/Meets Expectations" in all categories on the *Imagine, Plan, and Make* scoring device and on the *Composition* scoring device, and his work qualified as "Levels 1, 2, and 3" in the various categories on the *Evaluate to Refine* scoring device.

The beauty of the MCA, for Sean, was in the way it helped him bridge the connection between the expressive intent of his film and the musical decisions he made in response. He wrote, "What my group did was make music that made sense to our video. Our music was happy at first, then it was scary and augmented, and finally it was sad. We made it that way because the person was happy, then scared, and then sad at the very end. I loved this project." Because the *Imagine, Plan, and Make* worksheet drew a distinction between these two entities—expressive intent and musical ideas—yet required students to draw connections between them, Sean was guided in how to engage in the thought process of a composer by making informed decisions. "This project made me feel like I could create music a lot easier and still be good. I thought it was hard at first, because I am not that good at making music. [But] I would change the project to make it even more challenging."

Authentic assessment is not about recalling concepts discretely "but rather connecting information to achieve understanding" (Campbell, 2000, p. 406). Sean's engagement with the assessment indicates that the MCA in creating can serve as an authentic means of assessment in its requirement that learners synthesize knowledge across content areas in order to demonstrate understanding.

The bulk of the project was reinforcing the acting through music that would bring the emotions out and make them all too real. . . . The music would tell the story.

—Chris

According to Miller, Knips, and Goss (2013), a hallmark of an authentic assessment is that it requires students to not only prove they *have* content knowledge and skills, but also to *use* that knowledge and set of skills. Chris's work on the MCA in creating serves as an example of how those differ and why it's important to assess both.

Chris scored lower marks on the MCA's linguistic-based assessment measures. On the *Imagine, Plan, and Make* scoring device, Chris scored "Level 2/Approaches Expectations" in the "expressive intent" category and "Level 1/Emerging" in the "music ideas" category, both of which assessed his ability to describe, in words, his musical choices. Chris, however, scored "Level 3/Meets Expectations" in the "effective crafting of musical ideas into initial draft" category. This latter category was scored according to the first draft of the musical score Chris wrote and recorded. Similarly, Chris earned scores of "Level 1 and 2" across categories on the *Evaluate to Refine* rubric, which was based entirely on the written content he turned in. He scored "Level 4/Exceeds Expectations" in both categories on the *Composition* scoring device, which was based entirely on how he applied the assessed musical concepts in the final draft of his composition.

Chris's performance on the MCA in creating exemplified two important tenets of authentic assessment. First, whereas more traditional assessments—"tests"—require students to recognize and recall information out of context, authentic assessments "require students to be effective performers with acquired knowledge" (DeCastro-Ambrosetti & Cho, 2005, p. 58) in real-life contexts such as those of the composer or film scorer. Second, authentic assessment requires that students go beyond memorizing discrete pieces of knowledge, instead synthesizing these pieces of knowledge to form a final product whose sum is greater than its parts.

We had the freedom to make whatever kind of music and video we wanted.

—Ian

From an achievement standpoint, Ian demonstrated growth during the MCA in creating process and mastery upon its completion. The first draft of his composition scored "Level 3/Meets" across the board according to the *Imagine, Plan, and Make* scoring device. After going through the revision process as guided by peer and teacher feedback, his final draft and presentation scored "Level 4/Exceeds Expectations" according to the *Composition* scoring device and the *Evaluate to Refine* rubric.

According to Ochanji (2000), authentic assessment measures allow the teacher to "measure students' performance against their own abilities" (p. 27) in order to work toward narrowing the gap. In this way, engaging in authentic assessment is a dynamic process rather than merely a static measure. There are varied means by which this is achieved. One means is the onus placed on students to be self-directed learners (Lines, 1994). Ian felt that the freedom afforded in the MCA in creating allowed him space to do this: "We could create a video and a piece of music on what we wanted and without too specific of guidelines to follow." Another means by which the MCA, in creating, fostered a dynamic process was in the opportunity to receive peer and teacher feedback and make subsequent draft revisions. Ian wrote, "We got to learn from other classmates." Moon, Brighton, Callahan, and Robinson (2005) pointed out that this is a great strategy for middle school students in particular, because it creates a classroom community in which "relations with adults and peers are considered fundamental for intellectual development and personal growth" (p. 120) during a period in which social structures take center stage.

In one sense, the MCA in creating served as a means of summative assessment that helped the music teacher determine curriculum alignment. In another sense, the MCA served as a means of formative assessment that helped high-achieving students, such as Ian, narrow the gap between performance and ability using peer and teacher feedback.

ADAPTING THE MCAS TO VARIOUS SCHOOL SETTINGS AND PRACTICES

The grade 8 MCA in creating could be administered in its published form or adapted by the teacher to fit the nuances of each classroom, curriculum, or individual learner. Assessment Strategy 1, for example, could be completely improvisatory or formally composed. It could be addressed by an individual or a small group of students. The focus could be on a particular musical concept or element being studied in one's class, or it could be open-ended with the music being created for a film clip, poem, story, or simple keywords (e.g., "scary," "joyous"). The presentation could be performed on a student's primary instrument or using software instruments performed via the digital interface. Student responses could be provided in writing, verbally, or via other tools such as emotion cards for English Language Learners or students with special needs.

One Teacher's Adaptation

> *I, personally, found it easy to adapt each assessment strategy for use with my students. My school promotes cross-curricular work. The MCA was presented as a joint*

project between eighth graders' music and drama classes. Rather than using a teacher-selected poem or film clip, the students wrote their own scenes for drama class under the guidance of their drama teacher. In conjunction with their study of the anatomy of a scene, they wrote their scenes in three parts: introduction, climax, and conclusion (or beginning, middle, and end in the published MCA). In conjunction with their study of pantomime, their scenes were silent, so students used facial expressions and body language to convey their expressive intent. Next, in their music classes with me, the students furthered their exploration of the clips' expressive intent through the soundtracks they composed and performed in groups of two or three.

Assessment Strategy 1 was completed over the course of five class periods. The students were allowed to compose using real instruments and/or software instruments. Most opted to use GarageBand software instruments to create their composition. Premade loops and sound effects were not allowed; all material was required to be students' original work. The students joined their composition draft to their film using iMovie. Each group traded their draft with another group, and they used the Peer Assessment Worksheet to leave written feedback for each other. Each student filled out an Imagine, Plan, and Make Worksheet individually and submitted it to me, and I, too, left written feedback for each student. While the feedback given to group members about the composition itself was the same for each member, requiring the students to complete each worksheet as individuals allowed me to assess individual students' understanding of the material and to intervene appropriately.

Assessment Strategy 2 was completed over the course of two class periods. After each group received their written peer and teacher feedback, they revised their soundtrack accordingly and exported the final composition draft to iMovie. Each group prepared a verbal introduction describing their emotional intent and how they achieved it, including this in the presentation of their finished project before their peers. Each student filled out an Evaluate to Refine Worksheet individually, again allowing me to better assess individual achievement.

Teacher's Concluding Thoughts on the Creating MCA

From my perspective, that of a practicing music educator, the eighth-grade MCA in creating is a valuable means of authentic assessment. The MCA proved an invaluable resource for use in my classroom for a number of reasons:

1. The MCA allowed me to easily facilitate performance with acquired knowledge among my students, going beyond simple recollections of acquired knowledge.
2. The MCA allowed my students the opportunity to do this through real-world applications, following the same creative thought processes and musical procedures as professional film scorers.
3. The MCA called for a final product that was greater than the sum of its discrete parts; my students may have exercised much of the same skill set if they had completed chord-building and melody-voicing worksheets and responded to questions regarding chord quality and mood on a multiple-choice test, but I know they would not have had the same sense of accomplishment from these activities that they did from watching their own and their peers' films with accompanying original soundtracks.

4. *The MCA facilitated a feedback loop between students, their peers, and myself. Engagement in that feedback loop necessitated that students rethink and revise their work, ultimately resulting in not only a more polished product but also opportunities to think critically about their work and make more informed choices.*
5. *The MCA served not only as a means of assessing my students but also as a platform for student learning. This point is closely tied to the feedback loop in that in order to revise one's work and polish one's product, each student needed to continuously narrow the gap between their "at-the-moment" performance and their capability. In this way, the target keeps moving, allowing more growth to occur. This dynamic process plays an integral role in fostering a desire for lifelong learning and stands in contrast to the traditional "test" model, in which mastery can be achieved and learning deemed complete when a score of 100% is obtained. Students also retain knowledge most readily when acting as teachers themselves, and the MCA in creating facilitates this process when students are enlisted as peer editors of their classmates' work and must critique the work and offer solutions.*
6. *The MCA made it simple for me to facilitate the synthesis of areas of knowledge and skill among my students. On one level, it was a ready-made project I brought to my school's drama instructor and that she was happy to utilize in her own classroom in order for us to complete this assessment as a cross-curricular project. On a more specific level, my students needed to synthesize abstract content regarding mood, atmosphere, and emotional response with concrete content regarding chord progressions and form in order to engage in the composition process associated with the MCA in creating.*

As with any effective assessment, the MCA provided me a snapshot of what learning had taken place among my students. There were times, as evidenced in Chris's case study, when I might not have known the full extent of learning and/or where the gaps in understanding lay if not for the multiple modes of expression employed in the MCA in creating. For example, had I just had Chris write about how he would utilize various musical elements, I might not have known the depth of understanding that he displayed in his recorded composition; on the other hand, if I had only listened to Chris's recording and not asked for the written component, I might not have known that he required more guidance in how to articulate musical elements through language.

One thing I often catch my teaching colleagues and myself saying is, "If only I had more time— " and so another inherent benefit of the eighth-grade MCA in creating is that it serves so many functions at once, maximizing students' time in the classroom. All at once, it allows for application, demonstration, synthesis, feedback, revision, assessment, creation, and accomplishment. Its adaptability also ensures that teachers can integrate central tenets of the MCA with their existing curricula and/or with other subject areas through cross-curricular projects. For example, if completing a unit on program music, the MCA can be adapted to have no visual component, only program notes, perhaps in response to a conflict students are learning about in their social studies classes. If one would like to work with the physical education instructor in their building, the students could compose music to facilitate a warmup, workout, and cool-down, researching the varying tempos and other factors that might play into these musical choices. Whether choosing the ready-made version or adapting it to fit one's unique classroom and curriculum, the MCA is another resource to be accessed to maximize student learning.

Concluding Thoughts on the Students' Perspectives

The teacher found that the students who completed the MCA overall enjoyed the process. Teachers of adolescents know how important *buy-in* is to classroom engagement, and the MCA, in creating, appeared to have buy-in among students. When the students were asked to reflect on the project and potential changes to be made, here were some of their responses:

Asaan: "To be honest, I wouldn't change anything. I like everything about this project from the music to the filming. I never had days when I wished I wasn't doing the project."

Chris: "I think that this project was fine as is and is a really nice way to demonstrate understanding of music."

James: "I wouldn't make any changes, since you learn everything you need to know before or during the project. Also, there is the perfect amount of class time to do in class."

John: "I believe that the project is already perfect for our grade."

Jonah: "I think that the project is very straightforward from the rubric, guidelines, instructions, and examples. It is just up on you to follow instructions and perform well. I think that it is already very meaningful."

Joshua: "I don't have any suggestions for this project. I believe that this project was effective and helped us learn how to correctly compose music and how to use tools that help and allow us to create the music."

Michael: "None. Everything was simple and self-explanatory."

Noah: "There aren't really any changes that need to be made. This project is really well planned out and gives us more than enough time to make and finalize the piece."

Oliver: "Nothing. This project is fab."

Rayan: "It was really fun."

Sam: "Honestly, I think the project went perfectly just as it was. We had the perfect amount of time to do it, you responded to us, which really helped us, and our classmates responded to our piece, which gave us great constructive criticism."

As shared by the teacher: "I loved seeing how much my *students* genuinely enjoyed their engagement with the MCA, but of course, seeing the musical growth and sharpened critical-thinking skills that came about throughout the process was what allowed *me* to fully buy into the MCA's place in the eighth-grade classroom."

REFERENCES

Campbell, D. (2000). "Authentic Assessment and Authentic Standards." *The Phi Delta Kappan 81*(5), 405–407.

DeCastro-Ambrosetti, D., & Cho, G. (2005). Synergism in learning: A critical reflection of authentic assessment. *The High School Journal 89*(1), 57–62.

Lines, C. (1994). Authentic assessment at the middle level. *Middle School Journal 25*(4), 39–41.

Miller, S., Knips, M., & Goss, S. (2013). Changing the game of literature with authentic assessment: The promise of multimodal composing. *The English Journal 103*(1), 88–94.

Moon, T., Brighton, C., Callahan, C., & Robinson, A. (2005). Development of authentic assessments for the middle school classroom. *Journal of Secondary Gifted Education 16*(2/3), 119–135.

Ochanji, M. (2000). Rethinking the role of the science teacher: Eschewing standardized testing in favor of authentic assessment. *The Science Teacher 67*(5), 24–27.

Sweet, B. (2016). *Growing musicians: Teaching music in middle school and beyond.* New York: Oxford University Press.

Walker, M. (1997). Authentic assessment in the literature classroom. *The English Journal 86*(1), 69–73.

Six

The Model Cornerstone Assessments for Ensembles

Al D. Holcomb, Glenn E. Nierman, and Bret P. Smith

Much work has been done on developing valid and reliable achievement measures (primarily rubrics and rating scales) for individual, small-group, and large-group musical performance (for example, Cooksey, 1977; DeLuca & Bolden, 2014). Research on assessment of musical performance has consistently shown that, generally speaking, evaluators are able to accurately distinguish between levels of performance skill on multiple dimensions, and that as students gain experience and skill, they can accurately self-evaluate as well.

> The music education profession has devoted much time to the development of successful assessment and evaluation criteria, forms, publications, and tools related to assessment of students. By comparison, it has focused far less toward helping students learn to properly evaluate music performances. For students to grow into capable musical adults, they need to know how to make value judgments concerning their own performances, the performance of others, and the quality of musical compositions. (Hewett, 2013, p. 1)

Smartphones, iPads, and computers now can provide stakeholders with instant access to grades and assignments. Recordings of individual performances can be played back multiple times, allowing assessment of one performance dimension at a time. SmartMusic® (2017) software now allows teachers to access a student's portfolio of uploaded performances at any time, create custom rubrics that are specific to a state or region, and assign state standards to each assignment.

MODEL CORNERSTONE ASSESSMENTS FOR ENSEMBLES

It becomes clear that ensemble music educators, to the extent they choose to do so, are capable of, and confident in, assessing the relative sophistication of a student product (composition, improvisation) or musical performance. However, these products and performances are the result of a process of learning that can take widely different forms for individual learners and groups. Much has been said about the importance of formative assessment—often framed as *assessment for learning*—and the development of the metacognitive skills and motivated dispositions that underlie independent, informal, and lifelong learning. In approaching the National Core Arts Standards and Model Cornerstone Assessments (MCAs) from this viewpoint, the time was right to endeavor to reveal the step-by-step components of the artistic processes, always asking: *What do actual musicians do in non-school contexts?* and *How can evidence of a student's development of this aspect of the process be extracted?* Developed were models of tasks that authentically reflect the many dimensions specified in the standards, and to make them as flexible and widely applicable as possible. The word *suggested* has been used several times when describing aspects of each MCA. It cannot be over-emphasized that the MCAs are simply assessment templates to be modified by music educators to fit the literature, schedule, curricular objectives, and students in a particular program. MCAs neither specify the outcomes of a national curriculum nor signal the beginning of a national music exam.

Consideration was given to traditional ensembles (bands, choirs, orchestras) and their settings and routines, as well as more emergent ensembles such as jazz and improvisational groups that may not rely on standard music notation, various types of non-Western music ensembles, and group music-making that is facilitated by technology. Each of these applications could be embraced by the artistic processes that are elaborated in specific core arts standards.

The Model Cornerstone Assessments based on the Core Music Standards provide a framework into which teachers integrate their curriculum while using common learning expectations, with rubrics to monitor and document student growth. Ensemble MCAs have been developed for use in middle and high school settings and structured into strands of composing, improvising, performing, and responding to music. The MCAs are not tests but are tasks completed over time that reflect what musicians do in the real world. They encourage collaboration, flexibility, goal setting, inquisitiveness, openness and respect for the ideas and work of others, responsible risk-taking, self-reflection, self-discipline, and perseverance.

Ensemble directors commonly face the additional challenge of teaching (and assessing) students with different levels of prior experience, technical skill, and musical literacy in the same classroom. For this reason, they are divided into five skill levels: *Novice, Intermediate, Proficient, Accomplished,* and *Advanced. Novice* recognizes beginners of any age, equivalent to two years of study in an ensemble following a foundation of general music. *Intermediate* learners were seen as middle-level, or four years in an ensemble. *Proficient* is defined as the equivalent of one or more years of high school study (or to a level of five or more years of study), which in many states satisfies a graduation requirement. *Accomplished* students are those who exceed the average performance proficiency for high school study, with *Advanced* students as those preparing for collegiate study in music.

ASSESSING PERFORMING IN ENSEMBLES

The bulk of teacher activity in ensemble music is oriented toward whole-class teaching, with limited ability to focus on individual students to a great degree. When approaching the issue of individual practice, student-led ensembles, and sectional rehearsals in the ensemble classroom, the teacher is immediately confronted with constraints of time and space; most ensemble rehearsal rooms offer limited options with regard to private practice areas. The most effective design for a Model Cornerstone Assessment for ensemble classes consists of individual student experiences that are completed with whole-class preparation by the teacher, but primarily student directed and documented through written and audio/video evidence. This permits flexibility in allowing students to select repertoire for study from their solo, chamber ensemble, or full-ensemble literature, as well as to choose to work alone, in small mixed groups, or in sections. In all of these scenarios, students are asked to engage in the artistic process components of select, rehearse (analyze, interpret, rehearse, evaluate, and refine), and present.

The performing assessment task emphasizes the ability to listen actively to oneself, to one's section, and to the whole ensemble, with consideration of terminology appropriate for critiquing segments of a piece. Students must suggest and implement changes in the rehearsal strategy, develop appropriate technique, and expressively apply skills of musical performance. As students develop the listening skills necessary for constructive practice and expressive performance, they heighten understandings by reflecting on their performance and articulating observations.

A notable aspect of the performing MCA is that, regardless of students' prior experience or achievement level, big-picture ideas ensure that students are all involved in a similar task that authentically reflects the *cornerstone* nature of what musicians *do* when applying their skills and knowledge to prepare works for performance. Students consider the context, evaluate and select repertoire options in light of their own abilities, create and execute a rehearsal plan to achieve a high-quality result, and determine when the performance is ready to present. This process, with certain variations, endures regardless of musical style or the role of musical notation. The enduring understandings and essential questions that accompany the performing MCAs capture the essence of this process, and referring to them frequently is helpful when administering or adapting this assessment.

The enduring understandings for the performing MCA ask that students consider how performers' self-knowledge and knowledge of music guide their choices of repertoire when considered alongside the context of the performance. Musicians apply various strategies to prepare and refine their performance, evaluating their own progress toward specific goals and incorporating ideas and feedback from others. Depending on criteria that vary across time, place, and cultures, performers evaluate the success of their preparation and performance. These understandings are also framed in the form of the guiding essential questions, for example, *How do performers select repertoire? How do musicians improve the quality of their performance?* and *How do context and the way musical work is presented influence audience response?*

When designing the performing tasks and rubrics, three options were available to assess increasing achievement expectations and difficulty: Increased amount and difficulty of repertoire, increased *depth of engagement* with selected repertoire, and/or increased performance quality. All these elements are progressively included in the MCA within the same basic task. At one end of the spectrum, a novice student selects appropriate (Difficulty 1–2) repertoire and prepares one piece, while at the other end, an advanced student selects challenging (Difficulty 5–6) repertoire for a 15- to 20-minute recital demonstrating sophisticated analytical and interpretive ability. With students' continuing involvement in ensemble music over a period of years, this progression of assessments can be motivating for students within the familiar ensemble process. The MCA sequence enables music teachers to document student growth in all these dimensions on a task. The rubric scoring devices are designed with a progression where "Exceeds Expectations" at one level reflects "Meets Expectations" at the next. This is an important feature allowing for students to progress, regardless of what "grade" they may be in. For example, a grade 9 student can be assessed as *meeting* the expectations of the novice level across several dimensions.

The performing MCA is grouped into three tasks/levels for ease of use: one for *Novice/Intermediate*, one for *Proficient*, and one for *Accomplished/ Advanced*. Regardless of skill level, the MCA addresses the same three process components. The first component, select, asks that students review and choose three contrasting pieces or sections of music and provide insight into their choices through a written worksheet that is evaluated by the teacher using a common scoring rubric. Selections can be, for the novice, lines from a method book, segments of ensemble music, or solo pieces. As students advance, it is anticipated that students will be approaching repertoire that is more technically and musically challenging (difficulty levels are suggested). Students are asked to identify these challenges in preparation for the next process component.

The second process component asks that students create a rehearsal plan for one of the selected pieces that involves analysis, interpretation, rehearsal, self-evaluation (and optional peer evaluation), and refinement. Each of these aspects is represented as a prompt on a written worksheet and is evaluated by the teacher using a scoring rubric. As students increase their knowledge of musical structure and the performing technique of their instrument or voice, it is anticipated that students at the more advanced levels will bring increasing depth and precision to their reflections (musical thinking). When the student believes that the selection is ready to present, he or she records a performance (this can be in class, in a formal recital, or individually recorded), and both teacher and student complete a performance evaluation rubric that focuses on the familiar criteria of tone, rhythm/pulse, pitch/intonation, and expression/interpretation. Within these common criteria, students can observe and receive feedback at appropriately more demanding performance expectations. It is important to recognize that specific skill development is only assessed in general terms. Music teachers continue to administer skill assessments appropriate for the means of performance.

ASSESSING COMPOSING AND IMPROVISING IN ENSEMBLES

Music educators who lead ensembles are typically quite skilled in evaluating the quality of musical performances and the corresponding levels of musical achievement. After all, they have had experience in doing these tasks, starting early in their own development. The subjective task of assessing students' creative processes and products—achievement in the realm of composing, arranging, and improvising—is less familiar for many ensemble directors. The National Music Standards, with their inclusion of composing, arranging, and improvising as basic content standards, raised music educators' awareness that knowledge and skills in these areas should be expected and that all students should know and be able to do them, in addition to performing (MENC, 1994). Assessment of the artistic process of creating (composing, arranging, and improvising) remains challenging for music educators using the Revised National Core Music Standards (National Association for Music Education [NAfME], 2014). Now music educators who teach in ensemble settings are asked not only to assess students' creative products, but to assess the processes of creating, arranging, and improvising as well.

Early research into the assessment of the creativity of high school musicians was completed by Gorder (1976) and Webster (1977). Both devised measures to assess the improvisational abilities of high school students. These contributions to the literature are important, not only because of their success in meeting statistical thresholds for measurement, but because they helped to solidify a framework for defining the basic components of the artistic process of creating. Hickey (1999), a leader in the area of composition assessment today, suggests that "Teachers need concrete criteria to aid them—and their students—in recognizing what is good or not so good about the compositions produced" (p. 27). Furthermore, she suggests that rubrics are an excellent way to provide this feedback to students, and that three general criteria for use in any composition assessment are aesthetic appeal, creativity, and craftsmanship.

ASSESSING THE PROCESS OF
CREATING IN AN ENSEMBLE SETTING

As with all MCA tasks, the MCA ensemble creating/improvising tasks are designed to promote musical literacy, defined as "the knowledge and understanding required to participate authentically in the music" (National Coalition for Core Arts Standards [NCCAS], 2013, p. 10). This process orientation fits nicely into the educational context espoused by the P21 (Partnership for 21st Century Skills, 2004) group and others that emphasized the development of creativity, communication, critical thinking, and collaboration.

The creating assessment tasks are grounded in the philosophical framework for creativity provided by Peter Webster, who defined creativity in music as "the engagement of the mind in the active, structured process of thinking in sound for the purpose of producing some product that is new for the creator" (2002, p. 26). His work was very much influenced by the work of Margery Vaughn (1977), who completed the first significant attempts to measure creative thinking in music between 1969 and 1976. Webster's revised "Model of Creating Thinking Process in Music" (p. 27) shows that creative thinking is "a dynamic process of alternation between divergent and convergent thinking, moving in stages over time, enabled by certain skills (both innate and learned), and by certain conditions, all resulting in a final product" (p. 26). Webster's model and the process components of the artistic process of creating in the music standards themselves form the framework for the MCA ensemble: creating assessment tasks. These tasks emphasize the importance of revision and reflection in order to realize a creative product—composed music scores/recorded performances or recorded improvisations.

There are two ensemble Model Cornerstone Assessments that focus on creating as an artistic process: (1) creating and (2) improvising. As Burnard (2000) points out, improvising (i.e., creating spontaneous, single-event performances) and composing (i.e., creating revised pieces), while distinguished as being oriented toward time, body, relations, and space, could be considered two sides of the same *creative coin*. Because of the close theoretical relationship between these two creative processes (seen particularly in the medium of jazz) and because of chapter space limitations, the description of the ensemble: creating MCAs has been limited to the presentation of the ensemble—creating MCA.

There are four assessment strategies in the ensemble: creating MCA, one for each of the basic components of the artistic process of creating—imagine, plan and make, evaluate and refine, and present. Each strategy is grounded in a framework that includes the enduring understanding statement and the essential question(s) that are articulated in the National Music Standards, and the strategies are designed to meet specific performance standards, as presented in the teacher scoring rubrics for each of the basic components. Each of the scoring rubrics provide *suggested* descriptions for evaluating student work related to the performance standard—emerging, approaches, meets, and exceeds expectations—for each achievement stage (*novice, intermediate, proficient, accomplished,* and *advanced*). Furthermore, each strategy contains essential information for the teacher to implement the strategy. This information includes (1) prerequisite skills and knowledge (for the strategy), (2) teacher preparation instructions, (3) assessment environment setup, and (4) assessment (responsibilities of the teacher). There are also *suggested* worksheets for student use for the first three assessment strategies. The remainder of this section briefly describes each of the four creating assessment strategies in terms of their framework (enduring understandings/essential question(s), the student worksheets, and the teacher scoring rubrics.

Strategy 1: Imagine. Mozart was reported to have been able to see the finished creative product as a whole in his mind, so that for him, the creative process involved merely writing down the parts, as if taking dictation! Few, if any, students will approach the creative process in this way. The imagine strategy is designed to help the students imagine (i.e., to *generate musical ideas for various purposes and contexts*). The essential understanding for students in the basic component of imagining is *The creative ideas, concepts, and feelings that influence musicians' work emerge from a variety of sources*, and the essential question is *How do musicians generate creative ideas?*

Through the imagine worksheets, students are invited to begin with something that is known to them, for example, a motif or a short phrase from one of the ensemble pieces that is appropriate to their performance medium. They are then to record the motif or phrase—first in its original form and then in its *reimagined form*. In order to assist students in how the motif/phrase might be reimagined, students are presented with a *compositional device menu* that includes suggestions for reimagining at the achievement level of the student (novice through advanced). Some of these compositional device suggestions include things such as incorporating silence and using dynamic contrasts for novice learners and incorporating variations (meter changes, syncopation) for advanced learners.

Students are further asked to explain their choice of compositional devices with the aid of question prompts that are appropriate to their achievement level and to submit this explanation, along with a recording of the reimagined musical motif/phrase, to the teacher. The teacher then assesses the students' level of achievement of the imagining process using the rubric (or a modified version) provided in the MCA.

Strategy 2: Plan and Make. Now the real work and fun begins. Students are taught to sketch a plan for their musical creation and to actually begin making a prototype. Again, the enduring standards statement, *Musicians' creative choices are influenced by their expertise, context, and expressive intent* and the essential question *How do musicians make creative decisions?* guides the design of this strategy.

Using the worksheets provided with this strategy, the students, working alone or with a peer, use a *measure organizer* (at the beginning levels) and some categorical prompts (at the advanced levels) to develop their creative ideas. Students are then asked to submit their worksheet, along with a recording or their notational work (iconic or traditional) to the teacher for assessment.

The rubric for assessing the students' level of achievement of the plan/make process allows the assessor to select from descriptions at each achievement level that describes ever-increasingly sophisticated levels of being able to master the plan/make component. For example, at the proficient level, a student who meets the criterion has developed a clear draft of two phrases from contrasting historic styles that demonstrates a "clear connection to the contrasting historical styles of the pieces [*sic* phrases]."

Strategy 3: Evaluate to Refine. The third basic component of the artistic process of creating involves evaluating and refining (i.e., the ability to reflect on the strengths and weaknesses of the composition and to make appropriate adjustments). For this assessment activity, it is suggested that the teacher place students in groups of four students to facilitate productive feedback. Furthermore, it is suggested that the students use the final composition rubric as the basis for a discussion of how the composition could be moved to a higher rubric standard.

There are two worksheets in this assessment strategy task: a peer assessment worksheet and an evaluate to refine worksheet. The peer assessment worksheets, completed by each individual student in the group, are to be returned to the composer/arranger after his or her composition has been discussed by the group. The individual composer/arranger then uses these comments as the basis for completing the evaluate to refine worksheet, which is then assessed by the teacher using the evaluate to refine scoring device.

Strategy 4: Present. There is relatively little detail provided in this final MCA assessment strategy because when the composition is presented/performed, this final component of the creating process is the most familiar to both students and teachers. Nevertheless, the essential question—*When is a creative work ready to share?*—seems particularly relevant because it is an area that is often difficult for a young musician/composer to master.

A final composition scoring device is provided for the teacher's use in assessing the student's final composition. This form could be used as presented or modified by the teacher to meet the particular needs and available resources of a particular learning setting.

ASSESSING RESPONDING IN AN ENSEMBLE SETTING

Assessment of student ability to respond to (select, analyze, interpret, evaluate) music is frequently neglected in ensemble settings. If included, it is often limited to evaluation of performance of concert music being prepared, which is a process component of performing. Ensemble directors report a lack of time, resources, training, and interests as the reasons for not teaching and assessing these skills (Holcomb, 2002). Holcomb, Kruse, and Minear (2011) investigated assessment practices of secondary vocal and instrumental ensemble directors ($n = 478$) in Michigan, Florida, and Texas. While 95% of directors reported regular assessment of music-reading skills, less than 46% of the directors reported to regular assessment of student understanding of how to analyze or evaluate music.

The artistic process of responding to music often begins with selection of music to experience. This is followed by an aural analysis of the music through which the listener attempts to understand what is happening in the music and interprets the artistic decisions made by the creator and/or performer. As a result of analysis and interpretation, the listener is then able to evaluate the quality of the music and its performance.

The responding core standards guide instruction toward assisting students to select, hear, and understand music. The performance standards are based on responding anchor standards that provide continuity across grade and experience levels for curriculum development, instruction, and assessment of responding to music.

RESPONDING MODEL CORNERSTONE ASSESSMENT FOR ENSEMBLES

Ensemble directors, or students, choose the responding MCA most appropriate for an ensemble or individual student's level of achievement or years of ensemble experience, ranging from novice to advanced and based on the difficulty performance standards reflected in each scoring device. Like the other Model Cornerstone Assessments, the responding MCA is designed so that it can be administered within one instructional sequence or unit, or teachers may choose to spread the component parts of one MCA across multiple units or projects or use it as an extension to the performing or creating MCA or to other aspects of the ensemble rehearsal. When implementing the responding MCA, students working individually or collaboratively select musical works to compare. A responding worksheet is provided to assist with this task. Students are asked to choose one or more musical works, depending on which of the five achievement levels is selected (novice, intermediate, or proficient select one work to analyze; accomplished, two works, and advanced, three works) from performing ensemble literature or music outside of the ensemble to study. After locating recorded performance examples of the literature selected and researching the composer and the cultural/historical context of the music, students compare the performances by analyzing expressive and interpretive qualities. They then complete the *responding worksheet* and submit it to the teacher, who assesses it using the provided *scoring devices* with four possible scoring levels: Level 4—*Exceeds Expectations*, Level 3—*Meets Expectations*, Level 2—*Approaches Expectations*, and Level 1—*Emerging*.

Enduring understandings and essential questions are provided for each anchor standard. Together, they provide ensemble directors and students with broad learning focus and promote critical thinking for process component of responding to music. Anchor standards for responding include (1) students choose music appropriate for specific purposes and contexts; (2) students analyze how the structure and context of varied musical works inform the response; (3) students support interpretations of musical works that reflect creators'/performers' expressive intent; and (4) students support evaluations of musical works and performances based on analysis, interpretation, and established criteria. Essential questions represent the important questions that are not easily answered when thinking about how one engages in the process components of responding to music. Enduring understandings communicate big-picture ideas, such as *Individuals' selection of musical works is influenced by their interests, experiences.* Ensemble performance standards were developed for each experience level, novice–advanced, and describe what students at each level should be able to do.

PILOT STUDIES AND CASE STUDIES

The ensemble: creating, performing, and responding MCAs were introduced to choral and instrumental educators through the NAfME website in

Table 6.1. Demographic Information for the Ensemble MCA Pilot Study

	<20%	21–40%	41–60%	62–80%	>81%	
Socioeconomic Status (SES) as defined by percentage of students receiving free or reduced-cost lunch.	27%	21%	31%	7%	14%	
District Type	Inner-City	Suburb	Small City	Small Town	Rural	
	10%	18%	26%	24%	22%	
Region	Eastern	North Central	Northwest	Southern	Southwest	Western
	45%	28%	8%	4%	9%	6%
Teaching Experience	1–10 yrs.	11–30 yrs.	>30 yrs.			
	34%	53%	12%			
Levels	Middle School	High School				
	60%	40%				

fall 2014, and a call for participation in field testing resulted in the collection of initial student work samples and detailed feedback from teachers on implementation and suggestions for improvement. A second and third round of piloting followed in winter 2015 and spring 2016. In fall 2016, research advisors (RAs) asked piloting teachers to upload student work to a data-collection website and participate in the scoring of their peers' students. In all of these field tests, these advisors sought representation from middle and high school band, orchestra, and choir teachers at all skill levels from the 57 classrooms involved (see Table 6.1).

WHAT WAS LEARNED FROM THE PILOT STUDY?

Did the MCAs Reflect Music Teachers' Expectations of Student Learning?

The ensemble performance (intermediate) and ensemble perform (proficient) MCAs demonstrated overall strong construct validity as demonstrated by the reasonable parameter separation for each of the considered parameters. The parameters considered were (a) student work, (b) scorers, (c) scoring type, and (d) criteria. Reasonable parameter separation indicates that one set of parameters (the performance achievement of student work, for example) can be estimated without any interference from any of the other parameters (the severity of the raters or difficulties of the criteria, for example). Results indicated that the rank ordering of criteria by difficulty (from most difficult to least difficult) was (1) selection of varied program, (2) awareness of technical challenges, (3) evaluate/refine, (4) interpretation, (5) expressive qualities, (6) analysis, (7) rehearsal plan, (8) rhythm/pulse accuracy, (9) tone production, (10) pitch/intonation accuracy, and (11) awareness of expressive qualities. For ensemble perform (proficient), results indicated that the rank ordering of criteria by difficulty (from most difficult to least difficult) was (1) analysis, (2) pitch/intonation accuracy, (3) evaluate/refine, (4) awareness of expressive qualities, (5) expressive qualities, (6) rehearsal plan, (7) awareness of technical challenges, (8) selection of varied program, (9) rhythm/pulse accuracy, (10) interpretation, and (11) tone production. All criteria were found to be appropriate and meaningful in their overall functioning within the context of measuring the *intermediate and proficient ensemble performance construct.*

In general, teachers participating in the pilot studies reported that the MCAs for ensembles were appropriate for a variety of student needs, accurately reflecting the content of the national standards. Their survey data showed that they believed that the performing MCAs could most easily fit into typical teaching plans for ensembles and that they reflect appropriate expectations of students. Responses of this nature were endorsed as *agree* or *strongly agree* by 80–90% of teachers piloting performing MCAs, regardless of level or context. Participants commented that the performing MCA was similar to projects that they already implement with students and could be helpful with regard to district-level assessment data requirements. Some even stated that the MCA could be a part of a required graduation portfolio. It appears that the MCA was viewed as a meaningful reflection of student achievement relative to authentic, standards-based performance tasks. While some participants questioned the process rather than product orientation of the standards and MCA, believing that they did not adequately reflect the development of specific performance skills, others commented that the performance skills were already part of their curriculum. Teachers continue to assess specific technical and performance skills appropriate for the means of performance. Although statistical analysis of teacher responses toward the creating and responding MCAs was not possible due to an insufficient number of participants, anecdotal feedback from participating teachers suggests that we can have some level of confidence in the MCAs as valid assessments in these areas.

To What Extent Can the MCAs Be Administered and Scored with Consistency across Settings?

For the fourth field test as part of the pilot study, participating teachers were asked to submit all student written and audio-visual performances and score the student work on a data-collection website. Participants were also asked to blind-score student work submitted by other pilot teachers in order to attain two and, in some cases, three scores for each piece of student work. This enabled researchers to determine an overall measure of scorer consistency and to provide a measure of scorer leniency/severity based specifically on whether teachers were scoring their own students' work or student work from another unidentified teacher. In general, it appeared that the rubric scales that accompany the process component tasks of the performing at the intermediate (137 student work samples) and proficient (84 student work samples) levels were able to reliably separate student work at various achievement levels, as intended, with reliability of separation statistics of .88 ($n = 6$) and .99 ($n = 3$) respectively. As expected, scorers varied in their relative leniency or severity in their rubric use; however, they also provided high-quality ratings within their own use of the scales (as evidenced by reasonable fit statistics and low standard of error for all but one rater). The MCAs are intended to be flexible in that teachers are free to adapt the procedures, worksheets, and scoring rubrics to suit the needs of their students; from this perspective, the rubrics as field-tested provide a valid and reliable starting point for such modification.

How Effectively Can the MCAs Identify Student Achievement?

We were able to analyze rubric scores assigned by participating teachers to their own students, as well as scores assigned to students of other participants. This data set permitted a deeper look at each rubric element (considered as an independent measurement scale of an underlying construct) and allowed us to specifically inquire as to the coherence of the scale and its interpretation to the scorers. Based on responses to the model generated, it became consistently clear that the scorers were inconsistent in their use of the third and fourth levels of the scales—those that defined *met criterion* and *exceeded criterion*. From a purely statistical and psychometric point of view, the distinctions described in the rubrics as piloted appear to be without a difference. From that vantage point, a teacher implementing these rubrics may wish to consider collapsing these two levels into a single *met* or *exceeded* cell.

However, retaining a four-level rubric throughout the ensemble MCAs may be justified on motivational grounds, as well as lending coherence to the MCAs if they are to be implemented multiple times over several years in an ensemble program. The first rationale is simple—it is important to be able to acknowledge a student whose efforts resulted in an achievement on any component that could be termed *higher than expected* or simply, *exceeded expectations*. This acknowledges a job well done, and could provide a stimulus for the student to attempt a more difficult task next time (for example, in the case of the ensemble: performing MCA, choosing to approach the proficient level next time, after having exceeded the expectations outlined in the novice or intermediate handbooks). RAs also feel that there is value in viewing the continuum of achievement across the levels of the ensemble: performing MCA as a whole, in that what is considered to meet the defined details of a higher level would clearly be seen to exceed the expectation at a level below it. This illustrates what is well known to all serious musicians: one is never done refining and improving one's skills and insights into musical performance and its preparation.

How Do Teachers Adapt the MCAs to Coincide with Current Practice?

After the first field test in 2014, many participants noted the need to revise the instructions and worksheets for the performing MCA to be more *student-friendly* in their vocabulary and age-appropriate as to developmental level. One participant commented on challenges experienced by students "at the extremes" of levels of skills and knowledge and believed that the assessment had the potential to overwhelm and defeat lower-achieving students. Many participants stated that the scope and time necessary to assess every student on all three artistic processes was simply too much, and that students were not used to doing so much writing in their performance-based ensemble classes. A common challenge was access to recording technology for the implementation of the MCA. Most teachers made a variety of modifications based on their own technological situations (for example, modifying the forms to be usable online or on laptops).

How Might Implementing the MCAs Affect the Educational Experiences of Music Students?

Based on survey responses and comments, teachers participating in the field studies were positive in their evaluation of the ensemble MCAs. One middle school choir teacher noted: "It is at once the most simple and most difficult teaching strategy I have ever tried, and possibly the most effective." Others repeated this sentiment, and many observed that students enjoyed and were engaged in working individually or in small groups on their personal musical goals. The use of cornerstone assessments modifies the ensemble paradigm from performance-driven to student-centered. Teachers become facilitators of musical independence through enhanced literacy rather than singularly focusing on skill development.

IMPLEMENTATION IN DIFFERENT REHEARSAL SETTINGS

The ensemble MCAs were used differently in a variety of classroom settings. In some cases, the MCAs were modified to adapt to teachers' philosophical frameworks for working in ensemble settings. In others, modifications occurred because of limitations in students' learning environment—scheduling, facilities, and available equipment. Some teachers found the ensemble MCAs to be ready to use with little modification. For the fourth field study, teachers were given a list of questions to ask students after they had completed the performing MCA. Seventh- and eighth-grade orchestra students responded positively in one classroom with comments such as "This made me feel more capable because I practice[d] more often [, which] made me feel more prepared"; "It made me feel like I can play without someone telling me the notes and rhythm"; and "Yes, it made me feel more capable to play in front of others because I did pretty good even though [my teacher] didn't help." Some students were less positive, noting "I find it better if I get more feedback from a teacher" and "I would like it if I could have played with my whole section," and one student was clear: "I found it unuseful for us, maybe it was good for teachers [but] not me." In the same class, another student noted, "The most meaningful part was being able to work by myself and notice how different I sound when not in a group." Considering student comments like these, it seems important that teachers consider how context and purpose of the MCA are presented to students. One might think that, overall, students will be interested in applying their skills to learn music they choose if they see it as an opportunity to demonstrate their learning and get useful feedback on their progress. If this progress is framed relative to the standards (or prior individual achievement) rather than relative to others, it may be expected that students will engage more positively with the assessment process (Pintrich, 2000).

Likewise, student responses to the creating: ensemble tasks were positive overall. For example, in one of the pilot seventh-grade band setting, students were asked to choose a motif from a piece of music they were rehearsing. The selected motif was entered into Noteflight, an online music-writing application that allows students to create, view, print, and hear the results of professional-quality music notation, where the teacher directed students to modify the motif by changing pitches, dynamics, rhythms, and/or articulations. The students were then placed in pairs to evaluate and refine their musical compositions, before performing them for the class.

Student response, as reported, was positive to this activity. One student responded: "It made me feel like I can make my own music, like my piece that I thought was pretty good." Another commented, "I feel more capable because I felt inspired when I created it. I was proud knowing I was the one who created it." There was some concern expressed by the students, however, that the worksheet for *plan and make* was confusing.

The teacher who modified the creating ensemble assessment task for her seventh-grade band commented that "the students were interacting and working together in ways I had never tried before. I especially enjoyed the peer feedback process; even though their written comments were not as detailed as I would like, the students responded well to this part of the project." She continued, "A negative aspect of the project was the amount of in-class time I used to implement the project and have students practice and record. If I were to repeat the project, I would give more thought as to how I would navigate this as part of my curriculum."

Overall, what was learned about the creating ensemble MCA from an implementation standpoint was that the teacher needs to spend some time teaching students how to work in groups and the dispositions necessary to be a meaningful collaborator, such as "accept criticism graciously and praise humbly." This preparation was written into the *teacher preparation* section of each assessment activity.

Furthermore, the differences in the students' learning environment—scheduling, facilities, and available equipment—make large differences in how the assessment activity can be implemented. For example, some teacher piloters did not have technological resources available for students to hear how their compositions sounded when various alterations were made, nor did they have appropriate acoustical space to accommodate the reproduction of students' compositional ideas.

LESSONS LEARNED: PREPARING AND SCORING

Although adjustments were made during the two years of piloting the MCA ensemble activities, teachers in the field continued to be frustrated with two primary aspects of the ensemble MCAs: (1) students' lack of verbal facility to describe and to justify changes as they were involved when working with the *analyze*, the *interpret*, and the *evaluate/refine* components and (2) the lack of meaningful distinctions as articulated in rubric descriptions at various levels. A brief discussion of each of these aspects follows.

Students were often frustrated with the *plan and make* and the *evaluate and refine* worksheets. Comments such as "The worksheets were confusing," or "I didn't understand what my partner was telling me needed to be improved" were common. Perhaps rather than open-ended worksheets, the designers need to consider rubrics written with common language descriptors (short and separated; smooth and connected) rather than musical descriptors (staccato; legato) to help students focus on various components of the compositional or performing artistic process. This may be an indication of an instructional need to enhance student knowledge and communication skills of musical vocabulary and the conceptual understandings of musical language.

In addition, teachers commented about the lack of meaningful distinctions as articulated in levels of the rubrics. For example, on completion of the novice level activity of the ensemble performing MCA, one teacher asked, "In 'Reasons for selecting pieces,' how does one define the terms *general* and *specific*? In other words, how does one decide when a student moves from level 2 to level 3?" Another example: "For Level 1, only 'Interpretation' was 'not evident' yet the other 3 criteria required a student to have something written to achieve Level 1. For example, I had a student write 'I don't know' for *Analysis* but could not give him a Level 1 for his response; however, had he written 'I don't know' for *Interpretation* I would have been able to grade him at a Level 1." The rubric descriptions were checked thoroughly for inconsistencies before being finalized for publication.

FUTURE USE OF THE MCAs IN ENSEMBLE SETTINGS

Early on in the project, a decision was made to abandon the idea of having separate MCAs for nontraditional ensembles (steel-drum bands, popular music ensembles, etc.) distinct from MCAs for traditional ensembles (wind bands, orchestras, choruses). Regardless of whether traditional notation or no notation is used in a particular ensemble setting, the ensemble MCAs are written in such a way that they could be used in both traditional and nontraditional ensemble settings. The pilot sites, several of which included nontraditional ensembles, had no trouble adapting the assessment activities, at least for the performing artistic process. A limitation of the study was that the creating, improvising, and responding MCA activities pilots were not completed in any nontraditional performance settings. There were no data to examine for the efficacy of the ensemble: creating and responding MCAs in these settings. As nontraditional ensembles become more commonplace in the music curriculum, it will be easier to gather this important data.

Furthermore, students are becoming accustomed to using laptops for writing about events and recording information so that asking them to complete the worksheets in paper/pencil formats did not seem to create a positive culture to motivate students to complete some of the assessment tasks. Perhaps setting up a Google Classroom or similar online student access portal would help facilitate the recording of feedback for future MCA projects that could be shared easily among students.

As a final point regarding recommendations for future use, it should be noted that increased professional development opportunities are necessary if the MCAs are to be used efficiently and effectively with performing ensembles. These professional development opportunities should include time for teachers to develop multiple ideas for how the MCAs can be adapted for various rehearsal settings and levels and how they might be used with specific literature studied/performed by an ensemble.

It would be particularly valuable to assemble a series of case studies of examples of teachers' adaptations and implementations of the MCAs in various scenarios. Given the variety of school schedules, facilities and equipment, and overall approach to the ensemble curriculum, such examples could allow for teachers in particular settings to find sources of ideas specific to their needs and goals. The development and pilot process described in this chapter demonstrated that if the key elements of the core arts standards and artistic processes are used as a guide, teachers are able to provide valuable individual feedback to students and gather useful assessment data that can be used for a variety of purposes.

REFERENCES

Burnard, P. (2000). Examining experiential differences between improvisation and composition in children's music-making. *British Journal of Music Education, 17*(3), 227–224.

Cooksey, J. M. (1977). A facet-factorial approach to rating high school choral music performance. *Journal of Research in Music Education, 25*(2), 100–114.

DeLuca, C., & Bolden, B. (2014). Music performance assessment: Exploring three approaches for quality rubric construction. *Music Educators Journal, 101*(1), 70–76. doi:10.1177/0027432114540336

Gorder, W. (1976). *An investigation of divergent production abilities as constructs of musical creativity* (Doctoral dissertation). University of Illinois, Champaign-Urbana.

Hewitt, M. P. (2013). Evaluation and self-evaluation of musical performance. Unpublished manuscript.

Hickey, M. (1999). Assessment rubrics for music composition. *Music Educators Journal 85*(4), 26–52. doi:10.2307/3399530

Holcomb, A. D. (2002). An investigation of the concurrent validity of the discipline-based professional standards for teachers of music in Connecticut. (Doctoral dissertation). The Hartt School, University of Hartford, CT.

Holcomb, A. D., Kruse, N. B., & Minear, C. A. (2011, March). *Beyond music ensemble performance assessment.* Paper presented at the 3rd International Symposium on Music Education, Bremen, Germany.

Music Educators National Conference (MENC). (1994). *National standards for arts education: What every young American should know and be able to do in the arts.* Reston, VA: Music Educators National Conference.

National Association for Music Education (NAfME). (2014). *2014 music standards: Ensemble standards.* Retrieved from http://www.nafme.org/my-classroom/standards/core-music-standards/

National Association for Music Education. (2015). *Student assessment using model cornerstone assessments—Artistic process: Creating ensembles.* Retrieved from http://www.nafme.org/my-classroom/standards/mcas-information-on-taking-part-in-the-field-testing/

National Coalition for Core Arts Standards (NCCAS). (2013). *National core arts standards: A conceptual framework for arts learning.* Retrieved from http://nccas.wikispaces.com/Conceptual+Framework

Partnership for 21st Century Skills. (2004). Retrieved from http://www.p21.org/index.php?option=com_content&task=view&id=254&Itemid=120

Pintrich, P. R. (2000). Multiple goals, multiple pathways: The role of goal orientation in learning and achievement. *Journal of Educational Psychology, 92*(3), 544–555. doi:10.1037/0022-0663.92.3.544

Project Zero, Harvard Graduate School of Education. (1992). *Arts PROPEL: A handbook for music.* Cambridge, MA: Author.

SmartMusic. (2017). Retrieved from https://www.smartmusic.com/

Vaughn, M. (1977). Musical creativity: Its cultivation and measurement. *Bulletin of the Council of Research in Music Education, 50*, 72–77.

Webster, P. (1977). *A factor of intellect approach to creative thinking in music.* (Doctoral dissertation). Eastman School of Music, University of Rochester, Rochester, NY.
Webster, P. (2002). Creative thinking in music: Advancing the model. In T. Sullivan & L. Willingham (Eds.), *Creativity and music education* (pp. 16–34). Toronto, Ontario: Britannia Printers.

SEVEN

Harmonizing Instruments
Model Cornerstone Assessment

Wendy K. Matthews and Daniel C. Johnson

Harmonizing instruments include pianos, keyboards, Autoharps, steel drums, ukuleles, guitars, and similar tonal accompanying instruments. As instruments capable of playing chords, they offer great potential for supporting a wide range of musical ideas in classrooms. In addition, they frequently connect with students from a variety of cultures, ethnicities, and musical interests, thereby creating multiple opportunities for students to explore music. Their history embraces both classical and popular music genres, with widespread use in cultures globally. In addition, they often play a pivotal role in social music-making customs such as worship services, campfire songs, house concerts, and historical ballads.

In the preK–12 music curriculum, such harmonizing instruments often play a role in the general or non-performance classroom, beginning in the late elementary grades (Campbell & Scott-Kassner, 2014). During that time, students have sufficient dexterity and typically understand music fundamentals enough to be successful with these instruments. Depending on the school setting, harmonizing instruments can also feature prominently in non-performance or general music classes in middle and high school programs. For the purposes of this chapter on creating the Model Cornerstone Assessment (MCA) using harmonizing instruments, the focus is on using these instruments at the middle and high school levels.

Music education researchers have not studied middle school students to the degree they have investigated students in elementary general music and high school performing ensembles (Ebie, 2002). Only a few researchers have focused on middle school general music education. These studies have found that as students mature, they tend to have a less positive attitude toward school music instruction, and those attitudes are influenced by specific classroom activities (Mizener, 1993). They enjoyed playing instruments, rhythm games, and dancing; however, their least favorite activities included listening to orchestral recordings and reading music (Nolin, 1973; Vander Ark, Nolin, & Newman, 1980).

In 2004, Wayman explored eighth-grade general music students' beliefs about music education and found that students believed music was a fun class, but not a serious academic subject. In the study, students also believed that some of their peers were more naturally talented than others, suggesting that music instruction was more important for those students, and that music was primarily a passive activity, intended for entertainment. In another study, Davis (2009) found that middle-school students in non-performance music classes had meaningful and multifaceted musical experiences. In particular, they reported four central themes: careers, academic music, social interactions, and self-esteem. Students reported that they want to be actively engaged in "hands-on" music making. Contrary to earlier studies (Nolin, 1973; Vander Ark, Nolin, & Newman, 1980), Davis did find that middle school students valued the academic side of music class, for example, learning to read music. Students also experienced music class as a place to belong and to interact with peers as well as a place to develop their confidence.

With a focus on keyboard instruments, Boswell (1991) found that middle school students preferred improvising and playing the instruments. Conversely, the teachers' preferences were for the activities that students ranked as most unfavorable: singing and describing music. Similarly, Wig and Boyle (1982) reported that music instruction using a keyboard laboratory was more effective in terms of students' musical achievement, positive attitudes toward music, and their own musical skills than was traditional general music instruction.

Harmonizing instruments provide a range of creative and musical applications. In addition to the possibilities for realizing single-line melodies, they offer the harmonic accompaniments and chord progressions. Therefore, because creating is one of the least-emphasized artistic processes in American music education (Fowler, 2001; Johnson & Fautley, 2017), the authors of this chapter chose to design an MCA focused on creating in the context of harmonizing instruments. As described below, the particular tasks engage students in harmonizing a given melody using an iterative four-step process that includes improvisation/composition, notation, peer feedback, and performance skills. During each of the corresponding, sequential assessment strategies, students generate and refine their ideas through individual presentations and self-evaluations. When incorporated into curriculum, this MCA provides a path to teaching harmonization and a means to generate both formative and summative feedback from both the teacher and the student's peers. The MCA should be used neither to evaluate teachers nor to represent a prescribed national curriculum.

The essential questions and enduring understandings found in the new National Standards of Music Education put forth by the National Association for Music Education parallel the four steps of this MCA: imagine, plan and make, evaluate and refine, and present. The essential questions (questions students ask themselves to guide their learning) are:

1. How do musicians generate creative ideas?
2. How do musicians make creative decisions?
3. How do musicians improve the quality of their creative work? and
4. When is creative work ready to share?

Through this MCA, students attain the corresponding enduring understandings.

HARMONIZING INSTRUMENT MODEL CORNERSTONE ASSESSMENT—PROFICIENT FOR CREATING

This harmonizing instrument MCA is designed to assess students' creating of a harmonization for a melody. While supporting the corresponding enduring understandings and essential questions, this MCA serves as a guide for teachers in addressing the following anchor standards:

1. Generate and conceptualize artistic ideas and work (MU:Cr1.1.H.Ia—Imagine).
2. Organize and develop artistic ideas and work (MU:Cr2.1.H.Ia—Plan and Make).
3. Refine and complete artistic work (MU:Cr3.2.H.Ia—Evaluate, Refine, and Present).

The target student population for this MCA is middle and high school students, typically in their first or second year of a harmonizing instrument class at the proficient performance level. The context of each classroom regulates how teachers authentically incorporate this MCA while teaching harmonization. As discussed further in this chapter, the participating teachers in the pilot study adapted the MCA tasks to their particular student needs in a variety of ways. This MCA begins with students harmonizing a recorded major (*do*-based) pentatonic folk song by aurally analyzing the melody. Then, using previously learned chords, students individually plan a harmonic accompaniment that best fits the melody. Students then notate the harmonization using an analysis system (e.g., chord letter names or functional harmony) and incorporate the harmonization through a chosen rhythmic accompanying pattern (e.g., strumming patterns, block chords, and arpeggios). Finally, students present their harmonization to a peer or group of peers for feedback, revise their harmonizations based on the feedback, and then present their final version to the class.

In this MCA, teachers are to choose any melody that is relevant to their setting. As an example, the MCA offers the melody used in this pilot study: "Rocky Mountain." The MCA includes several worksheets to aid students in identifying the key and potential corresponding chords, revising their chord choices, assisting in peer evaluation, and preparing their final presentation and self-assessment. Before beginning work with this MCA, the teacher must ensure that the students have a basic understanding of key, meter, consonance, dissonance, and non-harmonic tones. Students should also be able to spell basic harmonic chords in a major key and be able to play at least three of these chords proficiently.

While adhering to school policies and procedures, teachers participating in the pilot study used this MCA in piano, guitar, and steel-drum classes, supplemented the MCA with technology, and adapted it to special learners. During the teaching process, they determined the time frame for each assessment component to reflect the practicality, available class time, and necessary accommodations.

FOUR STEPS OF THE MCA

There are four steps to guiding and assessing student learning in this harmonizing instrument MCA. Each step corresponds to one of the components of the artistic process of creating.

Step 1

Students imagine ideas for harmonization and accompaniment patterns. Using a starting chord, students use three or more chords and patterns to imagine an accompaniment. The imagine worksheet guides the student in this process. This step aids students in exploring and developing different potential chords and the order of those chords. Prior to starting the MCA, the teacher needs to address the following prerequisite skills and knowledge included in their regular curriculum: chord structure, function and notation in major keys, and rhythmic accompanying patterns. As the teacher performs the melody (or plays a recorded voice or a soprano recorder), students listen for melodic direction/repetition, formal structure, underlying beat, and rhythmic content. They also audiate possible chords to fit the melody. As an example, the folk-song melody "Rocky Mountain" is provided (http://www.k-state.edu/musiceducation/mca/harmonizationcreateproficient

/Rocky_Mountain-sheet-music.pdf). Teachers can, however, use a different melodic selection that best fits their curriculum. Students share their ideas through discussion, with the teacher's guidance, to consider different options. Then, individually or in small groups, students use the imagination sheet to generate and describe the possible strumming patterns (such as fingerpicking) or keyboard patterns (such as block or broken chords) that best fit the melody. Students should harmonize the melody to support the phrase structure and use chords that provide clear cadences while avoiding dissonance.

Step 2

Students experiment, improvise, and organize their harmonization using the harmonization worksheet. The teacher returns the students' imagination sheets, collected during step 1. He or she also provides students with recorded audio files of the selected melody, using a range of tempi (using software such as Audacity) so that students can coordinate their performances with the melody. Students independently experiment, improvise, and organize their harmonization using the harmonization plan worksheet. On this worksheet, the students (a) analyze key, meter, and mode; (b) notate their planned harmonization; and (c) describe why their harmonic accompaniment best fits the melody. Then, students rehearse and record the draft versions of their harmonization. The teacher collects the recorded and notated versions of their harmonization and the harmonization plan worksheet. He or she then scores those items along with the plan and make scoring device to guide further refinement. This may take several days or weeks.

Step 3

Students notate their harmonization to perform it for a classmate or peer group for peer feedback using a peer evaluation form. Then, students refine their harmonization using the presentation preparation worksheet. The teacher returns the student harmonization drafts collected during step 2. The students independently perform their harmonization for a classmate or peer group. The other student(s) evaluates the harmonic, melodic, and rhythmic fit of the student-created accompaniment to the melody, and provides feedback using the peer responding form. The harmonizing student then interprets the feedback from their peer(s) and from the teacher to guide a final refinement of their evolving draft. Each student independently prepares a legible, final draft of the harmonization using the presentation preparation worksheet in preparation for a final presentation.

Step 4

The teacher distributes the self-evaluation form and students present their completed harmonization. The teacher scores the presentation preparation worksheet, self-evaluation, and recorded presentation. Students present their harmonization to the class. The presentation should include announcing the title of the harmonization, persuasively describing why they chose their chords and accompaniment pattern, and performing their harmonization with the recorded melody for the class. The teacher simultaneously (or at a later time) scores the harmonization and presentation with the harmonization presentation scoring device. Following the presentation, students complete the harmonization self-evaluation form. The teacher collects both the presentation preparation worksheet and self-evaluation forms. The teacher scores these using the harmonization presentation scoring device by comparing the final notated/recorded performance to the earlier notated/recorded draft.

THE PILOT STUDY

Participants and Their Contexts

Six music teachers volunteered to participate in the pilot testing of this MCA during spring and fall 2016. The teachers taught across the United States, with two each in the eastern, western, and north central regions. Their teaching experience ranged from a first-year teacher to a 27-year veteran with the average teaching experience of all the participants being 11.6 years. The teachers met with students between 2 and 5 days per week (an average 3.3 days) for 40- to 75-minute class periods. The harmonizing instruments were mostly guitar; however, one teacher taught a piano class, one taught piano and guitar classes, and one teacher taught steel drums (with harmonizations realized in groups). Although most of the participating teachers had limited experience administering prescribed assessments, several were very experienced with assessing their students.

The teachers pilot-tested this MCA in two phases. Phase 1 took place in spring of 2016 and included three teachers who provided invaluable data and feedback that led to revisions of the rubrics and worksheets. Then, in fall of 2016, three more teachers piloted the MCA during phase 2. These teachers and their students provided essential insights about how others could use this MCA and provided additional constructive feedback. Table 7.1 indicates the range of school contexts along with pseudonyms and descriptors of the participating teachers.[1]

Table 7.1. School Contexts for the Harmonizing Instrument MCA Pilot

Pseudonym	Harmonizing Instrument	Socioeconomic Status (Percentage of Students Receiving Free or Reduced-Cost Lunch)	School Setting
Adrienne	Steel Drums	20% to 39%	High school, metropolitan suburban, public magnet school
Bridget	Guitar and Keyboard, (used GarageBand as accommodation for students)	60% to 79%	Middle school and high school, small town, public school with special education classes.
Ethan	Guitar and Keyboard	40% to 59%	High school, midsize city, public school, with English as a Second Language learners
John	Guitar (supplemented with GarageBand)	Less than 20%	High school rural, private school
Susan	Keyboard	40% to 59%	High school metropolitan, inner-city, public school, with second language learners
Terry	Guitar	Less than 20%	Middle school, metropolitan suburban, private school

Findings

Four questions frame the findings for this chapter, drawing on pre- and post-questionnaire data provided by participating teachers and their students completing the pilot tests.

1. To what extent do teachers recognize that the MCAs relate to their expectations of student learning?

At the beginning of the project, several teachers expressed their eagerness to be part of the MCA pilot process. Prior to beginning the MCA, 27.3% of participating teachers felt very confident that they could prepare their students for the MCA, followed by 72.8% feeling mostly or somewhat confident. As to instruction, 72.7% of teachers stated that the MCA clearly or mostly contributed to their curriculum, and 72.8% said that the MCA would improve student learning in their classroom.

The teachers also provided comments that reinforced their expectations for student learning and supported these numerical ratings. For example, one pilot teacher stated,

> I have been wanting to try out the new standards and this is the perfect opportunity. My classes are primarily novice and intermediate, but they do perform each semester. Getting them to think through the details required in this assessment will better prepare them and give them a sounder learning experience.

Many teachers were drawn to the artistic process of creating. John expressed it this way: "My main interest is adding composition to my performing ensemble. I have a strong interest in adding the creating component. . . . This will work well." Notably, Bridget decided to participate in the pilot of this MCA because she had negative experiences with other assessments that did not accommodate learners with special needs. Motivated by the desire to include special needs students in developing the MCAs, she stated,

> In many assessments, such as the regionally created ones, my students' abilities and the adaptations that I can put in place for them are often overlooked. . . . I want students with special needs to have a voice and be considered when making these assessments and measures.

2. To what extent can the MCAs be administered and scored with consistency across settings?

The researchers revised the current rubrics based on psychometric data gathered from teachers using the rubrics to assess their own students as well as other teachers' students. In phase 1, the harmonizing instrument MCA demonstrated overall strong construct validity. Therefore, considering the parameters of student work, scorers, scoring type, and criteria, readers can directly and meaningfully interpret each facet as a unique characteristic of the MCA. In order of difficulty from most to least difficult, the criteria were (1) development of harmonization, (2) interpretation, (3) craftsmanship, (4) recognition of notation, (5) verbal presentation, (6) imagining, and (7) analysis. Although researchers determined that all criteria were appropriate and meaningful in their overall roles, some of the levels in each criterion may be adjusted. For further details about these analyses, see the tables in chapter 12 of this book.

In phase 2, the revised harmonizing instruments MCA also demonstrated overall strong construct validity. As before, readers can directly and meaningfully interpret each facet as a unique characteristic of the MCA, based on the parameters of student work, scorers, scoring type, and criteria. The resulting order of difficulty was similar to that for the original version of this MCA. In order from most to least difficult, they were (1) documentation of harmonization, (2) development of harmonization, (3) melodic interpretation, (4) feedback, (5) imagining, and (6) recognition of notation. The development of harmonization criterion did not have a measurable predictive effect; therefore, it did not contribute meaningful information toward the measurement of student work. All other criteria were appropriate and meaningful in the revised MCA. As with the original version of this MCA, the data indicated some adjustments for greater usability and meaningfulness. Tables displaying all psychometric analyses for the harmonizing (revised) MCA are displayed in chapter 12.

3. How effectively can the MCAs identify student achievement as intended by the performance standards?

In the post-MCA surveys, 60% of teachers indicated that the MCA reflected what students should learn; however, 36.4% of teachers needed to modify the MCA to fit their curriculum. All of the participants (100%) agreed that the MCA reflected the expectations of the standards. A majority of the teachers (75%) believed that the MCA clearly and concisely conveyed instruction sequence and other information necessary to prepare students for success. Similarly, all teachers (100%) stated that the objectives were clear, concise, and measurable and linked to the standards. One teacher specifically commented that this MCA enhanced student learning in her class.

Three-fourths (75%) of the teachers agreed that the MCA accurately measured student learning, and 50% indicated that it was developmentally appropriate for their students. All teachers (100%) said they were able to integrate the assessments into their instruction, and 75% indicated that the scoring rubrics were appropriate for the students. As one teacher stated, "The assessments were well sequenced and was a wonderful way to expose students to songwriting." On the other hand, 9.1% of teachers indicated that the scoring measures were inappropriate for students. One teacher clarified this by commenting, "Some students in my program are unable to write and read without support. This may make things like writing notation a moot point for some of them. However, many of them have experience writing and reading iconic notation."

Several teachers modified the MCA to fit their context. One teacher did not make too many changes, but implemented the assessment differently between guitar and piano classes. Several teachers commented that they had concerns about the example folk song, provided as part of the MCA. They adapted the song into different keys and several chose other songs for their students. In addition, two teachers allowed the students to choose their own songs. The ability to choose song literature to fit their students' needs was especially important to teachers who taught second language learners or special needs students. For example, Susan commented, "The song selected for harmonizing instruments is not culturally relevant to my students. Approximately 80% of my students are new to the country and have limited English skills."

The teachers unanimously agreed that the MCA had a positive influence on their teaching, and most teachers (75%) indicated that they plan to reuse the MCA in the future. Two teachers commented that the students enjoyed the MCA, and that they themselves valued using the MCA in their classroom. Following the MCA pilot testing, all teachers (100%) indicated that the MCA reflected the expectations of the standards and fit into their current teaching plans. As to the usefulness of the MCA, 75% of the teachers were able to integrate it into their instruction, 100% believed that it had a positive influence on their teaching, and 75% plan to use or adapt for use in the future. As participating teacher Ethan commented,

> I really enjoyed being able to assign the steps to creation of music; it was really rewarding to see kids actually making music versus just kind of playing it. . . . Having the kids actually write music [was] very powerful and rewarding and makes for a great long-term project.

Responses from students in the post-MCA surveys were revealing as well. Overall, the students' post-project comments indicated that they were very happy with the progression and pacing of the project. Students indicated that they could describe the concepts and skills they learned through the MCA, including developing their performance proficiency and successfully reading and writing music notation.

When asked if they would suggest any changes to the MCA, most students said they would change nothing. Some students, however, suggested that they have more time to work on the project. Others wanted the opportunity to write their own melodies for the harmonization or wanted the opportunity to choose from a selection of songs. In the classrooms where the teacher supplemented the project with GarageBand, the students indicated that the technology helped them select chords that were interesting and allowed them to choose chords freely beyond their performance skills. Students also wanted the opportunity to learn more chords and notes, not just the ones that were used to harmonize "Rocky Mountain."

The students' responses to the question "What was the most meaningful part of this project?" were overall very positive and revealed their interest in creating the harmonization. Their responses also reflected the confidence they gained through the project. For example, one student wrote, "To me the most meaningful part was deciding the chords. This is because choosing the chords gives you the power to decide how you want the part of the song to be." Another student responded, "I feel that I am now able to write chords for a melody in any song. Not only will I be able to write the chords, but it will sound good." A third student reported, "This helped me create music easily and I felt more capable to perform. Overall, it helped me with my guitar skills."

4. How do in-service teachers in various school settings practically adapt the MCAs to coincide with current practice?

As shown with more detail in the descriptive multiple-case study section that follows, teachers adapted this MCA in a variety of ways, including changing the key of the provided melody, choosing or having students choose new melodies, allowing students to use iconic notation, and using technology such as GarageBand to facilitate performance. As part of this study, the six participating teachers responded to an additional postsurvey designed specifically for harmonizing instruments. It posed a variety of questions describing their experience with the MCA to explore musical and pedagogical benefits, as well as the corresponding challenges. These data allowed for a descriptive multiple-case study, examining within and between cases as teachers reflected on the authentic contexts in which they used the MCA (Yin, 2003). This process illuminated the participants' stories and their experiences. To understand the teachers' views and classroom settings, the researchers independently analyzed the written responses and found three emergent themes. As described below, those themes illustrated how the participants used this MCA in their classrooms in terms of benefits, challenges, and adaptations.

BENEFITS

Participating teachers indicated that they found the content and supporting documentation of the MCA very helpful, especially with respect to breadth, depth, and flexibility in teaching students to harmonize. They reported that the MCA provided a good sequence of material and flow of the information in teaching and using chords to harmonize a melody. The teachers in phase 1 provided valuable feedback, which allowed the researchers to revise the worksheets. As a result, all the teachers from phase 2 commented that the student worksheets were neatly organized and easy to use. For example, Terry wrote,

> The MCA was very comprehensive. It highlighted very important concepts pertaining to music theory, and guitar performance and the assessments were extremely helpful, and provided a great opportunity for designing a

class. . . . The MCA helped give my class direction, and very detailed goals. Without it, I think it would have been a very different class, with more of an emphasis on guitar playing. However, I think it was extremely benefi- cial to include composition and music theory as it is a large component of guitar playing. Having limited experience in teaching guitar and theory, it was helpful to have a pre-determined end goal (scoring exceeds standard in presentation preparation).

Several teachers indicated that the MCA introduced them to new ways to teach and reteach concepts, which made the pedagogy more successful and interesting in general. They also felt it provided a good mix of writing and performing activities. As John reflected,

> [The MCA was] positive, useful, guided me towards teaching in a new way with nicely sequenced activities. I was able to adapt to my students' abili- ties and prior knowledge. . . . It was refreshing to teach a large unit like this without having to reinvent the wheel myself, create all my worksheets and rubrics, etc. I learned that my students were able to harmonize a melody and discovered how chord progressions work, and took pride in their discover- ies, with feedback from students that said they learned a lot about what chords to play, and with what strumming style.

In addition, the teachers appreciated the multiple opportunities stu- dents had to explore and discover harmonic choices. As Susan wrote,

> The opportunity to explore is always important. The opportunity to create their own chord progressions is also important. I allowed the students to choose their own chord progressions, not based on how the chord functions and what "should" come next, but what they perceived to sound right and what they liked . . . creating and exploring are so important for the devel- opment of students' confidence in making musical decisions. I hope these continue to be present in assessments.

Many teachers commented on the positive aspects of the peer assess- ment. In particular, participating teachers believed the peer feedback step required students to analyze the works of others, which in turn supported their own learning. The teachers indicated that the rubrics included in the MCA helped them assess students and provide quick feedback.

CHALLENGES

Technology was a challenge for two teachers who did not have record- ing equipment. As a result, their students were not able to record them- selves, nor was the teacher able to provide the recording of the melody. In retrospect, quite a few teachers felt that they would like to spread the instruction over a longer period of time or strategically schedule this MCA during a different time in the school year. Several stated that they need more time than they had budgeted. Most of the teachers had classes 8–16 weeks in duration. In those settings, teachers had a variety of levels with most teaching exploratory or beginner classes. Most teachers taught the mechanics of their instrument before attempting the MCA. Even so, many expressed struggles in not having enough time to teach chord structure, keys, and different types of accompaniments. Terry expressed her challenges in this way:

> I had a very hard time making my students feel capable to complete the MCA. We began class with them not being able to read notes, and ended with them being able to write chords. This was an insane amount of information to cram into an eight-week class. I was faced with a huge obstacle of making intermediate material accessible to beginner-level students.

Several teachers noted that there were numerous skills to learn, such as theory knowledge, accompaniment styles, cadences, and general performance techniques. Although these were all pertinent skills, a number of their students had trouble with the mechanics of playing and this negatively affected their motivation. A few teachers felt that there were quite a lot of concepts and skills required at one time, and that the MCA would be better suited to their more advanced classes. As Ethan wrote,

> [The MCA is] great, but a bit advanced for a zero-level guitar/piano class. My students were learning to read music and melodies and had a hard time moving to chords and their titles, as well as the theory behind them and the key signatures. [It] felt a bit hefty for the first semester of guitar, and for most of my students their first real music class.

A few teachers indicated that it was difficult to have students recognize the theory behind their work. In those instances, students struggled with understanding why certain chords sounded more appropriate than others. To illustrate these challenges, Adrienne wrote,

> My students had so little background knowledge that they had trouble differentiating consonance and dissonance. This became problematic when they were writing their accompaniments; they had to focus more on note to chord matching, rather than relying on their ears.

ADAPTATIONS

The researchers designed this MCA to provide the framework for teaching harmonization at the middle and high school levels. Because there were a variety of settings for harmonizing instruments, the researchers expected that teachers would adapt the MCA to provide the best fit for their teaching situations. In this study, participating teachers were very responsive to their students' needs and used a variety of adaptations to expedite the instructional process. For instance, some teachers found that students' understanding of music theory outpaced their performance skills. In those cases, the teachers accommodated the learning process with technology such as GarageBand. For example, John described how he used technology to facilitate student learning:

> [A challenge was] being able to play the chords, record themselves, and have it sound good. We modified the activities and removed the performance part in some of the assessments, and focused on the theory. I used iPad GarageBand with SmartInstruments with my students so they could each create a harmony track for the melody. I gave them a pre-made session with the melody programmed in, and they could change the tempo, choose an "autoplay" strum pattern and just press on the correct chords at the correct time and hear what their harmonization sounded like. For my high school beginning guitar class, I changed the key of "Rocky Mountain" to G major so we could be comfortable with the diatonic chords. . . . I recorded the melody into GarageBand for my students. . . . My students have assigned iPads so we used GarageBand on the iPad for the imagine worksheet stage. . . . I gave them the melody on Track 1, and they experimented with the Smart Guitar (which automatically plays chords and strumming patterns) until they found a series of chords which sounded good to them. I found this to be a great resource for this work. My students were not proficient playing the chords on a guitar at the beginning of the project. So, the iPad allowed for immediate feedback for the harmonization.

Besides using GarageBand, several other adaptations included allowing students to choose their own songs to harmonize, playing the melody for the students while they performed the chords, and allowing students to use iconic notation. Allowing students to choose their own songs was also a prevalent adaptation in classes with special learners and with first-generation Americans. Those students' song choices included "This Land Is Your Land" and songs from their native lands, respectively. Several teachers who had second language learners found that the students struggled with words such as "tonic" and "dominant."

Adapting tasks to fit a school context is an important construct of the MCAs, in particular for students to demonstrate authentic artistic processes while reflecting their actual experiences. For example, Bridget explains her adaptations for her special education class:

> I needed to adapt the worksheets, rubric language and the final performance possibilities for my students. I teach special education so although this was

a middle school class, many of the students are functioning at a lower elementary developmental level. . . . I played the options measure-by-measure for some students so they could select chords that they felt sounded best. This allowed them to use their ears to select what they felt was the best answer . . . many students are unable to detect the difference in sound between major and minor and other students prefer the dissonance of minor chords with a major melody. In order to take out the dexterity requirement to play a piano or guitar accompaniment (which students learned for other songs in my class) and just focus on the design of what they created, I allowed them to use an iPad application (GarageBand) so that they could focus on playing the chord letter and the pattern they selected. This also allowed me to sing the melody into the application and AirDrop it to all of the students. Most of my students are males and they do not feel that singing is cool or for many they are unable to match pitch. My curriculum has a large emphasis on the modern band pedagogy . . . and super exciting and enticing for my students. . . . I realized when administering the MCA that the focus was less on performing and more on creating, which is lovely. I would like the ability to choose a popular song or melody for them to harmonize, not just a folk song. This would highly increase my ability for student participation in general, as well as pull in their prior knowledge and most likely give me more success (and them) in singing the melody and matching pitch. Most of my students were annoyed with the need for the melody to be a folk song and not a popular song, a tune in which they were interested.

CONCLUSION

As shown by the responses to the four research questions, this MCA satisfied its purposes and successfully supported student learning. Students responded very well to the MCA and were excited to begin to explore the essential questions reflecting how musicians generate creative ideas, make decisions about and refine their work, and prepare to share their work. Teachers' responses from the pilot tests were also positive. The setting for each teacher's report served as a case study and included several contextual factors. Circumstances such as variable contact time with the students played a part. In addition, these harmonizing instrument classes incorporated students with a wide range of prior experience while often providing the first organized music instruction after general music class. The teachers involved in the pilot were notably creative and able to use their particular resources to adapt the MCA to fit their students in a variety of ways.

Suggestions for future revisions of this MCA include building a more basic version that assumes no knowledge of musical terms, and includes a variety of difficulty levels in song choice. Another enhancement would be to provide MIDI files of the given songs choices, so that teachers could adapt the key and tempo to address students' skill and experience levels. One teacher suggested adding a pre-assessment of students' skills to help document how students have grown through the process. Other suggestions include allowing students to use their own harmonies based on sounds they liked, so that they are able to reflect and refine their decisions without adhering to traditional Western standards.

This harmonizing instrument MCA has several implications for music education, in part because a single musician can create multiple musical lines in this musical context. Guitar, keyboard, steel drum, and other classes offer engaging instruction leading to aesthetic experiences while exploring a range of creative musical possibilities. With appropriate professional development and support, music teachers can readily adapt harmonizing instruments instruction for special learners, English language learners, and students with limited musical experiences. Such pedagogy widens the opportunity and access for musical expression. As described in this chapter, this MCA supports teachers in their classrooms through a practical, standards-based instructional framework, introducing students to the creative process of making music with harmonizing instruments.

NOTE

1. Participant comments without pseudonyms indicate that the sources were general pre- and post-MCA questionnaires given to all participating teachers, whereas those with pseudonyms indicate that the source was a supplementary post-MCA questionnaire with open-ended responses, specifically designed for harmonizing instruments.

REFERENCES

Boswell, J. (1991). Comparisons of attitudinal assessments in middle and junior high school general music. *Bulletin of the Council for Research in Music Education, 108*, 49–57.

Campbell, P. S., & Scott-Kassner, C. (2014). *Music in childhood*. Stamford, CT: Schirmer.

Davis, V. W. (2009). The meaning of music education to middle school general music students. *Bulletin of the Council for Research in Music Education, 179*, 61–77.

Ebie, B. D. (2002). Characteristics of 50 years of research samples found in the *Journal of Research in Music Education*, 1953–2002. *Journal of Research in Music Education, 50*(4), 280–291. doi:10.2307/3345355

Fowler, C. B. (2001). *Strong arts, strong schools: The promising potential and short-sighted disregard of the arts in American schooling*. New York: Oxford University Press.

Johnson, D. C., & Fautley, M. (2017). Assessment of whole-class instrumental music learning in England and the United States of America: An international comparative study. *Education 3-13: International Journal of Primary, Elementary and Early Years Education, 45*(6), 1–9. doi:http://dx.doi.org/10.1080/03004279 .2017.1347131

Mizener, C. P. (1993). Attitudes of children toward singing and choir participation and assessed singing skill. *Journal of Research in Music Education, 41*(3), 233–245. doi:10.2307/3345327

Nolin, W. H. (1973). Attitudinal growth patterns toward elementary school music experiences. *Journal of Research in Music Education, 21*(2), 123–134. doi:10.2307/3344588

Vander Ark, S., Nolin, W., & Newman, I. (1980). Relationships between musical attitudes, self-esteem, social status, and grade level of elementary children. *Bulletin of the Council for Research in Music Education, 62,* 31–41.

Wayman, V. (2004). An exploratory investigation of three middle school general music students' beliefs about music education. *Bulletin of the Council for Research in Music Education, 160,* 26–37.

Wig, J., & Boyle, J. (1982). The effect of keyboard learning experiences on middle school general music students' music achievement and attitudes. *Journal of Research in Music Education, 30*(3), 163–172.

Yin, R. K. (2003). *Case study research: Design and methods.* Thousand Oaks, CA: SAGE Publications.

EIGHT

Composition/Theory Model Cornerstone Assessments

Patricia Riley

This chapter describes the three music composition/theory Model Cornerstone Assessments (MCAs), provides a summary of literature supporting assessment of student learning in the artistic process of creating, and reports on the MCA pilot project. It is intended to help music teachers understand and use these MCAs.

ASSESSING THE CREATING PROCESS IN MUSIC

Measuring achievement in creative processes might be a challenge, but it certainly is possible (Hickey & Webster, 2001). Deutsch writes, "the purpose of assessment in composition is to enable students to better achieve their aesthetic goals. Composition teachers must continually seek to understand their students' expressive intentions in order to provide instruction that makes this possible" (2016, pp. 53–54.) He recommends embedding assessment throughout the entire creating process.

> Assessment in the music composition program is formative. It helps the student and the teacher to form an opinion of what has been accomplished thus far and points to possible next steps. The primary purposes of assessment are to improve learning and determine progress. Assessment can also help determine the appropriateness and effectiveness of instruction. (Kaschub & Smith, 2009, p. 89)

Additionally, Hickey (2012) writes,

> Assessment comes in many forms and can aid in the learning process. It can be a nod of approval, a scathing critique, honest feedback, and evaluative mark such as a grade or a simple reward for a job well done. Whatever form we use, it must be used carefully because of the subjective and personal nature of music composition. (2012, p. 26)

Lierse (2012) recommends presenting tasks in novel ways so that students have something new to learn. She writes that students will find this enticing and exciting. Lierse suggests varying styles, forms, and combinations of sounds. In addition, Hickey recommends aligning assessment of tasks with task purposes. "If creative thinking is the main goal, then assessment should be flexible and process-oriented and the task holistic and authentic" (2013, p. 48). She suggests mixing up tasks and assessment types and recommends not assessing all compositions or assigning single-answer tasks.

Furthermore, Hickey espouses rubrics as an effective assessment tool. She states: "rubrics make evaluations concrete and objective, while providing students with detailed feedback and the skills to become sensitive music critics" (1999, p. 26).

Hickey and Webster (1995) examined the use of rating scales in the assessment of children's music compositions. They sought to compare rating scales with explicit (details expressed clearly and obviously, leaving no doubt as to intended meaning) and implicit design (not clearly and obviously stated; meaning is implied), and those rating specific and global aspects of "craftsmanship (technical skill), originality/creativity (imaginativeness), and aesthetic value (feelingful musical experience) of the children's compositions" (p. 29). Among their findings was that interjudge reliability was relatively high for both explicit and implicit designs, but that the implicit design tended to be higher; that explicit, specific designs related better to craftsmanship, and that implicit, global designs related better to originality/creativity and aesthetic value. They concluded that when designing rating scales to assess children's music compositions, it is important to keep in mind which aspects of the composition are being assessed (craftsmanship, originality/creativity, or aesthetic value), and design the implicit versus explicit and specific versus global aspects of the scales accordingly.

Hickey (2001) studied the creativity rating scale developed by Amabile in 1982, and asked who can most expertly and reliably assess children's music compositions: music teachers, composers, music theorists, seventh-grade children, or second-grade children. She found significant correlations between music teachers and theorists, and between seventh- and second-grade children; but only a moderate to low correlation between music teachers/theorists and children. A subgroup of general/choral music teachers had the highest rate of correlation with children. Hickey concluded that "it seems that the best 'experts,' or at least the most reliable judges, may be the very music teachers who teach the children" (p. 239).

Priest (2001) researched the extent to which assessment of creativity and craftsmanship in music compositions of others affects the level of creativity in students' own music compositions, finding that "teachers interested in fostering compositional creativity should help students become more aware of the relationship between temporal qualities inherent in musical composition and their relationship to global attributes" (p. 256). Similarly, Freed-Garrod (1999) investigated effects of children assessing their peers' and their own music compositions and found in part that the children's understanding of music concepts increased after composing and assessing their own and peers' music compositions.

Finally, Leung, Wan, and Lee (2009) studied assessing music compositions of undergraduate students to identify how student learning can be enhanced. They concluded that "both macro and micro aspects of assessing composition should be valued, and genuine feedback is effective in encouraging and sustaining students' interest in composing music" (p. 265). Student experience in creating music with feedback on all components of the process is a valuable component of student learning.

THE MCA ASSESSMENT ADDRESSING THE PROCESSES OF CREATING, PERFORMING, AND RESPONDING

The three composition/theory MCAs combine creating, performing, and responding into a singular task for each of three levels—proficient, accomplished, advanced. The composition/theory MCAs ask students to create a music composition, perform their own or a classmate's composition, and respond to classmates' creative work. In this way, they are different from the other MCAs.

The Composition/Theory MCA at the Proficient Level

The task for the proficient MCA asks students to create a composition to be considered for use as a jingle advertising a new smartphone. For this MCA, the compositions are through-composed and demonstrate how tempo, rhythm, dynamics, and timbre relate to the new phone. Students select their own or a classmate's jingle to perform, and each student responds to a classmate's jingle. The term *jingle* is used loosely in this context, because the composition might have words, or it might simply be a catchy instrumental piece.

The performance standards for each process-component in the proficient MCA, and the order in which they will be encountered are:

- Create/Imagine: Describe how sounds and short musical ideas can be used to represent personal experiences, moods, visual images, and/or story lines.
- Create/Plan and Make: Assemble and organize sounds or short musical ideas to create initial expressions of selected experiences, moods, images, or story lines.

- Create/Plan and Make: Identify and describe the development of sounds or short musical ideas in drafts of music within simple forms (such as one-part, cyclical, or binary).
- Perform/Analyze: Analyze how the elements of music (including form) of selected works relate to style and mood, and explain the implications for rehearsal or performance.
- Create/Evaluate and Refine: Identify, describe, and apply teacher-provided criteria to assess and refine the technical and expressive aspects of evolving drafts leading to final versions.
- Perform/Interpret: Develop interpretations of works based on an understanding of the use of elements of music, style, and mood, explaining how the interpretive choices reflect the creators' intent.
- Perform/Rehearse, Evaluate, and Refine: Create rehearsal plans for works, identifying repetition and variation within the form.
- Perform/Rehearse, Evaluate, and Refine: Identify and implement strategies for improving the technical and expressive aspects of multiple works.
- Create/Present: Share music through the use of notation, performance, or technology, and demonstrate how the elements of music have been used to realize expressive intent.
- Create/Present: Describe the given context and performance medium for presenting personal works, and how they influence the final composition and presentation.
- Perform/Present: Share live or recorded performances of works (both personal and others'), and explain how the elements of music are used to convey intent.
- Perform/Present: Identify how compositions are appropriate for an audience or context and how this will shape future compositions.
- Perform/Select: Identify and select specific excerpts, passages, or sections in musical works that express a personal experience, mood, visual image, or story line in simple form (such as one-part, cyclical, binary).
- Respond/Select: Apply teacher-provided criteria to select music that expresses a personal experience, mood, visual image, or story line in simple form (such as one-part, cyclical, binary), and describe the choices as models for composition.
- Respond/Analyze: Analyze aurally the elements of music (including form) of musical works, relating them to style, mood, and context, and describe how the analysis provides models for personal growth as composer, performer, and/or listener.
- Respond/Interpret: Develop and explain interpretations of varied works, demonstrating an understanding of the composers' intent by citing technical and expressive aspects and the style/genre of each work.

- Respond/Evaluate: Describe the effectiveness of the technical and expressive aspects of selected music and performances, demonstrating understanding of fundamentals of music theory.

The Composition/Theory MCA at the Accomplished Level

In the accomplished MCA, students create compositions to be considered for use as a theme song in a video documentary. The compositions consist of at least three related instrumental layers (including one percussion layer), and emphasize at least three of the following musical elements to represent the documentary's topic: beat, rhythm, pitch, melody, harmony, tone color, texture, form, tempo, dynamics, and/or articulation. Students then select their own or a classmate's composition to perform, and respond to a classmate's composition.

For each process component, the performance standards in the accomplished MCA and the order in which students will encounter these are:

- Create/Imagine: Describe and demonstrate how sounds and musical ideas can be used to represent sonic events, memories, visual images, concepts, texts, or story lines.
- Create/Plan and Make: Assemble and organize multiple sounds or musical ideas to create initial expressive statements of selected sonic events, memories, images, concepts, texts, or story lines.
- Create/Plan and Make: Describe and explain the development of sounds and musical ideas in drafts of music within a variety of simple or moderately complex forms (such as binary, rondo, or ternary).
- Perform/Analyze: Analyze how the elements of music (including form) of selected works relate to the style, function, and context, and explain the implications for rehearsal and performance.
- Create/Evaluate and Refine: Identify, describe, and apply selected teacher-provided or personally developed criteria to assess and refine the technical and expressive aspects of evolving drafts leading to final versions.
- Perform/Interpret: Develop interpretations of works based on an understanding of the use of elements of music, style, mood, function, and context, explaining and supporting how the interpretive choices reflect the creators' intent.
- Perform/Rehearse, Evaluate, and Refine: Create rehearsal plans for works, identifying the form, repetition and variation within the form, and the style and historical or cultural context of the work.
- Perform/Rehearse, Evaluate, and Refine: Identify and implement strategies for improving the technical and expressive aspects of varied works.

- Create/Present: Share music through the use of notation, solo or group performance, or technology, and demonstrate and describe how the elements of music and compositional techniques have been used to realize expressive intent.
- Create/Present: Describe the selected contexts and performance media for presenting personal works, and explain why they successfully impact the final composition and presentation.
- Perform/Present: Share live or recorded performances of works (both personal and others'), and explain how the elements of music and compositional techniques are used to convey intent.
- Perform/Present: Explain how compositions are appropriate for both audience and context and how this will shape future compositions.
- Perform/Select: Identify and select specific excerpts, passages, sections, or movements in musical works that express personal experiences, moods, visual images, concepts, texts, or story lines in simple form (such as binary, ternary, rondo) or moderately complex forms.
- Respond/Select: Apply teacher-provided or personally developed criteria to select music that expresses personal experiences and interests, moods, visual images, concepts, texts, or story lines in simple or moderately complex form, and describe and defend the choices as models for composition.
- Respond/Analyze: Aurally and/or by reading these scores of musical works, analyze the elements of music (including form), compositional techniques, and procedures, relating them to style, mood, and context, and explain how the analysis provides models for personal growth as composer, performer, and/or listener.
- Respond/Interpret: Develop and support interpretations of varied works, demonstrating an understanding of the composers' intent by citing the use of elements of music (including form), compositional techniques, and the style/genre and context of each work.
- Respond/Evaluate: Explain the effectiveness of the technical and expressive aspects of selected music and performances, demonstrating understanding of music theory and compositional techniques and procedures.

The Composition/Theory MCA at the Advanced Level

The task for the advanced MCA guides the students to create compositions to be considered for use as a theme and variations for a prime-time television show about sibling relationships. The compositions consist of a theme and three variations, in which one or more musical element (rhythm, meter, tempo, melody, dynamics, articulation, and/or phrasing) is used differently from the theme in each variation to affect the mood or style. As with the other composition/theory MCAs, the students then select their own or a classmate's composition to perform, and respond to a classmate's composition.

The performance standards for each process component in the advanced MCA and the order in which they will be encountered are:

- Create/Imagine: Describe and demonstrate multiple ways in which sounds and musical ideas can be used to represent extended sonic experiences or abstract ideas.
- Create/Plan and Make: Assemble and organize multiple sounds or extended musical ideas to create initial expressive statements of selected extended sonic experiences or abstract ideas.
- Create/Plan and Make: Analyze and demonstrate the development of sounds and extended musical ideas in drafts of music within a variety of moderately complex or complex forms.
- Perform/Analyze: Analyze how the elements of music (including form) and compositional techniques of selected works relate to the style, function, and context and explain and support the analysis and its implications for rehearsal and performance.
- Create/Evaluate and Refine: Research, identify, explain, and apply personally developed criteria to assess and refine the technical and expressive aspects of evolving drafts leading to final versions.
- Perform/Interpret: Develop interpretations of works based on an understanding of the use of elements of music (including form), compositional techniques, style, function, and context, explaining and justifying how the interpretive choices reflect the creators' intent.
- Perform/Rehearse, Evaluate, and Refine: Create rehearsal plans for works, identifying the form, repetition and variation within the form, compositional techniques, and the style and historical or cultural context of the work.
- Perform/Rehearse, Evaluate, and Refine: Identify, compare, and implement strategies for improving the technical and expressive aspects of multiple contrasting works.
- Create/Present: Share music through the use of notation, solo or group performance, or technology, and demonstrate and explain how the elements of music, compositional techniques, and processes have been used to realize expressive intent.
- Create/Present: Describe a variety of possible contexts and media for presenting personal works, and explain and compare how each could impact the success of the final composition and presentation.

- Perform/Present: Share live or recorded performances of works (both personal and others'), and explain and/or demonstrate understanding of how the expressive intent of the music is conveyed.
- Perform/Present: Explain how compositions are appropriate for a variety of audiences and contexts and how this will shape future compositions.
- Perform/Select: Identify and select specific sections, movements, or entire works that express personal experiences and interests, moods, visual images, concepts, texts, or story lines in moderately complex or complex form.
- Respond/Select: Apply researched or personally developed criteria to select music that expresses personal experiences and interests, visual images, concepts, texts, or story lines in moderately complex or complex form, and describe and justify the choices as models for composition.
- Respond/Analyze: Aurally and/or by reading these scores of musical works, analyze the elements of music (including form), compositional techniques, and procedures, relating them to aesthetic effectiveness, style, mood, and context, and explain how the analysis provides models for personal growth as composer, performer, and/ or listener.
- Respond/Interpret: Develop, justify, and defend interpretations of varied works, demonstrating an understanding of the composers' intent by citing the use of elements of music (including form), compositional techniques, and the style/genre and context of each work.
- Respond/Evaluate: Explain the effectiveness of the technical and expressive aspects of selected music and performances, demonstrating understanding of theoretical concepts and complex compositional techniques and procedures.

Each of these assessment tasks is to be incorporated into classroom instruction and used as is or adapted as desired for each teacher's particular students and teaching situation. The tasks include a variety of student worksheets and scoring-device rubrics to address each process component. The process components are sometimes addressed separately, and other times in combination. In order for students to complete the tasks, teachers provide printed task instructions, accompanying worksheets (sometimes called forms, and downloadable in editable form), pencils and erasers, a variety of instruments (e.g., guitars, piano/keyboard, band or orchestral instruments, barred classroom instruments, electronic instruments, computer or tablets, etc.), rehearsal spaces, and a digital audio recording device. The intent of the MCAs is for teachers to better understand the level of their students' knowledge, skills, and understanding in each of music's three artistic processes: creating, performing, and responding.

WHAT WAS LEARNED FROM THE PILOT STUDY

In the fall 2016 pilot project for the composition/theory MCA, three schools completed the project (one each from Connecticut, New York, and Vermont). Prior to the fall 2016 pilot project, four other schools completed the project and provided comments about the MCA with their students' reactions (one each from Connecticut and Wisconsin, and two from New York). Student work from the prepilot is not included in the data analysis, as the purpose was for task and rubric development. All schools piloted the proficient MCA. Schools were of various sizes and demographics, and teachers had a wide range of teaching experience. Interactions with the teachers occurred primarily via e-mail and included pilot protocol, necessary materials, and answers to questions and concerns. The following findings are not in the form of generalizable statistical results, but are descriptive and informative. Data were gleaned from e-mail correspondences, teacher pre- and postpilot survey responses, and student responses to the pilot project questionnaire. Data were analyzed via content analysis, guided by the Patton (2002) model.

Findings

Teachers in all three of the fall 2016 pilot schools reported that they felt confident they would be able to prepare their students for the MCA. Equally important is that they believed that the MCA is a positive contribution to their curriculum and improves student learning because of the observed engagement when administered in their classroom. One teacher stated,

> The students enjoyed the wide variety of compositions that were presented, often commenting on how they could combine, change or alter each others' to make them even better. The collaboration and free flow of ideas was tremendous and most of the process kept all students engaged at all times. A solid MCA has been established.

In addition, one teacher specifically commented that the performance task clearly represents the new standards and was appropriate for his class: "The materials were excellent, and I will be using them in the future."

Teachers indicated that the MCA reflects what they feel their students should learn and accurately measures the intended student learning. Through discussion it was clear that the pilot teachers felt the objectives are clear and measurable and linked to the performance standards. They felt that the scoring on the assessment rubrics was appropriate for their students and most expressed that they will use or adapt the MCA in the future. Because they felt the assessment task was developmentally appropriate, they appeared able to integrate the task into their instruction:

> Preparing students for this project was really exciting. I approached it using a business model, creating a "team" of composers writing and utilizing the tasks of the MCA and then reporting to the CEO of the company (teacher) as the process went along. We held team meetings for each step of the MCA and brainstorming sessions to stimulate ideas before working on the project. Overall, this process went pretty smoothly, and I am sure it will only yield a better process as the unit/project progresses in future years.

The assessment approach made it possible to address varied student needs. Their survey responses suggest that the assessment is free of bias (e.g., gender, ethnicity, race, socioeconomic), and that it allows for inclusion for all learners. The cross-curricular aspect of the MCA allowed for flexibility due to the student independence and ownership of the learning experience, as this teacher shares:

> Students enjoyed being able to pursue their own ideas and share them with others as the process went along. My administrator witnessed the process as well, and commented on the ability to teach this in a cross-curricular fashion with other departments in the future.

In discussion following the pilot project, teacher reflection exposed additional insights into the proficient MCA and its relevance in their classroom: "The task appeared to be perceived by the students as a real-world application of composing making the smartphone jingle an authentic task for assessment." Student experience with a task that seemed authentic in their classroom was also reflected in their responses to the postpilot project questionnaire, as stated by one of the students: "I created a jingle for a new product—this is how I would compose in a real-world situation." The following is a collection of thoughts from student responses describing their own experience with the proficient MCA:

> I completed a series of steps to generate ideas about how I could capture in music the qualities of the new product. This would hopefully make an audience interested in the product. . . . I used my musical skills to compose lyrics, rhythms, and pitches in a jingle for a new product. I liked using my creativity to explore ways to sell this product. I also liked collaborating with my peers in the steps. . . . I learned how to plan a small composition and carry it through to the production.

In the student response survey, students were given an opportunity to discuss how the projects helped them gain confidence in any of the three artistic processes of creating, performing, or responding to music. Many students shared their impressions of rehearsing and revising their compositions:

> After creating the piece, the rehearsing was new to me, so I learned how to revise my composition over time. . . . It was good for me to have several steps through which to develop my composition to a finished product. . . . Rehearsing the piece with my peers and rewriting parts so to make them sound better was one of the most meaningful things that I learned through the assessment.

It was clear through student responses that interaction with each other was an important component of the learning process, thus impacting how they demonstrated learning throughout the processes:

> We did a lot of discussing about our jingles and helped each other through the analysis. . . . For me the individual peer feedback was good. I enjoyed working with my peers to perform the piece and improve it from peer feedback; however, a class discussion in which each student presented their score was even more helpful.

In assessment, working individually is often the expectation, but when the process being assessed is applying theoretical knowledge through composing, interaction seems to be more than an instructional process. It enables students to fully demonstrate their learning and is essential as the students move through the process of composing. Said one student:

> I learned how to compose for different instruments, use motives, analyze form, and use harmonic functions. . . . This project made me more capable to respond to influences that could impact my composition and to analyze the components in my music. While I am not an expert at analyzing music, I think that I have a better understanding of how to go about it. . . . Writing the score was a real challenge for me, but I really improved.

When students shared what they felt was for them the most meaningful parts of the project, one of the strongest themes to emerge was that of making aesthetic decisions:

> What was most meaningful for me was learning to make the music I composed reflect the text and create a mood that was right for the phone. . . . Preparing for the performance using the video and then presenting it was a very meaningful task—we felt like real workers in a firm. It was really interesting how we composed so many different jingles for the same product. . . . The most meaningful part of this project was being able to expand my

knowledge of music. I learned more about artistic interpretation, and how [composers] want you to feel.

Statistical Validity and Reliability of the Scoring Rubrics

According to the statistical analysis of the fall 2016 pilot project, the composition/theory proficient MCA demonstrated overall strong construct validity, meaning that it measures what it intends to measure. All criteria were found to be appropriate and meaningful in their overall functioning within the context of measuring the composition/theory MCA. Results indicated that the rank order of criteria by difficulty (from most difficult to least difficult) was (1) recognizability, (2) imagine, (3) evaluation of time and effort, (4) analysis from the responding scoring device, (5) interpretation, (6) analysis from the plan, make, and analyze scoring device, (7) craftsmanship, (8) organization, (9) selection, (10) verbal, (11) strategies for improvement, and (12) feedback for refinement. All criteria were found to be appropriate and meaningful in their overall functioning within the context of measuring learning in this MCA. Scoring can be considered reliable and valid due to indications that one set of parameters (e.g., the performance achievement of student work) can be estimated without any interference from any of the other parameters (e.g., the severity of the raters or difficulties of the criteria). As a result, one can directly and meaningfully interpret the characteristics of each parameter as a unique characteristic of student learning. Revisions in the scoring devices (rubrics) encouraged from the analysis was addressed in the final versions published online on the NAfME website under standards (https://nafme.org/my-classroom/standards/mcas/).

DISCUSSION

The pilot-project teachers confirmed that the composition/theory MCA related well to their expectation of student learning and identified student achievement as intended by the performance standards. Teacher participants praised the authentic nature of the assessment task and the high quality of the materials; however, both teachers and students identified the abundance of paperwork involved in completing the MCA as repetitive and cumbersome. In one student's words,

> It was more paperwork than needed, the sheets were too repetitive. . . . It took [too] long to fill out the paperwork for this task and it was too much of the same thing. My [classmates and I] did a terrific job on the rehearsals, peer discussions, recording of the jingles and presentations. I don't believe the papers we handed in show the good work we did. . . . We should include

a copy of the score, and recording of the performance and presentation in the MCA collection instead of some of the paperwork.

In response to the pilot project, all three composition/theory MCAs have been revised. According to one teacher, "students thought the task itself was interesting and fun. They thought there was way too much paperwork for the planning." Another teacher stated, "The paper trail took away from the experience of creating and performing. Some writing and planning is of course needed, but it would not be a task I would do in my classroom normally due to the repetitive paperwork." Because of these and similar comments, the repetitive paperwork has been reviewed, and the rubrics have been condensed. It is also important to reinforce that a music teacher can often observe and assess student learning in ways that are not easily available in an externally administered assessment, as in the pilot. The rubrics can be used to assess student learning in some of the variety of ways students can demonstrate learning beyond writing about it. This is one of the valuable aspects of the Model Cornerstone Assessment framework. The measures (rubrics) allow students to demonstrate learning in multiple ways and the teacher to obtain assessment of these multiple demonstrations.

There is still quite a bit of writing involved in the MCAs due to the wording of the performance standards and that many processes are internal, requiring some form of student demonstration of what they are thinking. Many of the standards require students to engage through identifying, describing, explaining, citing, comparing, supporting, justifying, and defending what they are doing. In support of the reflective writing, one teacher stated, "I believe that all students enjoyed seeking the advice of their peers and the collaborative piece. The reflection seemed accepted also." Another teacher shared the following:

> I do most of the create tasks anyway, but I like the way the groups had to give feedback, so I will definitely incorporate this into my classroom. I will also begin to use the terminology more the way it was set up in the plan and make [process component]—hopefully it will help my students put the larger puzzle together in their heads.

Teachers who feel that there is too much writing in the MCAs (via worksheets and/or forms) can adapt them to their situation and students' needs by reducing the written components as they see fit. As an alternative, teachers might have students verbally identify, describe, explain, cite, compare, support, justify, and/or defend. An audio recording of these portions of the MCAs could serve as documentation.

In conclusion, the pilot-project teachers reported that the composition/ theory proficient MCA is developmentally appropriate and something that they were able to integrate into their instruction. They stated that it reflects what students should learn and accurately measures this learning. It is hoped that the three composition/theory MCAs will become useful additions to school curricula and will inform teaching and learning in this important music-subject strand.

REFERENCES

Deutsch, D. (2016). Authentic assessment in music composition: Feedback that facilitates creativity. *Music Educators Journal, 102*(3), 53–59. doi:10.1177/0027432115621608

Freed-Garrod, J. (1999). Assessment in the arts: Elementary-aged students as qualitative assessors of their own and peers' musical compositions. *Bulletin of the Council for Research in Music Education, 139,* 50–63. Retrieved from https://search-proquest-com.ezproxy.uvm.edu/docview/62313090?accountid=14679

Hickey, M. (1999). Assessment rubrics for music composition. *Music Educators Journal, 85*(4), 26–33. doi:10.2307/3399530

Hickey, M. (2001). An application of Amabile's consensual assessment technique for rating the creativity of children's musical compositions. *Journal of Research in Music Education, 49*(3), 234–245. doi:10.2307/3345709

Hickey, M. (2012). *Music outside the lines: Ideas for composing in K–12 music classrooms.* Oxford, UK: Oxford University Press.

Hickey, M. (2013). What to do about assessment. In D. Stringham & C. Randless (Eds.), *Musicianship: Composing in band and orchestra.* Chicago, IL: GIA Publications.

Hickey, M., & Webster, P. (1995). Rating scales and their use in assessing children's music compositions. *The Quarterly Journal of Music Teaching and Learning, 6*(4), 28–44.

Hickey, M., & Webster, P. (2001). Creative thinking in music. *Music Educators Journal, 88*(1), 19–23. doi:10.1177/0027432113500674

Kaschub, M., & Smith, J. (2009). *Minds on music: Composition for creative and critical thinking.* Lanham, MD: Rowman & Littlefield.

Leung, C. C., Wan, Y. Y., & Lee, A. (2009). Assessment of undergraduate students' music compositions. *International Journal of Music Education 27*(3), 250–268. doi:10.1177/0255761409337275

Lierse, S. (2012). The computer and composer in the classroom: How do we assess creativity? In T. S. Brophy (Ed.), *Music assessment across cultures and continents: The culture of shared practice. Proceedings of the 3rd International Symposium on Assessment in Music Education.* Chicago, IL: GIA Publications.

Patton, M. Q. (2002). *Qualitative research and evaluation methods* (3rd ed.). Thousand Oaks, CA: SAGE Publications.

Priest, T. (2001). Using creativity assessment experience to nurture and predict compositional creativity. *Journal of Research in Music Education, 49*(3), 245–258. doi:10.2307/3345710

NINE

Technology Model Cornerstone Assessment for Creating

Phillip Payne

ASSESSING LEARNING IN
TECHNOLOGY IN MUSIC EDUCATION

This chapter describes the development of the proficient level Model Cornerstone Assessments for technology (MCAT) from the prepilot phase through to the final piloting of the assessment. A general background of the topic and the MCAT's theoretical foundation is provided as well as thorough description of the MCAT and its implementation process. Due to a low response rate, combined with a high attrition, no usable data were collected to accurately measure the reliability of the scoring devices. However, through an extensive review of the literature and interactions with the piloters, the researcher has developed a set of next steps to guide the continued development of standards in music technology and suggestions for future research. Among the emerging topics of discussion were the existence of the standards, connections, the role of technology in music education, and equitable access to technology in the music classroom.

Many students in the United States today seem to be almost constantly connected to technology and even more so to their music through technology (Raiber, 2011). Consider walking down a street, through a hall at a high school, or on a university campus; many individuals have earbuds in or they are staring at the screen of a mobile device, be it a tablet or smartphone. People today have integrated technology into their lives whether of their own choosing or not; therefore, there it behooves educators to address technology integration in the classroom.

When approached about designing the Model Cornerstone Assessment (MCA) for technology (MCAT) in February 2014, I suggested that ideas about how technology is used in music classrooms had to be considered. Among considerations were (a) a definition of technology for music learning, (b) the pragmatism of including technology in music education, (c) the integration of technology in a music classroom, (d) equitable access, and (e) approaches to assessing music learning through technology. Each of these considerations played a significant role in shaping the MCA as it currently stands. Throughout this chapter, the foundation, development, implementation, results, and critique of the entire MCA process will be revealed. The chapter concludes with suggestions for strengthening the standards, an assessment model, and approach to technology in the music classroom in response to the current findings and considering current research.

Definition

Technology can be interpreted as a means by which a culture can be formed or changed (Borgmann, 2006). For purposes of this MCAT, technology will be defined as computers, software, and digital tools that can aid in enhancing and developing the music learning of an individual. Specifically, the digital sources will be digital audio workstations (DAWs; identified as GarageBand), computers, tablets, the Internet, MIDI input devices, keyboards, and any music-streaming software and/or devices.

Bauer (2014) described three considerations for technology in music education:

- *How we use this technology depends on our needs, the context, and current environment.* In a music classroom, the needs, context, and environment doesn't automatically reflect how students use technology in their world beyond schooling.
- *Technology is always shifting.* There is never a time where technology remains static. This is an issue when designing standards and curriculum because technological tools become obsolete by the time standards and assessments are developed. Therefore, there must be a way to make them flexible and focus on both the teaching and the learning of technology within the development of model assessments.
- *When using technology it is difficult to understand how learning occurs because the technology does a lot of the work.* We often press a button to make a specific task happen. If it does not happen, we often press other buttons or contact tech support. All this is external, and we are left not knowing exactly what happened. The assessment of technology needs to be able to shift and adapt to multiple contexts and environments due to these considerations.

Technology Standards

Beyond the NCCAS 2014 Standards for Technology in Music, there are several other sets of standards and guidelines that currently exist across a range of organizations. Among these are the International Society for Technology in Education (ISTE) standards for students, the Areas of Pedagogical Skill and Understanding (TAPSU) published by the Technology Institute for Music Educators, and the 11 competencies for technology in music education established by Webster and Williams (2014, 2015).

The ISTE standards (ISTE, 2016) describe how the students will (a) leverage technology to achieve their learning goals, (b) recognize the rights and functions of living in an interconnected world, (c) use technology to construct knowledge to produce meaningful learning experiences for them and others, (d) solve problems using technology in novel ways, (e) leverage technology to develop solutions to real-world problems, (f) use technology to creatively connect and communicate with one another, and (g) broaden their perspectives and collaborate with others to expand to communicating globally. Essentially, technology serves as a catalyst for stimulating creative thinking and applied problem-solving skills that will make students and future graduates more marketable in an ever-increasing global market. In each standard, technology is leveraged through the application of content, implying that students use technological knowledge, a pedagogical knowledge, and a content knowledge.

The Technology Institute for Music Educators (TI:ME) has created a set of skills and understandings that guide their mission as an entity and define the role of music technology in the classroom. As a group, they are ever-changing to match the fluidness with which technology changes. There is no assumption that using these skills results in student learning because they are intended as a set of skills "to be used alongside or in tandem with other sets of standards including those developed for general education, music education, and technology-based education" (TI:ME, n.d.). The contents are skills in music instruction software, computer music notation, multimedia development, electronic musical instruments, productivity tools, classroom and lab resources, electronic music production, and live sound reinforcement. Essentially, TI:ME has defined many ways that technology can function within a music classroom beyond your typical experiences with a digital audio workstation or notation software. Combined with the ISTE standards, they provide a strong framework from which to assemble and design a set of standards to integrate technology throughout music education.

From a series of studies (Webster & Williams, 2015) emerged a set of 11 competencies that help define what students should be able to do as they enter the workforce as music educators. These 11 competencies are (1) enter and edit music using notation software, (2) understand the basics of digital audio and how to edit digital audio files, (3) record and mix a performance with digital audio software, (4) demonstrate an understanding of copyright and fair use, (5) create a music presentation

with production software and appropriate hardware, (6) create a stream-
ing audio file (sharing recordings), (7) demonstrate an understanding
of MIDI and its applications, (8) demonstrate setting up a computer
music workstation/problem-solve technical issues, (9) demonstrate an
understanding of acoustics and audiology, (10) create and edit a simple
music video, and (11) use and manage a variety of social music sharing
tools (e.g., iTunes, Spotify, Pandora). These incorporate a great deal of
content and technological knowledge. Regardless, between ISTE, TI:ME,
and Webster and Williams (2015), there is a wealth of information and
a basis for a strong set of standards. Unfortunately, the 2014 NCCAS
standards did not address technological operations as components in the
three artistic processes. The MCA format was focused around the three
artistic processes of create, perform, and respond, thereby aligning with
the other MCA strands. Throughout the development of the MCAT, the
performance standards (NAfME, n.d.) were solely used to determine the
direction, scope, and function of the assessment framework. But throughout the development of the MCAT, these additional standards and guidelines (ISTE; TI:ME; Webster & Williams, 2015) were considered, albeit in
a smaller scope.

Pragmatism

In the initial development, the primary concern was to determine why
these standards were necessary and how an MCAT might be beneficial
to students. Williams (2007) describes music education in the public
schools as seeing gradually diminishing access. Essentially, students start
out their academic careers with musical opportunities for all. However,
as students continue in their education, if their interest deviates from
ensemble opportunities, their access and ability to participate in music
begins to decrease as they move into middle school or high school. Elpus
and Abril (2011) found that only about 20% of students in secondary
schools participated in music in some way. Could technology serve as a
bridging mechanism for the other 80%, and would an MCAT be able to
assess music learning for this population?

Dammers (2010) found that a technology course did have an impact
on attracting students from those who had not previously been enrolled
in secondary music. In a subsequent study, Dammers (2012) found that
nearly 14% of high schools in the United States had a technology-based
music class. The integration of technology in music learning has slowly
and steadily increased since 2000. Music education in the secondary
schools has explored technology access in meaningful ways beyond the
ensemble rehearsal (Elpus & Abril, 2011; Kratus, 2007; Williams, 2007,

2011), and technology seems to be a successful means of providing access to a music education.

Assessment Tasks

Defining a task through which students demonstrate the performance standards for technology is difficult because of the many ways that technology can be integrated. It seems that the performance standards were established with the process of creating in mind and focused on the student in the role of creator though composing and improvising. That may not be surprising because researchers have examined the role of technology in the classroom (Dammers, 2012; Dunbar, 2016; Studer, 2005; Webster, 2009) and found the primary roles that technology filled were through composition, improvisation, and as a tool for performing. However, Himonides and Purves (2010) noted that "music technology is a much broader concept than we [are] accustomed to, and does not necessarily translate [only] to the composition or manipulation of sound using popular software applications" (p. 137).

Composers have used digital and analog media for years to manipulate and organize sounds into new media and compositions. Software programs such as Band-in-a-Box, GarageBand, Soundtrap, and others have allowed performers to create grooves and backing tracks over which to perform an improvised solo. But most recently, a student was admitted into a university where his primary instrument will be a computer (Chen, 2016). We are beginning to observe technology serving a role beyond that of a compositional aid (e.g., as a teaching aid, performing aid, or instrument). With such a wide set of roles, designing an assessment to measure every role is not possible in three MCAs, and selecting a focus was a challenge. The question that had to be answered was to what extent the MCAT can reasonably and effectively assess creating, performing, and responding and address the multiple uses of technology.

MCAT Development

In designing the assessment, there were several considerations that had to be addressed. Among these considerations was the age of the students, the context for which the task was to be designed, and which task and assessment structure would best fit into a music classroom. The age of the participants was the first critical step to address when developing a useful and effective MCAT. This was critical; there are no novice or intermediate levels of the NCCAS standards for technology. The standards for the proficient level are published without preliminary sequential expectations.

There are no standards listed that can help guide instruction or assessment in this area.

Another important consideration was the classroom context; this is often dictated by access to hardware, software, and the Internet, to name a few. Differences in access range from schools where every student has an electronic device to schools where technology is limited to one computer lab or one per classroom. Software and Internet access are also very inconsistent in how they are used and accessed from district to district. Some schools have a large budget to supply students with a wide array of applications and opportunities, while others have basic e-mail and word processing capacity. Finally, with Internet access, the existence of firewalls and narrow bandwidths creates issues with access. Accordingly, each of these issues was taken into consideration when designing an MCAT that could be used in multiple settings.

Technology to Initiate Creating as a Process

Many researchers have investigated the process of creative thought when it comes to music and education (Bauer, 2014; Koehler & Mishra, 2009; Mlynczak, 2015; Webster, 2012). Bauer (2014) cites Wallas as a prime example of how to conceive and approach developing creativity. There is essentially a four-step process: (1) preparation, (2) incubation, (3) illumination, and (4) verification. Each of these four steps allows an individual to take an idea from a thought to a realization in sound. Webster (2012) views this same process through the constructivist lens and characterizes it through a combination of experiences containing convergent and divergent thoughts and activities. The students construct their own meanings and musical ideas. The context must allow time for creative thought to germinate, grow, expand, and be revised into refined expressions. The integration of technology as the means of experiencing each part of the MCAT became the means of measuring the process components of all three artistic processes.

The MCAT began to emerge as a composition project using a DAW and allowing for choices in personalizing the final product while maintaining the rigor of the standards. To remain current with research in integrating technology into a music classroom, *Music Learning Today: Digital Pedagogy for Creating, Performing, and Responding to Music* (Bauer, 2014) was reviewed as a guide to designing the task. The MCAT was designed as a non-notation approach, to allow greater student choice and to appeal to a wider group of participating schools. Students were provided a set of parameters through which they developed compositions using technology. Then, after being taught how to effectively critique musical works and use appropriate terminology, students provided self-assessment and peer feedback to aid in the creative choices made available through technology. Final projects were performed for an audience of the teacher's choosing. In sum, the goal was to develop an experience that integrated technology in a way that led students to a deeper musical understanding through all of the artistic processes.

MODEL CORNERSTONE ASSESSMENT FOR TECHNOLOGY

Overview

The MCAT fuses all three artistic processes through an interactive experience with music technology. It addresses the implementation of music technology at the proficient level as defined by the 2014 National Standards in Music Education. Through a series of revisions, the MCAT emerged as a four-phase design to be implemented over the course of a semester or academic year depending on the educational setting. In each phase, the students are led through a sequence of experiences that result to one of three final projects. The four phases are (1) a brainstorming session, (2) creating a draft of their project, (3) peer- and self-assessment opportunities, and (4) final performance and reflection of the process. The integration of technology and implementation of the MCAT relies on the student having some background and experience in music technology.

The MCAT encompasses the ability to create and experience music with the use of a DAW. It is not necessary to have a specific DAW to complete this task; in fact, teachers can use a variety of DAWs and still successfully complete this MCAT; most DAWs are designed the same way but operate on different platforms. The MCAT is presented and described using GarageBand; however, Soundtrap, Logic, or other DAWs will work just as well.

PHASE 1

The first phase establishes the foundation for idea generation. In this first task, students immerse themselves in songs that they might want to cover or that inspire them in some way. During this phase, students generate three potential project ideas based on their musical taste and interest. Following selection of potential songs, students brainstorm ways in which elements of each of their selections could be covered and/or altered. They might also consider how a song could inspire a new composition altogether. Here, they describe and analyze the musical components and discover which song will work best for the project. Among the concepts analyzed through listening and description are form, timbre, and harmony, among others. Following a detailed analysis of each of the songs, students are asked to *select* the song that provides the most opportunity for them to create a new version of the song. Along with this process, students are prompted to explain why they selected their specific song using prompting questions. Students conclude the first phase by listing ways in which they plan to use digital tools to alter or enhance their listed elements of music.

PHASE 2

For best results, students will need to explore and develop a working knowledge of the DAW that is available. Although not integrated into the MCAT, the best way to address this is by creating a series of assignments prior to implementing this MCAT that address the development of skills using a variety of techniques, including loop generation and manipulation, MIDI input, and recording. These prerequisite experiences are what would typically be included in novice and intermediate levels of the standards. A mixture of skills will be required for success in draft planning and creation. After receiving feedback on phase 1 from the teacher, students imagine ways in which they can use the DAW to create a cover or new sound for the song they have selected. For best results, spending time isolating the concepts and connecting their analyses with possible digital options will be critical. Addressing draft creation in its entirety can be overwhelming for both you and the students, so break this phase into small steps as necessary.

In the second phase, students list ways to use digital tools and software to manipulate various elements of music to design and compose their own version of the selected song. Students need plenty of time to consider options and experiment prior to draft creation. Guiding discussions with the group is a way to establish options for creatively addressing each of the musical concepts using the DAWs. Students will then outline, design, and construct a first draft of their musical creation. Depending on the skill level of the students, this phase could take the longest. Following the completion of the first draft, students will rationalize their use of digital technology and its role in the creation of the new piece, and develop an interpretation of musical decisions they are making during this experience.

One consideration is access to technology on several levels. When planning this section for instruction and practice, teachers should work to address access to technology, equal access to software, and necessary class time to complete the project. Students will become so immersed in these activities that they might get bogged down, so setting small goals or checkpoints along the way will be critical to success in the classroom.

Another consideration will be the school calendar. If there are going to be days that are missed, teachers should carefully consider these in the planning, because this is the most critical step in the MCAT and tasks.

PHASE 3

For phase 3 to be effective, students must be experienced in providing meaningful feedback and have a grasp of the terminology and pedagogical ideas that they will need. In this phase, students trade drafts with one another and provide constructive feedback on technological decisions. Using the critiques, a refinement plan is designed prior to making final decisions about technology use. Prior to the final presentation, students write liner notes describing the role of technology in their compositional process.

PHASE 4

In phase 4, students introduce and perform their technology-based cover songs and reflect on the use of technology throughout the entire process. This level of reflection allows the teacher to assess each of the artistic processes the students are using.

SUMMARY

This MCAT can be tailored in most classroom settings and seeks to develop the use of technology to guide critical listening, analysis, musicality, and performance. The MCAT was administered in classrooms from middle school to collegiate levels; however, preparation and skill development are paramount. This is not a novice-level assessment and those with developing knowledge and skills in music technology will struggle with this task. The MCAT demonstrates musical skills through the mastery of music technology while supporting existing musical goals of the current classroom with a flexibility that allows it to be segmented in across a class or expanded to become a stand-alone course in any program. This design was both surprising to and welcomed by the piloters.

Studying the Administration and Usefulness of the Measure

The first version of the proficient-level MCAT was designed and disseminated in August 2015. Although there was initial interest, there were no participants and little feedback. Therefore, the MCAT-Proficient was reassessed to determine why teachers might be avoiding implementing it in their classrooms. Music technology teachers shared concerns with the terminology and structure. Following revisions, the prepilot phase was readministered in July 2016 at a technology symposium to solicit feedback on its clarity, content, and process. Feedback from the symposium participants led to additional adjustments in the task and measures. On completion of the prepilot phase, the following adjustments were made to the MCAT: (a) rubrics were revised to allow for maximum differentiation and clarity, (b) phases were divided into distinct steps with more detail leading up to the assessment, (c) specific learning goals were emphasized, and (d) alignment between tasks and rubrics were clarified.

Three schools confirmed participation in fall 2016. Throughout the process, attrition resulted in insufficient data being collected to satisfactorily assess and categorize student work as well as measure the reliability of the assessment. Therefore, the focus of the results and discussion will center on what was discovered throughout the process and the next steps in the development of technology standards and assessments in the music education community.

Findings for Each of the Artistic Processes

The following vignettes resulting from interactions with piloting teachers are provided here as a basis for understanding what was learned and to establish alternative perspectives of music technology within a music classroom. These vignettes use pseudonyms and are written to explain the setting and illustrate the use of the MCAT.

Johnson Middle School

Johnson Middle School houses students in grades 6–8. The head director, Amy, "found this pilot to be useful but also very exposing to technology challenges." In her building, students are not 1-to-1 (that is, don't have a computer or iPad for each student) and only have access to one iPad cart on a variable basis. This iPad cart was available to the whole school, and several times, the students' projects were deleted due to repeated use of the iPads by other students in the school. Students were frustrated because they were not able to complete their projects due to delays between technology uses, which limited the scope of their projects. She describes the passion her students had for the project and how they wanted to present their best work, but the barriers were too great for many to overcome.

Schultz Middle School

Schultz Middle School (SMS) houses grades 6–8. It was the head director Stan's first year in this building. In the previous years, the school had not had any general or vocal music, and Stan's position was created to establish these programs at the site. Stan began the MCAT task; however, as the project unfolded in phases 1 and 2, it was apparent that students needed remediation of knowledge regarding musical terms and experiences. Once the remediation of base musical knowledge had occurred, they began to develop the technological skills to be successful on the remainder of the MCAT. But even with the adjustments and remediation, there were issues that precluded the students from moving through the project. The most profound issues were connection difficulties. SMS is the oldest building in the district and is separated from the main (and newer) building. These connection issues created a barrier between the students and their resources. To compound these challenges, the use of Chromebooks versus laptops hindered flexibility of technology for the music tasks. Students became increasingly frustrated when they were unable to complete their projects before the end of the scheduled course. Stan revealed that "this has been helpful for me to reflect on what changes I need to make for next semester to better serve the students and make the transitions easier from one software to another."

IRVING MIDDLE SCHOOL

Irving Middle School (IMS) primarily comprises seventh and eighth graders with a handful of sixth graders. The head director, Chuck, oversees all aspects of the music program. IMS is 1-to-1 Chromebooks and has two choirs, two bands, and a general music class. With the four performance ensembles, beginning instruction starts in seventh grade and builds into an advanced beginner group (typically eighth grade). There is also a class for those not involved with a music ensemble. Many of the students in this class were engaged in music outside of school but did not want to perform in an ensemble. The administrator was open to trying various approaches to engage these students as long as the standards were being addressed. The MCAT allowed the students to address expected learning through their choice of music. Chuck found that the students engaged in the task and found the experience to be "compelling." As a result of the enhanced student engagement, Chuck intends to use this task as a foundation for the course to teach music terminology and concepts. An important connection that emerged was that of popular music. Allowing for student choice appeared foundational for student engagement. This connection resulted in students wanting to work constantly on their projects. One moment that stood out to Chuck was when two seventh graders discovered that a chord progression and "hook" were exactly the same in both a Fallout Boy and Green Day song. Chuck described this as a "cool" moment to see the lightbulbs come on for students who might not otherwise have this opportunity.

Additionally, he found that the project revealed opportunities for student learning beyond what had been originally considered. He replied that "he must teach how to address technical issues, elements, and musicality" throughout the process and include "diagnostic assessment" of student skills throughout the project to keep it moving forward.

Among the drawbacks were access to sites, music, and other resources that lagged because of a lack of bandwidth and due to firewalls. This slowed progress in implementing some of the phases. But even with the challenges, Chuck felt that this was a great way to engage the nonensemble students in the "other 80%" and provided a way to establish ownership of personal music within the walls of a classroom, blurring the lines between school music and home music.

Conclusions

Several themes emerged from interactions with the directors. One of the most profound is that the use of technology strongly influences student engagement in musical tasks beyond traditional forms of performance. Among these challenges were helping students acquire sufficient knowledge and skills prior to administering technology-based assessment tasks, consistent access to technology resources, equity of technological proficiencies, and sufficient time for student completion of assessment tasks. In each case, students became frustrated when they could not complete projects due to challenges. The students became so engaged in the process that they wanted to spend more time with the project, but they were forced to end early because of the time constraints of the semester and the deadlines set forth by the district.

Foundational knowledge of musical terminology and technology skills were consistent issues. This was due to students not having technology knowledge/skills and specific musical knowledge of terminology prior to the administration of the MCA. Remedial projects had to be inserted to bridge these gaps. Another issue experienced at many sites was the availability of software and/or necessary hardware. Additional DAWs were sought to provide access to students, but again, the initial skills remained lacking due to the initial lack of access. Perhaps this is a sign that novice and intermediate levels of the technology standards are necessary as a curricular basis for student development. While the students might be digital natives, as described by Bauer (2014), their knowledge of music technology is not robust and still needs to be developed, as with any other technical skill. This would also be the same for teachers as digital immigrants (Bauer, 2014). While teachers might have high self-efficacy in using and implementing technology in the music classroom (Agnew, 2009), they don't have the access or the professional development necessary to be truly successful in the classroom. With the MCAT functioning as a summative assessment at the proficient level, access issues indicate that it might have to be implemented in the second semester of a yearlong course to provide sufficient experience to build the requisite knowledge and skills for student success. It will also be important to establish novice and intermediate levels of technology standards to guide expectations of developmental learning. Without addressing the introductory levels, the development of strong technological knowledge and skills is greatly challenged. While many of today's students might be digital natives, their proficiency and literacy in technology is mostly focused on social media, e-mail, and word processing (Bloom, 2014; Šorgo, Bartol, Dolničar, & Boh Podgornik, 2017).

CONNECTIONS WITH STUDENTS

Based on the interactions with teachers through the prepilots and pilots, we have drawn several conclusions about assessing the National Standards for Music using Technology. Similar to the findings of Dammers (2010, 2012), it was discovered that technology-based music classes have the capability to engage students in school music programs not typically motivated by ensemble participation. One director went out of his way to ensure that these students were engaging in ways beyond the typical school music program. The content seems to be appealing to many students. Engagement with the MCAT task also elicits a motivational ownership and connection with music exemplified by a desire to work more consistently than time allows. The students became so engaged with the process that they did not want the course to end, which indicates some level of connection that needs further study and documentation. Although not addressed in this MCAT, the development of digital portfolios to store students' work and share with both families and peers could be additional contributions and worthy of study.

Furthermore, there seems to be a lack of curricular attention on how to teach music with technology in ways that could prepare students for the MCAT. Learning can be hindered on a secondary level if technology integration is not addressed on the novice and intermediate levels (Dunbar, 2016). A comprehensive investigation into how to incorporate technology across the K–12 curriculum is suggested for the technology standards to determine how to best establish connections for learning development.

ROLE OF TECHNOLOGY IN MUSIC LEARNING

A revision of the current technology standards to better reflect and align with the ISTE standards and TAPSU by TI:ME is strongly recommended. It would be an excellent starting point for a discussion of the integration of music technology into creating, performing, and responding. Furthermore, the 11 competencies described by Webster and Williams (2014) might bridge the gap of skill development necessary for the profession. Greher (2011) promoted the idea of school–university partnerships to begin establishing the bridge between theory and practice when it comes to music technology integration. Expanding on the current standards to align with current practices of teachers using technology in their classrooms could conceivably expand consideration toward the student whose primary instrument is a computer (Chen, 2016).

ADDRESSING ACCESS TO TECHNOLOGY

Access was a large issue in the pilot as indicated in each of the three vignettes. Access to hardware, software, and the Internet were all issues that resulted in difficulties for administering this MCA. Every district was different in the access provided to students, from hardware to software to bandwidth. Some districts are 1-to-1 with technology, some have class sets that travel between classrooms, and some are only provided a lab for the entire school. Access time for students to learn and use the technology to the extent of their desired level of achievement was an unforeseen issue. The inequality of access in technology and time makes it difficult to establish a level of expectation that can be applied across all contexts. ISTE (2016) has established a set of essential conditions that outline what every site should have to fully integrate technology in a curriculum; among these conditions are equitable access, technical support, and consistent and adequate funding. However, the integration of technology throughout the pedagogical process and throughout a curriculum might address this access issue while enhancing creating, performing, responding, and connecting through musical activities. More investigation is needed in this area.

TECHNOLOGICAL COMPETENCE

An additional level of access concerned the teachers. There was a differentiation of teachers based on their comfort level with the technology and their technological pedagogical content knowledge. The more comfortable they were with the technology, the more they were willing to try new things and use the MCAT or at least adjust content and instruction as needed throughout the process. This seems to be consistent with the findings of Agnew (2009), who discovered that significant predictors of technology integration were availability and professional development. With the current pilot study, there was an assumption that the teachers were already teaching similar technology in class and had access to professional development that would enhance their technological and pedagogical knowledge. The lack of access to professional development created an issue in the pilot study. However, with technology, it is critical that both teacher and students constantly upgrade their skills and the knowledge of how they can be applied in the classroom. Adaptive expertise is definitely an area that needs to be addressed and explored further as we consider how to address the evolving nature of technology and access in the classroom.

Next Steps

Moving forward, the first conversation to be had is whether technology standards should be established at all, or if the current NCCAS 2014 Standards for Technology in Music might undergo substantial revision. In light of current research (Agnew, 2009; Bauer, 2014; Dunbar, 2016; Šorgo et al., 2017; Webster, 2009; Webster and Williams, 2015), technology is a set of knowledge and skills that enhance products and/or processes. It is a tool that allows for more efficiency in executing skills and processes. Technology is so vast in its conception and definition that narrowing a focus for the development of standards and authentic assessments is a near-impossible task. Considering the varied uses of technology we observe in the classroom, how do DAWs integrate into the classroom? What about iPad ensembles? What about recording equipment and practices? In each instance, technology allows access to all the artistic processes through a variety of functions. Within this consideration, assessing technology with unique standards is like measuring trumpet integration across the ensemble standards. The trumpet (like technology) is the vehicle by which creating, performing, and responding are demonstrated. Then, consider other technological tools such as Sibelius or GarageBand. Students compose and learning keyboard skills by using these technologies. Is the focus of the assessed learning the student use of the technology or the artistic process itself? This is a critical conversation and will determine the direction of the technology standards.

If technology standards are deemed necessary (or essential), among the first considerations for future research is to establish criteria in the dimensions of novice and intermediate. This will be critical to establishing a foundation of technological and content knowledge that will enable meeting the ISTE standards. Furthermore, consideration should be given to the 11 competencies revealed by Webster and Williams (2015), and to embedding the TAPSU provided by TI:ME in current music teacher education curricula.

Second, as a profession, we must expand the scope of the technology standards beyond working with a DAW or notation software for creating music; this is only a small segment of how our music students experience music through technology. Expanding the role of technology and its integration throughout the music classroom is critical, but this is only possible through a revision of the standards as a whole. Future work should be undertaken to establish a set of standards that aligns with the three artistic processes while merging the ISTE standards, TAPSU of TI:ME, and the 11 music technology competencies established by Webster and Williams (2014, 2015). This is a large task; however, it is one that will set a new level of expectation for music teaching at all levels.

REFERENCES

Agnew, S. M. (2009). *Factors influencing the implementation of technology in the music classroom* (Master's thesis). Available from ProQuest Dissertations & Theses Global. (304916815).

Bauer, W. I. (2014). *Music learning today: Digital pedagogy for creating, performing, and responding to music.* New York: Oxford University Press.

Bloom, A. (2014, August 15). How even digital natives get tangled up in the Web. *The Times Educational Supplement.* Retrieved from https://www.tes.com/news/tes-archive/tes-publication/how-even-digital-natives-get-tangled-web

Borgmann, A. (2006). Technology as a cultural force for Alena and Griffin. *Canadian Journal of Sociology, 31*(3), 351–360.

Chen, J. (2016, May 12). UMKC accepts its first music student whose instrument is the computer. *KCUR 89.3.* Retrieved from http://kcur.org/post/umkc-accepts-its-first-music-student-whose-instrument-computer#stream/0

Dammers, R. J. (2010). A case study of the creation of a technology-based music course. *Bulletin of the Council for Research in Music Education, 186,* 55–65.

Dammers, R. J. (2012). Technology-based music classes in high schools in the United States. *Bulletin of the Council for Research in Music Education, 194,* 73–90. doi:10.5406/bulcouresmusedu.194.0073

Dunbar, L. (2016). Music for music's sake and tech for tech's sake. *General Music Today, 30*(1), 38-40. doi:10.1177/1048371316658326

Elpus, K., & Abril, C. R. (2011). High school music ensemble students in the United States: A demographic profile. *Journal of Research in Music Education, 59*(2), 128–145.

Greher, G. R. (2011). Music technology partnerships: A context for music teacher preparation. *Arts Education Policy Review, 112*(3), 130–136.

Himonides, E., & Purves, R. (2010). *The role of technology.* In S. Hallam & A. Creech (Eds.), *Music education in the 21st century in the United Kingdom: Achievements, analysis and aspirations,* pp. 123–140. London, UK: Institute of Education.

International Society for Technology in Education (ISTE). (2016). Site page for the International Society for Technology in Education's Essential Conditions. Retrieved from https://www.iste.org/standards/tools-resources/essential-conditions

Koehler, M. J., & Mishra, P. (2009). What is technological pedagogical content knowledge? *Contemporary Issues in Technology and Teacher Education, 9*(1), 60–70.

Kratus, J. (2007). Centennial series: Music education at the tipping point. *Music Educators Journal, 94*(2), 42–48.

Mlynczak, J. (2015). Music technology lesson planning. *School band and orchestra, 18*(10), 39.

National Association for Music Education (NAfME). (n.d.). Home page for the National Core Arts Standards in Music. Retrieved from http://www.nafme .org/my-classroom/standards

Raiber, M. A. (2011). Getting to the "core" of the matter. *Oklahoma Music, 18*(1), 8, 16.

Šorgo, A., Bartol, T., Dolničar, D., & Boh Podgornik, B. (2017). Attributes of digital natives as predictors of information literacy in higher education. *British Journal of Educational Technology, 48*(3), 749–767. doi:10.1111/bjet.12451

Studer, K. (2005). Maximum technology in the music classroom: Minimum requirements. *Teaching Music, 13*(3), 44.

Technology. (n.d.). *Dictionary.com Unabridged*. Retrieved from http://www.dic tionary.com/browse/technology

Technology Institute for Music Educators (TI:ME). (n.d.). Webpage for disseminating the areas of pedagogical skill and understanding. Retrieved from https://ti-me.org/index.php/home/areas-of-tapsu.html

Webster, P. R. (2009). Music technology as a servant to real music experience. *The Orff Echo, 42*(1), 9–12.

Webster, P. R. (2012). Encouraging imaginative thought in music with students in classroom. (n.d.). Retrieved from http://peterrwebster.com/Present/Imaginative Thought.pdf

Webster, P. R., & Williams, D. B. (2014). *Defining undergraduate music technology competencies and strategies for learning: A fourth year followup—Exemplars.* Retrieved from https://coach4technology.net/teachMusicTech/musictech compssurvey2014_oc.pdf

Webster, P. R., & Williams, D. B. (2015). *Music technology competencies: An international perspective.* Retrieved from https://coach4technology.net/teachMusic Tech/internationaltechcompssurve.pdf

Williams, D. A. (2007). What are music educators doing and how well are we doing it? *Music Educators Journal, 94*(1), 18–23.

Williams, D. A. (2011). The elephant in the room. *Music Educators Journal, 98*(1), 51–57.

TEN

Methodology for Qualitative Data

Frederick Burrack

The primary questions that guided the pilot for the Model Cornerstone Assessment (MCA) development were:

1. To what extent do teachers recognize that the MCAs authentically reflect student learning expected at grade-level/proficiency strand?
2. How do practicing teachers in various school settings adapt the MCAs to usefully coincide with current practice?
3. In what ways do the MCAs modify the current paradigm of school music education and educational experiences of music students?
4. To what extent can the MCAs be administered and scored with consistency across settings?
5. How effectively can the MCAs identify student achievement as intended by the performance standards? and
6. Are there relationships of learning domains across settings, grade levels, and process components?

To cultivate a thorough understanding of teachers' experiences with the MCAs around these questions, it was essential to collect sufficient demographic data about the school context to be able to effectively analyze the data for the questions at hand. The following information was collected from every teacher who showed interest in piloting the MCAs: (a) school district (inner-city, suburban, mid-size city, small town, rural); (b) region in the United States (as defined by the National Association for Music Education (NAfME); (c) economic status of school (percentage of students receiving free or reduced-price lunches); (d) opportunity to learn (number of days per week of music class and number of minutes per class period); (e) teacher's experience administering outside assessments; and (f) initial attitudes toward the draft versions of the MCAs (perception of relevance to current curriculum, impressions of appropriateness for current students in their program, inference as to whether MCAs would need adaptations for administration in the class).

Data collected through the postpilot survey included (a) reflection on clarity and ease of administration of pilot protocol; (b) connection and usefulness within the current curriculum; (c) ways that the MCA was adapted to fit context; (d) observed student response; (e) curricular impact; (f) instruction administered to prepare students for the assessment; (g) changes in teacher perception of the MCAs and student learning; and (h) suggestions for enhancements made to the MCAs, rubrics, and/or protocols as appropriate. Information attained through selected response and open-ended questions were sorted and analyzed by grade level and the specific MCA administered. Of particular interest beyond the constructs in the postpilot questions was uniqueness within or among demographic groups. The demographic filters obtained through a pre-pilot survey included (a) region in the United States as designated at the National Association for Music Education (NAfME); (b) school district size; (c) socioeconomic status of students in the district as designated by percent of free and reduced lunches; and (d) student opportunity to learn, as designated by number of days per week the teacher meets with the students and number of minutes allocated per class period.

The researchers for each MCA additionally collected attitudinal responses from the piloting teachers through videoconference interview and e-mail interaction. Through the development and administration of the MCAs, field notes were taken to document teacher feedback pertaining to the assessment tasks, scoring devices, administration protocol, and interaction with students. Analysis of any quantitative item data was disaggregated by demographic characteristic to expose unique, as well as common, characteristics of the MCAs among various demographic contexts. This disaggregation was achieved using Microsoft PowerBI technology, with which each researcher selected filters to isolate and visualize the data through graphs and text dashboards.

Each researcher reviewed the disaggregated data filtered by their pilot teachers to analyze each data category comparing demographic groups, student achievement results, and individual feedback. The data were also analyzed holistically across the pilot to expose (a) the overall educational usefulness of the MCAs; (b) whether there is a relationship between student achievement scores and teacher concept of student learning; (c) if there was consistency of administration and scoring across multiple settings; (d) the perceived usefulness of Model Cornerstone Assessments in current practice; and (e) if there are relationships of learning domains across settings, grade levels, and processes. Data and inferences are reported in each chapter of this book, written in a format intended for transfer to school music classrooms and understanding by music teachers.

Eleven

Methodology for Examining the Psychometric Qualities of the Model Cornerstone Assessments

Brian C. Wesolowski

Classroom assessments and, more specifically, the measurement instruments used in classrooms, undergo little if any psychometric (e.g., validity, reliability, and fairness) evaluation. In the rare event that classroom assessments in the arts are evaluated for psychometric quality, the most used measurement model is based on classical test theory (CTT). CTT, or "true-score theory," uses raw scores gleaned from a pool of examinees to test their relative success or failure on individual items. Known for its relatively weak theoretical assumptions, the CTT measurement model assumes that the observed scores obtained from a measure comprise two parts: true score and measurement error. CTT analysis is usually limited to item-difficulty indices based on proportion-correct and reliability coefficients that summarize proportions of variance. In the case of polytomously scored items, such as those found in the Music Model Cornerstone Assessments (herein referred to as MCAs), adjusted proportion correct values (p-values) and correlation coefficients are used to indicate item difficulty and overall ability level of an examinee. The major disadvantage of using CTT as a means for analyzing performance assessment data is the sample and test dependency of estimated person parameter estimates (e.g., true scores) and item parameters (e.g., item discrimination and item difficulty). This limits the ability to develop valid and reliable measures and to make informed inferences related to examinee ability and item difficulty that extend beyond the context of the sample of student work or performances used in the assessment context.

In contrast, the Rasch family of measurement models offers a more grounded theory compared to CTT (Cavanagh & Waugh, 2011). Rasch measurement theory (Rasch, 1960/1980) is often preferred in scale development as well as in the measurement of latent traits in the behavioral, social, and health sciences (Engelhard, 2013). The major benefit of the Rasch model is that, when adequate fit to the model is observed, invariant measurement is achieved. In the context of assessments, invariant measurement implies that the measurement of persons is not influenced by the particular items that they happen to take, and the measurement of items is not influenced by the particular persons by whom they are measuring. Rasch measurement models use probabilistic distributions of responses as a logistic function of person and item parameters in order to define a latent trait; in contrast to CTT, where raw scores are directly used in the analyses, Rasch measurement theory converts raw scores to a log-odds scale using a logistic transformation. The transformed test-score data can then be conceptualized as a dependent variable with multiple independent variables (i.e., facets) of interest, including measures of scorer severity and leniency, criterion difficulty, and student performance achievement level. Hierarchies of difficulty for each relevant criterion, and each examinee's discrete item responses are mapped onto a single logit (log-odds units) scale. As a result of the mapping of facets onto a single, continuous, latent variable scale, it is possible to construct a variable map to use as a visual display for illustrating relative differences in locations among facets.

It is important to note that the property of invariant measurement that characterizes the Rasch model must be evaluated using empirical data. Invariant measurement is a hypothesis that must be confirmed or disconfirmed by evidence in a data set (Engelhard, 1994). Engelhard and Perkins (2011) provided a set of five requirements that can be used to determine the degree to which invariant measurement is obtained for persons and items. These requirements include (a) item-invariant measurement of persons (i.e., the measurement of persons must be independent of the particular items that happen to be used for the measurement); (b) non-crossing person response functions (i.e., a more able person must always have a better chance of success on an item than does a less able person); (c) person-invariant calibration of test items (i.e., the calibration of the items must be independent of the particular persons used for calibration); (d) non-crossing item response functions (i.e., any person must have a better chance of success on an easy item than on a more difficult item); and (e) variable map (i.e., items and person must be simultaneously located on a single underlying latent variable). Based on the difference in item and person locations on the variable map, items can be evaluated for their usefulness in providing information about persons' varying achievement levels. The benefit of Rasch approaches to measurement and construct modeling is the strong requirement that a set of items being used can measure a single construct (i.e., latent trait), the local independence of items, and sample-independent estimations of person and item parameters (i.e., invariant measurement).

On the occasion that scorers facilitate the assessment process, as is the case with the MCA pilot study, the Many Facet Rasch (MFR) model can be used to simultaneously define student ability, criterion difficulty, and scorer severity (Linacre, 1989/1994). The MFR model stems from the family of Rasch measurement models and can be used for both dichotomous or polytomous items (Wright & Mok, 2004). As pointed out by Engelhard (2013), the five requirements for invariant measurement can be extended to the context in which assessments are mediated by scorers: (a) scorer-invariant measurement of persons (i.e., the measurement of persons must be independent of the particular scorers that happen to be used for the measuring); (b) non-crossing person response functions (i.e., a more able person must always have a better chance of obtaining higher ratings from scorers than does a less able person; (c) person-invariant calibration of scorers (i.e., the calibration of the scorers must be independent of the particular persons used for calibration); (d) non-crossing scorer response functions (i.e., any person must have a better chance of obtaining a higher rating from lenient scorers than from more severe scorers; and (e) variable map (i.e., persons and scorers must be simultaneously located on a single underlying latent variable). When the data fit the requirements of the Rasch model, then it becomes possible to support invariant measurement that also implies scorer-invariant measurement of performances (Engelhard, 2013).

The purpose of the technical report in the following chapter is to investigate the psychometric properties (e.g., validity and reliability) of the National Association for Music Education's (NAfME) Music Model Cornerstone Assessment 2015–2016 Pilot Study. The MCAs investigated in this study include (a) Grade 2 create, (b) Grade 2 perform, (c) Grade 2 respond, (d) Grade 5 perform, (e) Grade 5 respond, (f) Grade 8 create, (g) composition/theory, (h) ensemble perform (intermediate), (i) ensemble perform (proficient), (j) harmonizing instruments, and (k) harmonizing instruments (revised). MCAs not investigated in this study involved challenges for the analysis for three possible reasons: (a) no data collected; (b) not enough data collected to warrant analysis; or (c) no cross-scoring occurred, resulting in student work confounding with the scorer. The specific research questions that guide this study include:

1. What is the overall psychometric quality (e.g., validity and reliability) of each of the model cornerstone assessments?
2. How well do the criteria fit the measurement model and how do they vary in difficulty?[1]
3. How does the rating-scale structure (i.e., levels) of each Model Cornerstone Assessment vary across individual criteria?

$$\ln\left[\frac{P_{nijmk}}{P_{nijmk-1}}\right] = \theta_n - \lambda_i - \delta_j - \gamma_m - \tau_{ik} \quad , \tag{1}$$

where

$\ln[P_{nijmk}/P_{nijmk-1}]$ = the probability that Student work n rated by Scorer i on Criterion j receives a rating in level k rather than level k-1,

  θ_n = the logit-scale location (e.g., achievement) of Student Work n,

  λ_i = the logit-scale location (e.g., severity) of Scorer i,

  δ_j = the logit-scale location (e.g., severity) of Scoring Type (e.g., peer- or self-scored) j,

  γ_m = the logit-scale location (e.g., achievement) of Criterion m,

  t_{ik} = the location on the logit scale where scale levels k and k-1 are equally probable for Scorer i.

Figure 11.1.

MEASUREMENT MODEL

The measurement model used in this study was the Multifaceted Rasch Partial Credit (MFR-PC) measurement model (Linacre, 1989/1994) (see Figure 11.1). The Partial Credit (PC) version of the model (Masters, 1982) adds an additional parameter to the model that allows for the investigation of the rating-scale structure across each of the criteria, thereby making it possible to test the null hypothesis of equidistant rating-scale levels across each criterion. The addition of this parameter provides construct evidence of the measure through the verification of an increasingly monotonic relationship between adjacent levels (i.e., the preservation of increasingly positive ordering that establishes an intended direction of "more achievement"), acceptable discrimination between performances, appropriate distribution of frequency use by scorers (i.e., multimodal use of all available rating-scale levels), and levels of acceptable randomness for the stochastic process of probabilistic modeling (i.e., acceptable levels of unsystematic variability for probabilistic processes; Linacre, 2002a). The PC model is specified as follows:

DATA ANALYSIS PROCEDURES

Examining Psychometric Quality

Table 11.1 presents a set of statistics and displays based on the MFR-PC model that can be used to examine the psychometric quality of musical performance assessments. Indices based on three distinct levels were examined: (a) logit-scale locations, (b) separation, and (c) model-data fit. Logit-scale locations provide a method for summarizing student work,

Table 11.1. Statistics and Displays Based on the MFR-PC Model

Level	Indicators and Displays based on the MFR-PC Model	Substantive Interpretation (Question)			
		Student Work Facet	Scorer Facet	Scoring-Type Facet	Criteria Facet
A. Logit-Scale Locations	1. Variable map	Where is the student work located on the construct being measured (criterion achievement)?	Where are the scorers located on the construct being measured (criterion achievement)?	Where are the scoring types located on the construct being measured (criterion achievement)?	Where are the criteria located on the construct being measured (criterion achievement)?
	2. Location of elements within the facet	What is the location of each student work (criterion achievement)?	What is the location of each scorer (severity/ leniency)?	What is the location of each scoring type (severity/ leniency)?	What is the location of each criterion (difficulty)?
	3. Standard error	How precisely has the location of each student work been estimated?	How precisely has the location of each scorer been estimated?	How precisely has the location of each scoring type been estimated?	How precisely has the location of each criterion been estimated?

(continued)

Table 11.1. (Continued)

Level	Indicators and Displays based on the MFR-PC Model	Substantive Interpretation (Question)				
		Student Work Facet	Scorer Facet	Scoring-Type Facet	Criteria Facet	
B. Separation	4. Reliability of separation statistic	How spread out are the scored performance locations on the logit scale?	How spread out are the scorer locations on the logit scale?	How spread out are the scoring-type locations on the logit scale?	How spread out are the criterion locations on the logit scale?	
	5. Chi-square statistic	Are the overall differences between student work locations significant?	Are the overall differences between scorer locations significant?	Are the overall differences between scoring-type locations significant?	Are the overall differences between criterion locations significant?	
C. Model-Data Fit	6. Mean Square Error (MSE) and standardized fit statistics	How consistently has each student work been interpreted by the scorers?	How consistently has each scorer interpreted the items and rating scale levels across the student work?	How consistently has each scoring type interpreted the items and rating scale levels across the student work?	How consistently has each criterion been interpreted by the scorers?	

scorer severity, scoring-type severity, and criterion difficulty on a single linear scale that represents the latent construct. Separation indicates the degree to which the elements within a facet can be reliably differentiated from one another. Elements refer to each piece of individual student work (within the student work facet), each individual scorer (within the scorer facet), each scoring type (within the scoring type facet), and each individual criterion (within the criterion facet). The separation statistic for student work can be interpreted similarly to Cronbach's alpha, indicating high reproducibility of relative measure locations. Separation statistics for scorers, scoring type, and criteria can be interpreted as the separation verification of the hierarchy for the elements within each facet (i.e., construct validity). Model-data fit indices describe how closely the raw score observations provided by the scorers approximate the useful, invariant properties of the Rasch model. Mean square error (MSE) fit statistics demonstrate the overall randomness within the model (Linacre, 2002b). Perfect predictability is represented by the value of 1.00. Values less than 1.00 indicate too much predictability/redundancy in the data (i.e., muted data). Values above 1.00 indicate too little predictability in the data (i.e., sporadic data). In particular, infit MSE fit statistics represent inlier-sensitive fit, where over- or under-fit for Guttman probabilistic patterns are detected. Outfit MSE fit statistics represent outlier-sensitive fit, where over-fit for observations of model variance are detected. When reasonable model-data fit to the model is observed, invariant measurement is achieved. At the parameter level, the reasonable mean-square range for infit and outfit is 0.50–1.50. The reasonable mean-square range for infit and outfit at the element level for *high stakes assessments* is 0.80–1.20. In the case of the MCAs, the data will be treated as *survey/rating-scale data* where the scorers are untrained. Therefore, the reasonable mean-square range for infit and outfit for the element level is 0.60–1.40. Standardized fit statistics (*Zstd*) are t-tests (reported as z-scores) that test the hypothesis of perfect model data fit for predictability of data. Less than the expected score of 0.00 indicates predictability, and values above 0.00 indicate lack of predictability. All data fitting in the range of −1.90 to 1.90 indicates reasonable predictability and good model data fit (Linacre & Wright, 2004). Fit statistics within the threshold indicate sufficient accuracy and predictability of model data fit, validity evidence for the construct, and good productivity for measurement (Linacre, 2002b).

Because the Rasch model is unidimensional, it is possible to display the location estimates for each facet on a single linear scale. The *variable map* is a useful method for visually displaying descriptions of student work, criteria, scorers, and other facets of interest in terms of a single, unidimensional latent variable. The usefulness of the variable map is a major factor in the adoption of Rasch modeling by many national and international assessments, including but not limited to the National Assessment of Educational Progress and the Program for International Student Assessment, for example. In the context of this study, the variable maps provide a graphical representation of the student work, scorer, score type, and criterion facets on a common "ruler."

Examining Rating-Scale Structure

Application of the Partial Credit Model (Wright & Masters, 1982) to Linacre's (1989/1994) MFR model extends the analysis to allow the distance between rating-scale level thresholds to vary across each criterion. Statistically, the process of freeing each criterion from a rating-scale grouping and allowing it to define its own partial credit scale allows for each ordered rating-scale level to be estimated. Substantively, the process indicates that in addition to each criterion having its own unique difficulty level as identified by its location on the logit scale, each rating-scale level within each item, too, has its own difficulty level as indicated by its own unique location on the logit scale. For polytomous items, such as those found in the MCAs, inter-adjacent-level discrimination indices (i.e., Rasch-Andrich thresholds) provide the location on the latent continuum where adjacent rating-scale levels are discriminated. In the instance where four levels are used for each criterion (e.g., Level 1 = "Emerging"; Level 2 = "Approaching Criterion"; Level 3 = "Meets Criterion"; Level 4 = "Exceeding Criterion"), the levels are modeled by a set of three discrimination indices that describe the location where (1) Level 1 and Level 2 are discriminated, (2) where Level 2 and Level 3 are discriminated, and (3) where Level 3 and Level 4 are discriminated. The substantive interpretation of the Rasch-Andrich thresholds, however, is based on adequate functioning and proper optimization of the rating-scale levels.

Linacre (2002b) indicates that methodological steps can be taken in order to optimize rating-scale level structures. Modification of the structure based on this empirical methodology provides more rigorous examination and precise estimation of performances, ultimately addressing and improving validity issues surrounding construct validity of the measurement instrument. Additionally, this post hoc investigation can clarify the meaning of the collected data and improve subsequent use of the scale. First, frequency counts for each of the four levels were examined. Uniformly distributed frequency counts across each of the rating-scale levels are optimal for the calibration of rating-scale difficulties. Any frequency count demonstrating less than 10% of the total level usage provides incentive to collapse the level into an adjacent level. Second, outfit MSEs were examined for values ≥2.0. Values greater than 2.0 indicate excessive noise in the ratings. More specifically, levels exhibiting MSE values ≥2.0 indicate that they have been used by scorers in unexpected contexts and warrant their collapse into an adjacent level. Third, average observed logit measures were examined for violations of monotonicity. Monotonicity can be described as the continuous advancement of threshold calibrations (Andrich, 1996). This is a requirement for inferential interpretability of the rating scale. In instances when incrementally higher measures were not observed, it is suggested that violating levels are to be collapsed into adjacent levels.

NOTE

1. Throughout this report, each component of the MCA (e.g., interpret, evaluate, etc.) is referred to as a *trait*. Each row of the MCA is referred to as a *criterion*, and the columns (emerging, approaching standard, meets standard, exceeds standard) are referred to as *levels*.

REFERENCES

Andrich, D. A. (1996). Measurement criteria for choosing among models for graded responses. In A. von Eye & C. C. Clogg (Eds.), *Analysis of categorical variables in developmental research* (pp. 3–35). Orlando FL: Academic Press.

Cavanagh, R. F., & Waugh, R. F. (2011). *Applications of Rasch measurement in learning environment research*. Rotterdam, The Netherlands: Sense Publishers.

Engelhard, G. (1994). Examining rater errors in the assessment of written composition with a many-faceted Rasch model. *Journal of Educational Measurement, 31*(2), 93–112.

Engelhard, G. (2013). *Invariant measurement: Using Rasch models in the social, behavioral, and health sciences*. New York: Routledge.

Engelhard Jr., G., & Perkins, A. F. (2011). Person response functions and the definition of units in the social sciences. *Measurement, 9*(1), 40–45.

Linacre, J. M. (1989/1994). *Many-facet Rasch measurement*. Chicago, IL: MESA Press.

Linacre, J. M. (2002a). Judge ratings with forced agreement. *Rasch Measurement Transactions, 16*(1), 857–858.

Linacre, J. M. (2002b). Optimizing rating scale level effectiveness. *Journal of Applied Measurement, 3*, 85–106.

Linacre, J. M., & Wright, B. D. (2004). Construction of measures from many-facet data. In E. V. Smith & R. M. Smith (Eds.), *Introduction to Rasch measurement: Theories, models, and applications* (pp. 296–321). Maple Grove, MN: JAM Press.

Masters, G. N. (1982). A Rasch model for partial credit scoring. *Psychometrika, 47*, 149–174.

Rasch, G. (1960/1980). *Probabilistic models for some intelligence and attainment tests*. Copenhagen, Denmark: Danish Institute for Educational Research. Expanded edition. (1980). Chicago, IL: University of Chicago Press.

Wright, B. D., & Masters, G. N. (1982). *Rating Scale Analysis*. Chicago: MESA Press.

Wright, B. D., & Mok, M. C. (2004). An overview of the family of Rasch measurement models. In E. V. Smith and R. M. Smith (Eds.), *Introduction to Rasch measurement: Theories, models, and applications* (1–24). Maple Grove, MN: JAM Press.

TWELVE

Examination of the Psychometric Qualities of the Model Cornerstone Assessments

Brian C. Wesolowski

In music and related behavioral sciences, psychological measurement is used as a method for inference. One fundamental distinction of psychological measurement from scientific measurement is that it is concerned with measuring abstract, latent properties that cannot be physically demonstrated. Accordingly, latent properties must be defined by secondary, observable behaviors. The purpose of the Model Cornerstone Assessment (MCA) Pilot Study was to develop criteria that provide formative and summative means to measure student achievement of performance standards in the National Core Music Standards. However, it is important to be aware that the development of criteria within the context of an assessment is, but perhaps more broadly, the process of developing a hypothetical, latent construct. In the broadest sense, the constructs are the processes directly associated with the National Core Music Standards. Therefore, the development of assessments is dualistic: (a) to provide a means for measuring students, and (b) to develop a hypothetical latent construct. Therefore, the results reported in this chapter not only provide information about student performance; more importantly, they provide diagnostic information about each of the latent constructs represented by the measurement instruments. Therefore, it is recommended that the suggestions provided here be strongly considered as a mechanism to re-develop and refine the hypothetical construct intended to be developed.

The MCAs investigated in this study include Grade 2: create, perform, respond; Grade 5: perform, respond; Grade 8: create; Composition/ Theory create, respond, perform (proficient level); Ensemble: perform (intermediate and proficient); and Harmonizing Instruments: create (proficient). Responses to research question 1, *"What is the overall psychometric quality (e.g., validity and reliability) of each of the Model Cornerstone Assessments?"* are provided under the summary statistics subheadings and depicted through the related variable maps. Responses to research question 2, *"How well do the criteria fit the measurement model, and how do they vary in difficulty?"* are provided under the calibrations of traits and calibration of criteria subheadings. Responses to research question 3, *"How does the rating-scale structure of each Model Cornerstone Assessment vary across individual criteria?"* are provided under the rating-scale-level diagnostics and inter-adjacent-level discrimination indices subheadings. Each MCA report includes *summary statistics, calibration of student work, calibration of scorer findings, calibration of scoring type, calibration of traits, calibration of criteria, rating-scale-level diagnostics,* and *inter-adjacent-level discrimination indices* and a *Findings* section.

PRECURSORY INFORMATION

In all reports that follow, the *calibration of student work* assumes that the student work facet was allowed to float (i.e., noncentered) relative to all other facets in the model. Common practice indicates that objects of measurement be allowed to float. All student work outside the reasonable mean-square range for infit and outfit (0.60–1.40) did not adequately fit the measurement model. It is suggested that first, these cases not be used as exemplars of student work, and second, that they be investigated qualitatively for indicators as to why they may not have demonstrated adequate model-data fit.

The *calibration of scorer findings* assumes that the scorer facet was centered on the logit scale (mean of 0.00 logits) to provide a frame of reference for the interpretation of the student work locations (i.e., objects of measurement), and as a result, means are reported in logits.

The *calibration of scoring type* assumes that student work was crossed-scored, providing two types of scoring: (a) peer scoring and (b) self-scoring. The scoring-type facet was centered on the logit scale (mean of 0.00 logits) to provide a frame of reference for the interpretation of the student work locations (i.e., objects of measurement).

The *calibration of traits* assumes that the trait facet was centered on the logit scale (mean of 0.00 logits) to provide a frame of reference for the interpretation of the student work locations (i.e., objects of measurement). Similarly, the *calibration of criteria* assumes that the student work facet was centered on the logit scale (mean of 0.00 logits) to provide a frame of reference for the interpretation of the student work locations (i.e., objects of measurement).

The *inter-adjacent-level discrimination* indices all assume that evidence exists to reject the null hypothesis of equidistant rating-scale levels. Prior to evaluating the inter-adjacent-level discrimination indices provided, any recommendations of collapsing levels under the *Rating-Scale-Level Di-*

agnostics subheading should be considered. Then, assuming acceptability of the related rating-scale-level diagnostics, the range of rating-scale Level 1 (emerging) is −∞ to the logit score indicated under the *Level 2 Threshold* subheading, minus the standard error. The range of rating-scale Level 2 (approaching) is the logit score listed under the *Level 2 Threshold* subheading, minus the standard error and the logit score listed under the *Level 3 Threshold* subheading, minus the standard error. The range of rating-scale Level 3 (meets) is the logit score listed under the *Level 3 Threshold* subheading, minus the standard error and the logit score listed under the *Level 4 Threshold* subheading, minus the standard error. The range of rating-scale Level 4 (i.e., exceeding) is the logit score listed under the *Level 4 Threshold* subheading, minus the standard error to ∞.

Construct validity is addressed in each report in the *Findings* section as demonstrated by the reasonable parameter separation for each of the considered parameters. The parameters considered for each MCA were (a) student work, (b) scorers, (c) scoring type, and (d) criteria. Reasonable parameter separation indicates that one set of parameters (the performance achievement of student work, for example) can be estimated without any interference from any of the other parameters (the severity of the raters or difficulties of the criteria, for example). As a result, one can directly and meaningfully interpret the characteristics of each parameter (e.g., the overall performance achievement of a student, the overall severity of the scorers, the overall severity of scoring types, and the overall difficulties of the level) as a unique characteristic to those parameters. This is a characteristic of fundamental measurement that is specifically underscored by properties of invariance that is expected in physical measurement, and a unique characteristic of the Rasch family of measurement models in the context of psychological measurement as applied here. As with the previous chapter and for the purposes of this chapter, each process component of the MCA (e.g., interpret, evaluate, etc.) is referred to as a *trait*. Each row of the MCA is referred to as a *criterion*, and the columns (Emerging, Approaching Standard, Meets Standard, Exceeds Standard) are referred to as *levels*. Tables and figures are found at http://nafme.org/wp-content/files/2017/10/Chapter-12-Data-Tables-and-Figures.pdf.

GRADE 2 CREATE MCA

Summary Statistics

Table 12.A1 provides the summary statistics for the MFR-PC model analysis of student work ($n = 333$), scorers ($n = 8$), scoring type ($n = 2$) and criteria ($n = 1$). The analysis indicated an overall good model data fit with significant differences between student work ($\chi^2_{(332)}$ = 841.90, p< .01), scorers ($\chi^2_{(7)}$ = 123.80, p< .01), scoring type ($\chi^2_{(1)}$ = 61.60, p< .01), and criteria ($\chi^2_{(10)}$ = 3821.20, p< .01). Reliability of separation statistics for all four facets are as follows: student work (*Rel* = .63), scorers (*Rel* = .71), scoring type (*Rel* = .97), and criteria (*Rel* = .99). See figure 12.I1 for the variable map.

Calibration of Student Work

Table 12.B1 provides student work calibration information. The mean of the student work was 0.89 logits with a range of 2.95 logits for the highest fit achieving student work (Student ID 4778) to –1.39 logits for the lowest fit achieving (Student ID 4802).

Calibration of Scorers

Table 12.C1 provides scorer calibration information. The mean of the scorers was 0.00 logits with a range of 0.39 for the most severe scorer (Scorer 8) to –0.43 for the most lenient scorer (Scorer 1). All scorers demonstrated adequate fit to the model based on the reasonable mean-square range for infit and outfit (0.60–1.40).

Calibration of Scoring Type

Table 12.D1 provides scoring-type calibration information. The mean of the scoring-type facet was 0.00 logits with a range of 0.15 for the most severe scoring type (peer score) to –0.15 for the most lenient scoring type (self score). Both scoring types demonstrated adequate fit to the model based on the reasonable mean-square range for infit and outfit (0.60–1.40).

Calibration of Traits

Table 12.E1 provides trait calibration information. The mean of the traits was 0.00 logits with a range of 0.60 for the most difficult trait (scoring device 1, part 2) to –0.25 for the least difficult trait (scoring device 1, part 1). All traits demonstrated adequate fit to the model based on the reasonable mean-square range for infit and outfit (0.60–1.40).

Calibration of Criteria

Table 12.F1 provides criterion calibration information. The mean of the criteria was 0.00 logits with a range of 2.76 for the most difficult criterion (rhythmic complexity) to –1.05 for the easiest criterion (uniqueness of response). All criteria demonstrated adequate fit to the model based on the reasonable mean-square range for infit and outfit (0.60–1.40).

Rating-Scale-Level Diagnostics

Rating-scale diagnostics can be found in table 12.G1. Three steps were taken in order to evaluate the rating-scale-level structure. First, frequency counts for each level were evaluated for usage under 10%. Results indicated that four levels did not reach the prescribed 10% usage: (a) Level 1 of criterion 2, (b) Level 1 of criterion 7, (c) Level 1 of criterion 8, and (d) Level 2 of criterion 9. It is therefore recommended that all first levels be collapsed into their respective adjacent Level 2 and be rewritten, and Level 2 of criterion 9 be collapsed into its adjacent Level 1 and be rewritten. Second, outfit mean squares (MSE) were examined for values ≥ 2.0. Results indicated that no levels were found to have an MSE value ≥ 2.0. Third, average observed logit measures were examined for violations of monotonicity. Results indicated no violations of monotonicity.

Inter-Adjacent-Level Discrimination Indices

Rasch-Andrich thresholds can be found in table 12.H1 for each criterion within the respective trait.

Findings

The Grade 2 Create MCA demonstrated overall strong construct validity as demonstrated by the reasonable parameter separation for each of the considered parameters.

Results indicated that the rank order of traits by difficulty (from most difficult to least difficult) was (1) scoring device 1, part 2, (2) scoring device 2, and (3) scoring device 1, part 1. All criteria were found to be appropriate and meaningful in their overall functioning within the context of measuring the *Create* construct for second grade. An analysis of the usability and meaningfulness of the levels across each criterion indicated some evidence for suggested revisions. The labels associated with each criterion are found in table 12.G1. Based on the analysis, the following is recommended: (a) Level 1 of criterion 2 should be collapsed with Level 2 of criterion 2 and be rewritten; (b) Level 1 of criterion 7 should be collapsed with Level 2 of criterion 7 and be rewritten; (c) Level 1 of criterion 8 should be collapsed with Level 2 of criterion 8 and be rewritten; and (d) Level 2 of criterion 9 should be collapsed with Level 1 of criterion 9 and be rewritten. The tables displaying all psychometric analyses for the Grade 2 Create MCA include tables 12.A1, 12.B1, 12.C1, 12.D1, 12.E1, 12.F1, 12.G1, and 12.H1. The variable map can be found in figure 12.I1 (http://nafme.org/wp-content/files/2017/10/Chapter-12-Data-Tables -and-Figures.pdf).

GRADE 2 PERFORM

Summary Statistics

Table 12.A2 provides the summary statistics for the MFR-PC model analysis of student work (n = 222), scorers (n = 9), scoring type (n = 2) and criteria (n = 7). The analysis indicated an overall good model data fit with significant differences between student work ($\chi^2_{(221)}$ = 1649.30, p< .01), scorers ($\chi^2_{(8)}$ = 184.80, p< .01), scoring type ($\chi^2_{(1)}$ = 5.00, p< .01), and criteria ($\chi^2_{(6)}$ = 1115.30, p< .01). Reliability of separation statistics for all four facets are as follows: student work (Rel = .86), scorers (Rel = .94), scoring type (Rel< .00), and criteria (Rel = .99). See figure 12.I2 for the variable map.

Calibration of Student Work

Table 12.B2 provides student work calibration information. The mean of the student work was 0.70 logits with a range of 3.86 logits for the highest fit achieving student work (Student ID 4934) to –3.53 logits for the lowest fit achieving (Student ID 4343).

Calibration of Scorers

Table 12.C2 provides scorer calibration information. The mean of the scorers was 0.00 logits with a range of 0.68 for the most severe scorer (Scorer 5) to –0.49 for the most lenient scorer (Scorer 6). All scorers demonstrated adequate fit to the model based on the reasonable mean-square range for infit and outfit (0.60–1.40).

Calibration of Scoring Type

Table 12.D2 provides scoring-type calibration information. The mean of the scoring-type facet was 0.00 logits. Because separation of reliability was low (0.00), both scoring types demonstrated logit measures 0.00, indicating that student performances were not separated based on scorers' affiliation to a scoring type.

Calibration of Criteria

Table 12.F2 provides criterion calibration information. The mean of the criteria was 0.00 logits with a range of 1.46 for the most difficult criterion (expressive quality) to –1.55 for the easiest criterion (rhythm). All criteria demonstrated adequate fit to the model based on the reasonable mean-square range for infit and outfit (0.60–1.40).

Rating-Scale-Level Diagnostics

Rating-scale diagnostics can be found in table 12.G2. Three steps were taken in order to evaluate the rating-scale-level structure. First frequency counts for each level were evaluated for usage under 10%. Results indicated that two levels did not reach the prescribed 10% usage: (a) Level 1 of criterion 2, and (b) Level 4 of criterion 7. It is therefore recommended that Level 1 of criterion 2 be collapsed into its respective adjacent Level 2 and be rewritten, and Level 4 of criterion 7 be collapsed into its adjacent Level 3 and be rewritten. Second, outfit mean squares (MSE) were examined for values ≥2.0. Results indicated that one level was found to have an MSE value ≥2.0: Level 3 of criterion 1. It is therefore recommended that Level 3 be examined and rewritten. Third, average observed logit measures were examined for violations of monotonicity. Results indicated no violations of monotonicity.

Inter-Adjacent-Level Discrimination Indices

Rasch-Andrich thresholds can be found in table 12.H2 for each criterion within the respective trait.

Findings

The Grade 2 Perform MCA demonstrated overall strong construct validity as demonstrated by the reasonable parameter separation for each of the considered parameters.

Results indicated that the rank order of criteria by difficulty (from most difficult to least difficult) was (1) expressive quality, (2) tonal center, (3) intonation/pitch, (4) starting pitch, (5) singing voice, (6) tempo, and (7) rhythm. All criteria were found to be appropriate and meaningful in their overall functioning within the context of measuring the *Perform* construct for second grade. An analysis of the usability and meaningfulness of the levels across each criterion indicated some evidence for suggested revisions. The labels associated with each criterion are found in table 12.G2. Based on the analysis, the following is recommended: Level 1 of criterion 2 be collapsed into its respective adjacent Level 2 and be rewritten, and Level 4 of criterion 7 be collapsed into its adjacent Level 3 and be rewritten, Level 3 be rewritten with more specificity. The tables displaying all psychometric analyses for the Grade 2 Perform MCA include tables 12.A2, 12.B2, 12.C2, 12.D2, 12.E2, 12.F2, 12.G2, and 12.H2. The variable map can be found in figure 12.I2.

GRADE 2 RESPOND

Summary Statistics

Table 12.A3 provides the summary statistics for the MFR-PC model analysis of student work ($n = 261$), scorers ($n = 8$), scoring type ($n = 2$) and criteria ($n = 3$). The analysis indicated an overall good model data fit with significant differences between student work ($\chi^2_{(260)} = 714.60$, $p< .01$), scorers ($\chi^2_{(7)} = 124.40$, $p< .01$), scoring type ($\chi^2_{(1)} = 10.40$, $p< .01$), and criteria ($\chi^2_{(2)} = 33.20$, $p< .01$). Reliability of separation statistics for all four facets are as follows: student work ($Rel = .65$), scorers ($Rel = .94$), scoring type ($Rel = .81$), and criteria ($Rel = .91$). See figure 12.I3 for the variable map.

Calibration of Student Work

Table 12.B3 provides student work calibration information. The mean of the student work was –1.12 logits with a range of 4.69 logits for the highest fit achieving student work (Student ID 2596) to –6.06 logits for the lowest fit achieving (Student ID 3808).

Calibration of Scorers

Table 12.C3 provides scorer calibration information. The mean of the scorers was 0.00 logits with a range of 1.73 for the most severe scorer (Scorer 5) to –0.29 for the most lenient scorer (Scorer 6). Scorer 3 demonstrated muted rating patterns as evidenced by an infit MSE less than 0.60.

Calibration of Scoring Type

Table 12.D3 provides scoring-type calibration information. The mean of the scoring-type facet was 0.00 logits with a range of 0.26 for the most severe scoring type (peer score) to –0.26 for the most lenient scoring type (self score). Both scoring types demonstrated adequate fit to the model based on the reasonable mean-square range for infit and outfit (0.60–1.40).

Calibration of Traits

Table 12.E2 provides trait calibration information. The mean of the traits was 0.00 logits with a range of 0.16 for the most difficult trait (evaluate) to –0.31 for the least difficult trait (interpret). All traits demonstrated adequate fit to the model based on the reasonable mean-square range for infit and outfit (0.60–1.40).

Calibration of Criteria

Table 12.F3 provides criterion calibration information. The mean of the criteria was 0.00 logits with a range of 0.51 for the most difficult criterion (cite musical reasons) to –0.31 for the easiest criterion (movement). All criteria demonstrated adequate fit to the model based on the reasonable mean-square range for infit and outfit (0.60–1.40).

Rating-Scale-Level Diagnostics

Rating-scale diagnostics can be found in table 12.G3. Three steps were taken in order to evaluate the rating-scale level structure. First frequency counts for each level were evaluated for usage under 10%. Results indicated that three levels did not reach the prescribed 10% usage: (a) Level 4 of criterion 1, and (b) Level 4 of criterion 2, and (c) Level 4 of criterion 3. It is therefore recommended that each of these levels be collapsed into their respective Level 3s and be rewritten. Second, outfit mean squares (MSE) were examined for values ≥2.0. Results indicated that one level was found to have an MSE value ≥2.0: Level 4 of criterion 3. Because Level 4 of criterion 3 additionally did not reach the minimum level usage, it is recommended that this level be collapsed into Level 3. Third, average observed logit measures were examined for violations of monotonicity. Results indicated one level that violated the rule of monotonicity: Level 4 of criterion 4. Because Level 4 of criterion 3 did not reach the minimum frequency use and was found to have an MSE value ≥2.0, it is recommended to collapse Level 4 into the adjacent Level 3.

Inter-Adjacent-Level Discrimination Indices

Rasch-Andrich thresholds can be found in table 12.H3 for each criterion within the respective trait.

Findings

The Grade 2 Respond MCA demonstrated overall strong construct validity as demonstrated by the reasonable parameter separation for each of the considered parameters.

Results indicated that the rank order of criteria by difficulty (from most difficult to least difficult) was (1) cite musical reasons, (2) verbal response, and (3) movement. All criteria were found to be appropriate and meaningful in their overall functioning within the context of measuring the *Respond* construct for second grade. An analysis of the usability and meaningfulness of the levels across each criterion (i.e., emerging, approaches standard, meets standard, exceeds standard) indicated some evidence for suggested revisions. The labels associated with each criterion are found in table 12.G3. Based on the analysis, the following is recommended: (a) Level 4 of criterion 1 should be collapsed with Level 3 of criterion 1 and be rewritten, and (b) Level 4 of criterion 2 should be collapsed with Level 3 of criterion 2 and be rewritten, and (c) Level 4 of criterion 3 should be collapsed with Level 3 of criterion 3 and be rewritten. The tables displaying all psychometric analyses for the Grade 2 Respond MCA include tables 12.A3, 12.B3, 12.C3, 12.D3, 12.E3, 12.F3, 12.G3, and 12.H3. The variable map can be found in figure 12.I3.

GRADE 5 PERFORM

Summary Statistics

Table 12.A4 provides the summary statistics for the MFR-PC model analysis of student work ($n = 43$), scorers ($n = 3$), scoring type ($n = 2$) and criteria ($n = 12$). The analysis indicated an overall good model data fit with significant differences between student work ($\chi^2_{(42)} = 356.80$, $p< .01$), scorers ($\chi^2_{(2)} = 99.00$, $p< .01$), and criteria ($\chi^2_{(11)} = 172.40$, $p< .01$). Non-significance was found for score type ($\chi^2_{(1)} = 2.20$, $p = .55$). Reliability of separation statistics for the three significant facets are as follows: student work ($Rel = .85$), scorers ($Rel = .97$), and criteria ($Rel = .94$). See figure 12.I4 for the variable map.

Calibration of Student Work

Table 12.B4 provides student work calibration information. The mean of the student work was –0.12 logits with a range of 3.46 logits for the highest fit achieving student work (Student ID 3058) to –3.16 logits for the lowest fit achieving (Student ID 5132).

Calibration of Scorers

Table 12.C4 provides scorer calibration information. The mean of the scorers was 0.00 logits with a range of 0.71 for the most severe scorer (Scorer 1) to –0.97 for the most lenient scorer (Scorer 3). All scorers demonstrated adequate fit to the model based on the reasonable mean-square range for infit and outfit (0.60–1.40).

Calibration of Traits

Table 12.E3 provides trait calibration information. The mean of the traits was 0.00 logits with a range of 0.59 for the most difficult trait (performance) to –0.91 for the least difficult trait (music selection). All traits demonstrated adequate fit to the model based on the reasonable mean-square range for infit and outfit (0.60–1.40).

Calibration of Criteria

Table 12.F4 provides criterion calibration information. The mean of the criteria was 0.00 logits with a range of 1.05 for the most difficult criterion (expressive quality) to –2.36 for the easiest criterion (P interest). All criteria demonstrated adequate fit to the model based on the reasonable mean-square range for infit and outfit (0.60–1.40).

Rating-Scale-Level Diagnostics

Rating-scale diagnostics can be found in table 12.G4. Three steps were taken to evaluate the rating-scale-level structure. First frequency counts for each level were evaluated for usage under 10%. Results indicated that eight levels did not reach the prescribed 10% usage: (a) Level 1 of criterion 1, (b) Level 1 of criterion 2, (c) Level 1 of criterion 10, (d) Level 1 of criterion 11, (e) Level 1 of criterion 12, (f) Level 4 of criterion 3, (g) Level 4 of criterion 5, and (h) Level 4 of criterion 6. It is therefore recommended that each Level 1 be collapsed into its respective adjacent Level 2 and be rewritten, and each Level 4 of criterion be collapsed into its adjacent Level 3 and be rewritten. Second, outfit mean squares (MSE) were examined for values ≥2.0. Results indicated that one level was found to have an MSE value ≥2.0: Level 2 of criterion 4. It is therefore recommended that this level be examined, collapsed into Level 1, and rewritten. Third, average observed logit measures were examined for violations of monotonicity. Results indicated no violations of monotonicity.

Inter-Adjacent-Level Discrimination Indices

Rasch-Andrich thresholds can be found in table 12.H4 for each criterion within the respective trait.

Findings

The Grade 5 Perform MCA demonstrated overall strong construct validity as demonstrated by the reasonable parameter separation for each of the considered parameters. Results indicated that the rank order of criteria by difficulty (from most difficult to least difficult) was (1) expressive quality, (2) accuracy, (3) technical ability, (4) quality of interpretation, (5) appropriateness, (6) context, (7) considerations of personal performance, (8) analyze, (9) consideration of feedback, (10) performance decorum, (11) consideration of teacher-provided criteria and peer feedback, and (12) personal interest. All criteria were found to be appropriate and meaningful in their overall functioning within the context of measuring the *Perform* construct for fifth grade. An analysis of the usability and meaningfulness of the levels across each criterion (i.e., emerging, approaches standard, meets standard, exceeds standard) indicated some evidence for suggested revisions. The labels associated with each criterion are found in table 12.G4. Based on the analysis, the following is recommended: (a) Level 1 of criterion 1 should be collapsed with Level 2 of criterion 1 and be rewritten, (b) Level 1 of criterion 2 should be collapsed with Level 2 of criterion 2 and be rewritten, (c) Level 1 of criterion 10 should be collapsed with Level 2 of criterion 10 and be rewritten, (d) Level 1 of criterion 11 should be collapsed with Level 2 of criterion 11 and be rewritten, (e) Level 1 of criterion 12 should be collapsed with Level 2 of criterion 12 and be rewritten, (f) Level 4 of criterion 3 should be collapsed with Level 3 of criterion 3 and be rewritten, (g) Level 4 of criterion 5 should be collapsed with Level 3 of criterion 5 and be rewritten, and (h) Level 4 of criterion 6 should be collapsed with Level 3 of criterion 6 and be rewritten. The tables displaying all psychometric analyses for the Grade 5 Respond MCA include tables 12.A4, 12.B4, 12.C4, 12.D4, 12.E4, 12.F4, 12.G4, and 12.H4. The variable map can be found in figure I4.

GRADE 5 RESPOND MCA

Summary Statistics

Table 12.A5 provides the summary statistics for the MFR-PC model analysis of student work ($n = 110$), scorers ($n = 6$), scoring type ($n = 2$) and criteria ($n = 5$). The analysis indicated an overall good model data fit with significant differences between student work ($\chi^2_{(109)} = 587.10$, $p < .01$), scorers ($\chi^2_{(5)} = 30.90$, $p < .01$), scoring type ($\chi^2_{(1)} = 48.10$, $p < .01$), and criteria ($\chi^2_{(4)} = 64.80$, $p < .01$). Reliability of separation statistics for all four facets are as follows: student work ($Rel = .83$), scorers ($Rel = .78$), scoring type ($Rel = .96$), and criteria ($Rel = .92$). See figure 12.I5 for the variable map.

Calibration of Student Work

Table 12.B5 provides student work calibration information. The mean of the student work was −0.98 logits with a range of 3.41 logits for the highest fit achieving student work (Student ID 3229) to –5.36 logits for the lowest fit achieving (Student ID 4331).

Calibration of Scorers

Table 12.C5 provides scorer calibration information. The mean of the scorers was 0.00 logits with a range of 0.26 for the most severe scorer (Scorer 3) to –0.63 for the most lenient scorer (Scorer 4). All scorers demonstrated adequate fit to the model based on the reasonable mean-square range for infit and outfit (0.60–1.40).

Calibration of Scoring Type

Table 12.D5 provides scoring-type calibration information. The mean of the scoring-type facet was 0.00 logits with a range of 0.38 for the most severe scoring type (peer score) to –0.38 for the most lenient scoring type (self score). Both scoring types demonstrated adequate fit to the model based on the reasonable mean-square range for infit and outfit (0.60–1.40).

Calibration of Criteria

Table 12.F5 provides criterion calibration information. The mean of the criteria was 0.00 logits with a range of 0.64 for the most difficult criterion (selecting best representation Q2) to –0.56 for the easiest criterion (interpreting qualities Q1). All criteria demonstrated adequate fit to the model based on the reasonable mean-square range for infit and outfit (0.60–1.40).

Rating-Scale-Level Diagnostics

Rating-scale diagnostics can be found in table 12.G5. Three steps were taken in order to evaluate the rating-scale-level structure: First, frequency counts for each level were evaluated for usage under 10%. Results indicated that one level did not reach the prescribed 10% usage: Level 4 of criterion 3. It is therefore recommended that Level 4 be collapsed into its respective adjacent Level 3 and be rewritten. Second, outfit mean squares (MSE) were examined for values ≥2.0. Results indicated that no levels were found to have an MSE value ≥2.0. Third, average observed logit measures were examined for violations of monotonicity. Results indicated no violations of monotonicity.

Inter-Adjacent-Level Discrimination Indices

Rasch-Andrich thresholds can be found in table 12.H5 for each criterion within the respective trait.

Findings

The Grade 5 Respond MCA demonstrated overall strong construct validity as demonstrated by the reasonable parameter separation for each of the considered parameters. Results indicated that the rank order of criteria by difficulty (from most difficult to least difficult) was (1) selecting best representation Q2, (2) reflection Q2, (3) interpreting qualities Q3, (4) connections Q4, and (5) interpreting qualities Q1. All criteria were found to be appropriate and meaningful in their overall functioning within the context of measuring the *Respond* construct for fifth grade. An analysis of the usability and meaningfulness of the levels across each criterion (i.e., emerging, approaches standard, meets standard, exceeds standard) indicated some evidence for suggested revisions. The labels associated with each criterion are found in table 12.G5. Based on the analysis, the following is recommended: Level 4 should be collapsed with Level 3 of criterion 3 and be rewritten. The tables displaying all psychometric analyses for the Grade 5 Respond MCA include tables 12.A5, 12.B5, 12.C5, 12.D5, 12.E5, 12.F5, 12.G5, and 12.H5. The variable map can be found in figure 12.I5.

GRADE 8 CREATE

Summary Statistics

Table 12.A6 provides the summary statistics for the MFR-PC model analysis of student work ($n = 40$), scorers ($n = 2$), scoring type ($n = 2$) and criteria ($n = 8$). The analysis indicated an overall good model data fit with significant differences between student work ($\chi^2_{(39)} = 204.90$, $p< .01$), scorers ($\chi^2_{(1)} = 30.60$, $p< .01$), scoring type ($\chi^2_{(1)} = 4.50$, $p< .01$), and criteria ($\chi^2_{(7)} = 111.20$, $p< .01$). Reliability of separation statistics for all four facets are as follows: student work (*Rel* = .83), scorers (*Rel* = .93), scoring type (*Rel* = .55), and criteria (*Rel* = 93). See figure 12.I6 for the variable map.

Calibration of Student Work

Table 12.B6 provides student work calibration information. The mean of the student work was –0.71 logits with a range of 1.74 logits for the highest fit achieving student work (Student ID 4518) to –3.77 logits for the lowest fit achieving (Student ID 3530).

Calibration of Scorers

Table 12.C6 provides scorer calibration information. The mean of the scorers was 0.00 logits with a range of 0.61 for the most severe scorer (Scorer 1) to –0.61 for the most lenient scorer (Scorer 2). All scorers demonstrated adequate fit to the model based on the reasonable mean-square range for infit and outfit (0.60–1.40).

Calibration of Scoring Type

Table 12.D6 provides scoring-type calibration information. The mean of the scoring-type facet was 0.00 logits with a range of 0.41 for the most severe scoring type (peer score) to –0.41 for the most lenient scoring type (self score). Both scoring types demonstrated adequate fit to the model based on the reasonable mean-square range for infit and outfit (0.60–1.40).

Calibration of Criteria

Table 12.F6 provides criterion calibration information. The mean of the criteria was 0.00 logits with a range of 1.14 for the most difficult criterion (applying criteria) to –1.48 for the easiest criterion (craftsmanship). All criteria demonstrated adequate fit to the model based on the reasonable mean-square range for infit and outfit (0.60–1.40).

Rating-Scale-Level Diagnostics

Rating-scale diagnostics can be found in table 12.G6. Three steps were taken in order to evaluate the rating-scale-level structure: First, frequency counts for each level were evaluated for usage under 10%. Results indicated that eight levels did not reach the prescribed 10% usage: (a) Level 1 of criterion 1, (b) Level 1 of criterion 2, (c) Level 1 of criterion 8, (d) Level 4 of criterion 3, (e) Level 4 of criterion 4, (f) Level 4 of criterion 5, (g) Level 4 of criterion 6, and (h) Level 4 of criterion 7. It is therefore recommended that each Level 1 be collapsed into its respective adjacent Level 2 and be rewritten, and each Level 4 of criterion be collapsed into its adjacent Level 3 and be rewritten. Second, outfit mean squares (MSE) were examined for values ≥2.0. Results indicated that one level was found to have an MSE value ≥2.0: Level 1 of criterion 1. Because Level 1 of criterion 1 additionally did not reach the minimum level usage, it is recommended this level be collapsed into Level 2. Third, average observed logit measures were examined for violations of monotonicity. Results indicated one level that violated the rule of monotonicity: Level 2 of criterion 1. It is recommended to collapse Level 2 into the adjacent Level 1.

Inter-Adjacent-Level Discrimination Indices

Andrich thresholds can be found in table 12.H6 for each criterion within the respective trait.

Findings

The Grade 8 Create MCA demonstrated overall strong construct validity as demonstrated by the reasonable parameter separation for each of the
considered parameters. Results indicated that the rank order of criteria by
difficulty (from most difficult to least difficult) was (1) applying criteria,
(2) rational for refinement, (3) evaluation, (4) music ideas, (5) expressive
intent from the Imagine Plan and Make Worksheet, (6) effective crafting,
(7) expressive intent from the composition scoring device, and (8) craftsmanship. All criteria were found to be appropriate and meaningful in their
overall functioning within the context of measuring the *Create* construct
for eighth grade. An analysis of the usability and meaningfulness of the
levels across each criterion (i.e., emerging, approaches standard, meets
standard, exceeds standard) indicated some evidence for suggested revisions. The labels associated with each criterion are found in table 12.G6.
Based on the analysis, the following is recommended: (a) Level 1 of criterion 1 should be collapsed with Level 2 of criterion 1 and be rewritten,
(b) Level 1 of criterion 2 should be collapsed with Level 2 of criterion 2
and be rewritten, (c) Level 1 of criterion 8 should be collapsed with Level
2 of criterion 8 and be rewritten, (d) Level 4 of criterion 3 should be collapsed with Level 3 of criterion 3 and be rewritten, (e) Level 4 of criterion 4
should be collapsed with Level 3 of criterion 4 and be rewritten, (f) Level 4
of criterion 5 should be collapsed with Level 3 of criterion 5 and be rewritten, (g) Level 4 of criterion 6 should be collapsed with Level 3 of criterion
6 and be rewritten, and (h) Level 4 of criterion 7 should be collapsed with
Level 3 of criterion 7 and be rewritten, (i) Level 2 of criterion 1 should be
collapsed with Level 1 of criterion 1 and be rewritten. The tables displaying all psychometric analyses for the Grade 8 Create MCA include tables
12.A6, 12.B6, 12.C6, 12.D6, 12.E6, 12.F6, 12.G6, and 12.H6. The variable
map can be found in figure 12.I6.

COMPOSITION/THEORY:
CREATE, RESPOND, PERFORM—PROFICIENT

Summary Statistics

Table 12.A7 provides the summary statistics for the MFR-PC model
analysis of student work ($n = 40$), scorers ($n = 3$), scoring type ($n = 2$) and
criteria ($n = 12$). The analysis indicated an overall good model data fit
with significant differences between student work ($\chi^2_{(86)} = 225.20$, $p< .01$),
scorers ($\chi^2_{(2)} = 72.80$, $p< .01$), scoring type ($\chi^2_{(1)} = 1.70$, $p< .01$), and criteria
($\chi^2_{(11)} = 153.50$, $p< .01$). Reliability of separation statistics for all four facets
are as follows: student work ($Rel = .86$), scorers ($Rel = .77$), scoring type
($Rel<.01$), and criteria ($Rel = .93$). See figure 12.I7 for the variable map.

Calibration of Student Work

Table 12.B7 provides student work calibration information. The mean of the student work was 0.20 logits with a range of 3.86 logits for the highest fit achieving student work (Student ID 5075) to –2.42 logits for the lowest fit achieving (Student ID 5096).

Calibration of Scorers

Table 12.C7 provides scorer calibration information. The mean of the scorers was 0.00 logits with a range of 0.87 for the most severe scorer (Scorer 2) to –0.95 for the most lenient scorer (Scorer 1). All scorers demonstrated adequate fit to the model based on the reasonable mean-square range for infit and outfit (0.60–1.40).

Calibration of Scoring Type

Table 12.D7 provides scoring-type calibration information. The mean of the scoring-type facet was 0.00 logits with a range of 0.14 for the most severe scoring type (peer score) to –0.14 for the most lenient scoring type (self score). Both scoring types demonstrated adequate fit to the model based on the reasonable mean-square range for infit and outfit (0.60–1.40).

Calibration of Traits

Table 12.E4 provides trait calibration information. The mean of the traits was 0.00 logits with a range of 1.38 for the most difficult trait (imagine) to –0.27 for the least difficult trait (process). All traits demonstrated adequate fit to the model based on the reasonable mean-square range for infit and outfit (0.60–1.40).

Calibration of Criteria

Table 12.F7 provides criterion calibration information. The mean of the criteria was 0.00 logits with a range of 1.38 for the most difficult criterion (imagine) to –1.47 for the easiest criterion (strategies for improvement). The recognizability criterion and the feedback for refinement criterion both demonstrated sporadic rating patterns as evidenced by an infit MSE greater than 1.40. Therefore, it is recommended that both criteria should be either rewritten and further tested or removed.

Rating-Scale-Level Diagnostics

Rating-scale diagnostics can be found in table 12.G7. Three steps were taken in order to evaluate the rating-scale-level structure: First, frequency

counts for each level were evaluated for usage under 10%. Results indicated that 14 levels did not reach the prescribed 10% usage: (a) Level 1 of
criterion 2, (b) Level 1 of criterion 4, (c) Level 1 of criterion 5, (d) Level 1 of
criterion 7, (e) Level 1 of criterion 8, (f) Level 1 of criterion 10, (g) Level 1 of
criterion 11, (h) Level 1 of criterion 12, (i) Level 2 of criterion 11, (j) Level 4
of criterion 1, (k) Level 4 of criterion 6, (l) Level 4 of criterion 7, (m) Level
4 of criterion 8, and (n) Level 4 of criterion 9. It is therefore recommended
that each Level 1 be collapsed into its respective adjacent Level 2 and be
rewritten, and each Level 4 of criterion be collapsed into its adjacent Level
3 and be rewritten. In the case of criterion 11 where both Levels 1 and 2
demonstrated insufficient usage, the collapsing of both levels into each
other would render sufficient usage. However, considering the large per-
centages of their respective Levels 3 and 4, it is recommended to consider
removing both Levels 1 and 2. Second, outfit mean squares (MSE) were
examined for values ≥2.0. Results indicated that one level was found to
have an MSE value ≥2.0: Level 1 of criterion 4. Because Level 1 of criterion
4 additionally did not reach the minimum level usage, it is recommended
this level be collapsed into Level 2 and be rewritten. Third, average observed logit measures were examined for violations of monotonicity. Results indicated two levels that violated the rule of monotonicity: (a) Level
2 of criterion 6, and (b) Level 2 of criterion 11. It is recommended that both
levels be collapsed into their adjacent Level 1 and be rewritten.

Inter-Adjacent-Level Discrimination Indices

Rasch-Andrich thresholds can be found in table 12.H7 for each criterion
within the respective trait.

Findings

The composition/theory MCA demonstrated overall strong construct
validity as demonstrated by the reasonable parameter separation for each
of the considered parameters. Results indicated that the rank order of
criteria by difficulty (from most difficult to least difficult) was (1) recognizability, (2) imagine, (3) evaluation of T&E, (4) analysis from the responding
scoring device, (5) interpretation, (6) analysis from the plan, make, and
analyze scoring device, (7) craftsmanship, (8) organization, (9) selection,
(10) verbal, (11) strategies for improvement, and (12) feedback for refinement. All criteria were found to be appropriate and meaningful in their
overall functioning within the context of measuring the *composition/theory
construct*. An analysis of the usability and meaningfulness of the levels
across each criterion (i.e., emerging, approaches standard, meets standard,
exceeds standard) indicated some evidence for suggested revisions. The

labels associated with each criterion are found in table 12.G7. Based on the analysis, the following is recommended: (a) Level 1 of criterion 2 should be collapsed with Level 2 of criterion 2 and be rewritten, (b) Level 1 of criterion 4 should be collapsed with Level 2 of criterion 4 and be rewritten, (c) Level 1 of criterion 5 should be collapsed with Level 2 of criterion 5 and be rewritten, (d) Level 1 of criterion 7 should be collapsed with Level 2 of criterion 7 and be rewritten, (e) Level 1 of criterion 8 should be collapsed with Level 2 of criterion 8 and be rewritten, (f) Level 1 of criterion 10 should be collapsed with Level 2 of criterion 10 and be rewritten, (g) Level 1 of criterion 11 should be collapsed with Level 2 of criterion 11 and be rewritten, (h) Level 1 of criterion 12 should be collapsed with Level 2 of criterion 12 and be rewritten, (i) Level 2 of criterion 11 should be collapsed with Level 1 of criterion 11 and be rewritten, (j) Level 4 of criterion 1 should be collapsed with Level 3 of criterion 1 and be rewritten, (k) Level 4 of criterion 6 should be collapsed with Level 3 of criterion 6 and be rewritten, (l) Level 4 of criterion 7 should be collapsed with Level 3 of criterion 7 and be rewritten, (m) Level 4 of criterion 8 should be collapsed with Level 3 of criterion 8 and be rewritten, (n) Level 4 of criterion 9 should be collapsed with Level 3 of criterion 9 and be rewritten, and (o) Level 2 of criterion 6 should be collapsed with Level 1 of criterion 6 and be rewritten. The tables displaying all psychometric analyses for the composition/theory MCA include tables 12.A7, 12.B7, 12.C7, 12.D7, 12.E4, 12.F7, 12.G7, and 12.H7. The variable map can be found in figure 12.I7.

ENSEMBLE PERFORM (INTERMEDIATE)

Summary Statistics

Table 12.A8 provides the summary statistics for the MFR-PC model analysis of student work ($n = 137$), scorers ($n = 6$), scoring type ($n = 2$) and criteria ($n = 11$). The analysis indicated an overall good model data fit with significant differences between student work ($x^2_{(136)} = 685.50$, $p < .01$), scorers ($x^2_{(5)} = 55.40$, $p < .01$), scoring type ($x^2_{(1)} = 7.90$, $p < .01$), and criteria ($x^2_{(10)} = 203.40$, $p < .01$). Reliability of separation statistics for all four facets are as follows: student work ($Rel = .82$), scorers ($Rel = .88$), scoring type ($Rel = .75$), and criteria ($Rel = .95$). See figure 12.I8 for the variable map.

Calibration of Student Work

Table 12.B8 provides student work calibration information. The mean of the student work was −0.89 logits with a range of 1.44 logits for the highest fit achieving student work (Student ID 2416) to −4.84 logits for the lowest fit achieving (Student ID 2571).

Calibration of Scorers

Table 12.C8 provides scorer calibration information. The mean of the scorers was 0.00 logits with a range of 0.50 for the most severe scorer (Scorer 4) to –0.46 for the most lenient scorer (Scorer 1). All scorers demonstrated adequate fit to the model based on the reasonable mean-square range for infit and outfit (0.60–1.40).

Calibration of Scoring Type

Table 12.D8 provides scoring-type calibration information. The mean of the scoring-type facet was 0.00 logits with a range of 0.12 for the most severe scoring type (peer score) to –0.12 for the most lenient scoring type (self score). Both scoring types demonstrated adequate fit to the model based on the reasonable mean-square range for infit and outfit (0.60–1.40).

Calibration of Traits

Table 12.E5 provides trait calibration information. The mean of the traits was 0.00 logits, with a range of 0.27 for the most difficult trait (rehearsal) to –0.31 for the least difficult trait (perform). All traits demonstrated adequate fit to the model based on the reasonable mean-square range for infit and outfit (0.60–1.40).

Calibration of Criteria

Table 12.F8 provides criterion calibration information. The mean of the criteria was 0.00 logits with a range of 0.79 for the most difficult criterion (selection of varied program) to –0.98 for the easiest criterion (awareness of Exp Qual). All criteria demonstrated adequate fit to the model based on the reasonable mean-square range for infit and outfit (0.60–1.40).

Rating-Scale-Level Diagnostics

Rating-scale diagnostics can be found in table 12.G8. Three steps were taken in order to evaluate the rating-scale-level structure: First, frequency counts for each level were evaluated for usage under 10%. Results indicated that 10 levels did not reach the prescribed 10% usage: (a) Level 4 of criterion 1, (b) Level 4 of criterion 2, (c) Level 4 of criterion 3, (d) Level 4 of criterion 4, (e) Level 4 of criterion 5, (f) Level 4 of criterion 6, (g) Level 4 of criterion 7, (h) Level 4 of criterion 9, (i) Level 4 of criterion 10, and (j) Level 4 of criterion 11. It is therefore recommended that each Level 4 be collapsed into its respective adjacent Level 3 and be rewritten. Second, outfit mean squares (MSE) were examined for values ≥2.0. Results indicated that no levels were found to have an MSE value ≥2.0. Third, average observed logit measures were examined for violations of monotonicity. Results indicated one level that violated the rule of monotonicity: it is recommended that Level 4 criterion be collapsed into its adjacent Level 3 and be rewritten.

Inter-Adjacent-Level Discrimination Indices

Rasch-Andrich thresholds can be found in table 12.H8 for each criterion within the respective trait.

Findings

The ensemble perform (intermediate) MCA demonstrated overall strong construct validity as demonstrated by the reasonable parameter separation for each of the considered parameters. Results indicated that the rank order of criteria by difficulty (from most difficult to least difficult) was (1) selection of varied program, (2) awareness of technical challenges, (3) evaluate/refine, (4) interpretation, (5) expressive qualities, (6) analysis, (7) rehearsal plan, (8) rhythm/pulse accuracy, (9) tone production, (10) pitch/intonation accuracy, and (11) awareness of expressive qualities. All criteria were found to be appropriate and meaningful in their overall functioning within the context of measuring the *Intermediate Ensemble Perform* construct. An analysis of the usability and meaningfulness of the levels across each criterion (i.e., emerging, approaches standard, meets standard, exceeds standard) indicated some evidence for suggested revisions. The labels associated with each criterion are found in table 12.G8. Based on the analysis, the following is recommended: (a) Level 4 of criterion 1 should be collapsed with Level 3 of criterion 1 and be rewritten, (b) Level 4 of criterion 2 should be collapsed with Level 3 of criterion 2 and be rewritten, (c) Level 4 of criterion 3 should be collapsed with Level 3 of criterion 3 and be rewritten, (d) Level 4 of criterion 4 should be collapsed with Level 3 of criterion 4 and be rewritten, (e) Level 4 of criterion 5 should be collapsed with Level 3 of criterion 5 and be rewritten, (f) Level 4 of criterion 6 should be collapsed with Level 3 of criterion 6 and be rewritten, (g) Level 4 of criterion 7 should be collapsed with Level 3 of criterion 7 and be rewritten, (h) Level 4 of criterion 9 should be collapsed with Level 3 of criterion 9 and be rewritten, (i) Level 4 of criterion 10 should be collapsed with Level 3 of criterion 10 and be rewritten, and (j) Level 4 of criterion 11 should be collapsed with Level 3 of criterion 11 and be rewritten. The tables displaying all psychometric analyses for the ensemble perform (intermediate) MCA include tables 12.A8, 12.B8, 12.C8,

12.D8, 12.E5, 12.F8, 12.G8, and 12.H8. The variable map can be found in figure 12.I8.

ENSEMBLE PERFORM (PROFICIENT)

Summary Statistics

Table 12.A9 provides the summary statistics for the MFR-PC model analysis of student work ($n = 84$), scorers ($n = 3$), scoring type ($n = 2$) and criteria ($n = 11$). The analysis indicated an overall good model data fit with significant differences between student work ($\chi^2_{(83)} = 586.20$, $p < .01$), scorers ($\chi^2_{(5)} = 298.40$, $p < .01$), scoring type ($\chi^2_{(1)} = 115.10$, $p < .01$), and criteria ($\chi^2_{(10)} = 210.10$, $p < .01$). Reliability of separation statistics for all four facets are as follows: student work ($Rel = .87$), scorers ($Rel = .99$), scoring type ($Rel = .90$), and criteria ($Rel = .95$). See figure 12.I9 for the variable map.

Calibration of Student Work

Table 12.B9 provides student work calibration information. The mean of the student work was −1.42 logits with a range of 1.22 logits for the highest fit achieving student work (Student ID 2635) to −3.68 logits for the lowest fit achieving (Student ID 2650).

Calibration of Scorers

Table 12.C9 provides scorer calibration information. The mean of the scorers was 0.00 logits with a range of 0.75 for the most severe scorer (Scorer 3) to −1.04 for the most lenient scorer (Scorer 1). All scorers demonstrated adequate fit to the model based on the reasonable mean-square range for infit and outfit (0.60–1.40).

Calibration of Scoring Type

Table 12.D9 provides scoring-type calibration information. The mean of the scoring-type facet was 0.00 logits with a range of 0.48 for the most severe scoring type (peer score) to −0.48 for the most lenient scoring type (self score). Both scoring types demonstrated adequate fit to the model based on the reasonable mean-square range for infit and outfit (0.60–1.40).

Calibration of Traits

Table 12.E6 provides trait calibration information. The mean of the traits was 0.00 logits with a range of 0.18 for the most difficult trait (rehearsal) to –0.19 for the least difficult trait (perform). All traits demonstrated adequate fit to the model based on the reasonable mean-square range for infit and outfit (0.60–1.40).

Calibration of Criteria

Table 12.F9 provides criterion calibration information. The mean of the criteria was 0.00 logits with a range of 0.92 for the most difficult criterion (analysis) to –1.43 for the easiest criterion (tone production). The selection of a varied program criterion demonstrated sporadic rating patterns as evidenced by an infit MSE greater than 1.40. Therefore, it is recommended that this criterion be either rewritten and further tested or removed.

Rating-Scale-Level Diagnostics

Rating-scale diagnostics can be found in table 12.G9. Three steps were taken in order to evaluate the rating-scale-level structure: First, frequency counts for each level were evaluated for usage under 10%. Results indicated that 11 levels did not reach the prescribed 10% usage: (a) Level 4 of criterion 1, (b) Level 4 of criterion 2, (c) Level 4 of criterion 3, (d) Level 4 of criterion 4, (e) Level 4 of criterion 5, (f) Level 4 of criterion 6, (g) Level 4 of criterion 7, (h) Level 4 of criterion 8, (i) Level 4 of criterion 9, and (j) Level 4 of criterion 10, and (k) Level 4 of criterion 11. It is therefore recommended that each Level 4 be collapsed into its respective adjacent Level 3 and be rewritten. Second, outfit mean squares (MSE) were examined for values ≥2.0. Results indicated that one level was found to have an MSE value ≥2.0: Level 4 of criterion 1. Because Level 4 of criterion 1 additionally did not reach the minimum level usage, it is recommended this level be collapsed into Level 3 and be rewritten. Third, average observed logit measures were examined for violations of monotonicity. Results indicated one level that violated the rule of monotonicity: Level 4 of criterion 10. It is therefore recommended this level be collapsed into its adjacent Level 3 and be rewritten.

Inter-Adjacent-Level Discrimination Indices

Rasch-Andrich thresholds can be found in table 12.H9 for each criterion within the respective trait.

Findings

The ensemble perform (proficient level) MCA demonstrated overall strong construct validity as demonstrated by the reasonable parameter separation for each of the considered parameters. Results indicated that the rank order of criteria by difficulty (from most difficult to least difficult) was (1) analysis, (2) pitch/intonation accuracy, (3) evaluate/refine, (4) awareness of expressive qualities, (5) expressive qualities, (6) rehearsal plan, (7) awareness of technical challenges, (8) selection of varied program, (9) rhythm/pulse accuracy, (10) interpretation, and (11) tone production. All criteria were found to be appropriate and meaningful in their overall functioning within the context of measuring the *Proficient Ensemble Perform* construct. An analysis of the usability and meaningfulness of the levels across each criterion (i.e., emerging, approaches standard, meets standard, exceeds standard) indicated some evidence for suggested revisions. The labels associated with each criterion are found in table 12.G9. Based on the analysis, the following is recommended: (a) Level 4 of criterion 1 should be collapsed with Level 3 of criterion 1 and be rewritten, (b) Level 4 of criterion 2 should be collapsed with Level 3 of criterion 2 and be rewritten, (c) Level 4 of criterion 3 should be collapsed with Level 3 of criterion 3 and be rewritten, (d) Level 4 of criterion 4 should be collapsed with Level 3 of criterion 4 and be rewritten, (e) Level 4 of criterion 5 should be collapsed with Level 3 of criterion 5 and be rewritten, (f) Level 4 of criterion 6 should be collapsed with Level 3 of criterion 6 and be rewritten, (g) Level 4 of criterion 7 should be collapsed with Level 3 of criterion 7 and be rewritten, (h) Level 4 of criterion 8 should be collapsed with Level 3 of criterion 8 and be rewritten, (i) Level 4 of criterion 9 should be collapsed with Level 3 of criterion 9 and be rewritten, (j) Level 4 of criterion 10 should be collapsed with Level 3 of criterion 10 and be rewritten, and (l) Level 4 of criterion 11 should be collapsed with Level 3 of criterion 11 and be rewritten. The tables displaying all psychometric analyses for the ensemble perform (proficient) MCA include tables 12.A9, 12.B9, 12.C9, 12.D9, 12.E6, 12.F9, 12.G9, and 12.H9. The variable map can be found in figure 12.I9.

HARMONIZING INSTRUMENTS:
CREATE (PROFICIENT LEVEL)

Summary Statistics

Table 12.A10 provides the summary statistics for the MFR-PC model analysis of student work ($n = 20$), scorers ($n = 2$), scoring type ($n = 2$) and criteria ($n = 7$). The analysis indicated an overall good model data fit with significant differences between student work ($\chi^2_{(19)} = 46.60$, $p< .01$), scorers ($\chi^2_{(1)} = 48.30$, $p< .01$), scoring type ($\chi^2_{(1)} = 19.20$, $p< .01$), and criteria ($\chi^2_{(6)} = 69.90$, $p< .01$). Reliability of separation statistics for all four facets are as follows: student work ($Rel = .79$), scorers ($Rel = .96$), scoring type ($Rel = .90$), and criteria ($Rel = .91$). See figure 12.I10 for the variable map.

Calibration of Student Work

Table 12.B10 provides student work calibration information. The mean of the student work was 0.07 logits with a range of 4.86 logits for the highest fit achieving student work (Student ID 3517) to –1.66 logits for the lowest fit achieving (Student ID 3479).

Calibration of Scorers

Table 12.C10 provides scorer calibration information. The mean of the scorers was 0.00 logits with a range of 0.83 for the most severe scorer (Scorer 2) to –0.83 for the most lenient scorer (Scorer 1). All scorers demonstrated adequate fit to the model based on the reasonable mean-square range for infit and outfit (0.60–1.40).

Calibration of Scoring Type

Table 12.D10 provides scoring-type calibration information. The mean of the scoring-type facet was 0.00 logits with a range of 0.47 for the most severe scoring type (self score) to –0.47 for the most lenient scoring type (peer score). Both scoring types demonstrated adequate fit to the model based on the reasonable mean-square range for infit and outfit (0.60–1.40).

Calibration of Traits

Table 12.E7 provides trait calibration information. The mean of the traits was 0.00 logits with a range of 0.42 for the most difficult trait (plan/ make) to –0.99 for the least difficult trait (imagine). All traits demonstrated adequate fit to the model based on the reasonable mean-square range for infit and outfit (0.60–1.40).

Calibration of Criteria

Table 12.F10 provides criterion calibration information. The mean of the criteria was 0.00 logits with a range of 2.06 for the most difficult criterion (development of harmonization) to –1.21 for the easiest criterion (analysis). All criteria demonstrated adequate fit to the model based on the reasonable mean-square range for infit and outfit (0.60–1.40).

Rating-Scale-Level Diagnostics

Rating-scale diagnostics can be found in table 12.G10. Three steps were taken in order to evaluate the rating-scale-level structure: First, frequency counts for each level were evaluated for usage under 10%. Results indicated that three levels did not reach the prescribed 10% usage: (a) Level 1 of criterion 3, (a) Level 4 of criterion 1, and (b) Level 4 of criterion 2. It is therefore recommended that each Level 1 be collapsed into its respective adjacent Level 2 and be rewritten and Level 4 be collapsed into its respective adjacent Level 3 and be rewritten. Second, outfit mean squares (MSE) were examined for values ≥2.0. Results indicated that one level was found to have an MSE value ≥2.0: Level 4 of criterion 2. Because Level 4 of criterion 2 additionally did not reach the minimum level usage, it is recommended this level be collapsed into Level 3 and be rewritten. Third, average observed logit measures were examined for violations of monotonicity. Results indicated one level that violated the rule of monotonicity: Level 4 of criterion 2. It is therefore recommended that Level 4 be collapsed into its adjacent Level 3 and be rewritten.

Inter-Adjacent-Level Discrimination Indices

Rasch-Andrich thresholds can be found in table 12.H10 for each criterion within the respective trait.

Findings

The harmonizing instruments MCA demonstrated overall strong construct validity as demonstrated by the reasonable parameter separation for each of the considered parameters. Results indicated that the rank order of criteria by difficulty (from most difficult to least difficult) was (1) development of harmonies, (2) interpretation, (3) craftsmanship, (4) recognition of notation, (5) verbal presentation, 6) imagine, and (7) analysis. All criteria were found to be appropriate and meaningful in their overall functioning within the context of measuring the *Harmonizing Instruments* construct. An analysis of the usability and meaningfulness of the levels across each criterion (i.e., emerging, approaches standard, meets standard, exceeds standard) indicated some evidence for suggested revisions. The labels associated with each criterion are found in table 12.G10. Based on the analysis, the following is recommended: (a) Level 1 of criterion 3 should be collapsed with Level 2 of criterion 3 and be rewritten, (b) Level 4 of criterion 1 should be collapsed with Level 3 of criterion 1 and be rewritten, and (c) Level 4 of criterion 2 should be collapsed with Level 3 of criterion 2 and be rewritten. The tables displaying all psychometric analyses for the harmonizing MCA include tables 12.A10, 12.B10, 12.C10, 12.D10, 12.E7, 12.F10, 12.G10, and 12.H10. The variable map can be found in figure 12.I10.

HARMONIZING INSTRUMENTS:
CREATE—PROFICIENT (REVISED)

Summary Statistics

Table 12.A11 provides the summary statistics for the MFR-PC model analysis of student work ($n = 49$), scorers ($n = 4$), scoring type ($n = 2$) and criteria ($n = 6$). The analysis indicated an overall good model data fit with significant differences between student work ($\chi^2_{(48)} = 536.10$, $p < .01$), scorers ($\chi^2_{(3)} = 31.90$, $p < .01$), and criteria ($\chi^2_{(5)} = 154.00$, $p < .01$). Nonsignificance was found for score type ($\chi^2_{(1)} = .30$, $p = .58$). Reliability of separation statistics for the three significant facets are as follows: student work ($Rel = .89$), scorers ($Rel = .91$), and criteria ($Rel = .95$). See figure 12.I11 for the variable map.

Calibration of Student Work

Table 12.B11 provides student work calibration information. The mean of the student work was 0.60 logits with a range of 4.96 logits for the highest fit achieving student work (Student ID 4588) to −6.51 logits for the lowest fit achieving (Student ID 5136).

Calibration of Scorers

Table 12.C11 provides scorer calibration information. The mean of the scorers was 0.00 logits with a range of 0.54 for the most severe scorer (Scorer 3) to −1.30 for the most lenient scorer (Scorer 1). Scorer 4 demonstrated sporadic rating patterns as evidenced by an infit MSE greater than 1.40.

Calibration of Traits

Table 12.E8 provides trait calibration information. The mean of the traits was 0.00 logits with a range of 1.20 for the most difficult trait (plan/make) to −0.80 for the least difficult trait (imagine). All traits demonstrated adequate fit to the model based on the reasonable mean-square range for infit and outfit (0.60–1.40).

Calibration of Criteria

Table 12.F11 provides criterion calibration information. The mean of the criteria was 0.00 logits with a range of 2.42 for the most difficult criterion (documentation of harmonization) to −0.99 for the easiest criterion (recognition of notation). All criteria demonstrated adequate fit to the model based on the reasonable mean-square range for infit and outfit (0.60–1.40). The development of harmonization criterion demonstrated muted rating patterns as evidenced by an infit MSE less than 0.50. Therefore, it is recommended that this criterion be either rewritten and further tested or removed.

Rating-Scale-Level Diagnostics

Rating-scale diagnostics can be found in table 12.G11. Three steps were taken in order to evaluate the rating-scale-level structure. First, frequency counts for each level were evaluated for usage under 10%. Results indicated that eight levels did not reach the prescribed 10% usage: (a) Level 1 of criterion 1, (b) Level 1 of criterion 4, (c) Level 1 of criterion 5, (d) Level 2 of criterion 2, (e) Level 2 of criterion 4, (f) Level 4 of criterion 1, (g) Level 4 of criterion 2, and (h) Level 4 of criterion 3. It is therefore recommended that each Level 1 be collapsed into its respective adjacent Level 2 and be rewritten, each Level 2 be collapsed into its respective adjacent Level 1 and be rewritten, and each Level 4 be collapsed into its respective adjacent Level 3 and be rewritten. In the case of criterion 4 where both Levels 1 and 2 demonstrated insufficient usage, the collapsing of both levels into each other would still not render sufficient usage. Therefore, it is recommended to consider removing both Levels 1 and 2 and rewriting Levels 3 and 4. Second, outfit mean squares (MSE) were examined for values ≥2.0. Results indicated that one level was found to have an MSE value ≥2.0: Level 1 of criterion 3. It is examined that this level be examined and rewritten. Third, average observed logit measures were examined for violations of monotonicity. Results indicated no violations of monotonicity.

Inter-Adjacent-Level Discrimination Indices

Rasch-Andrich thresholds can be found in table 12.H11 for each criterion within the respective trait.

Findings

The harmonizing instruments (revised) MCA demonstrated overall strong construct validity as demonstrated by the reasonable parameter separation for each of the considered parameters. Results indicated that the rank order of criteria by difficulty (from most difficult to least difficult) was (1) documentation of harmonization, (2) development of harmonization, (3) melodic interpretation, (4) feedback, (5) imagine, and (6) recognition of notation. The development of harmonization criterion was found to be too predictable, therefore not contributing meaningful information toward the measurement of student work. Therefore, it is recommended that this criterion be either rewritten and further tested or removed. All other criteria were found to be appropriate and meaningful in their overall functioning within the context of measuring the *Harmonizing Instruments* (revised) construct. An analysis of the usability and meaningfulness of the levels across each criterion (i.e., emerging, approaches standard, meets standard, exceeds standard) indicated some evidence for suggested revisions. The labels associated with each criterion are found in table 12.G11. Based on the analysis, the following is recommended: (a) Level 1 of criterion 1 should be collapsed with Level 2 of criterion 1 and be rewritten, (b) Level 1 of criterion 4 should be collapsed with Level 2 of criterion 4 and be rewritten, (c) Level 1 of criterion 5 should be collapsed with Level 2 of criterion 5 and be rewritten, (d) Level 2 of criterion 2 should be collapsed with Level 1 of criterion 2 and be rewritten, (e) Level 2 of criterion 4 should be collapsed with Level 1 of criterion 4 and be rewritten, (f) Level 4 of criterion 1 should be collapsed with Level 3 of criterion 1 and be rewritten, (g) Level 4 of criterion 2 should be collapsed with Level 3 of criterion 2 and be rewritten, and (h) Level 4 of criterion 3 should be collapsed with Level 3 of criterion 3 and be rewritten. The tables displaying all psychometric analyses for the Harmonizing (revised) MCA include tables 12.A11, 12.B11, 12.C11, 12.D11, 12.E8, 12.F11, 12.G11, and 12.H11. The variable map can be found in figure 12.I11.

REFERENCE

Rasch, G. (1960/1980). *Probabilistic models for some intelligence and attainment tests.* Copenhagen, Denmark: Danish Institute for Educational Research. Expanded edition. (1980). Chicago, IL: University of Chicago Press.

THIRTEEN

A Case for
Validity and Reliability

Frederick Burrack

Classroom assessments and the scoring devices used in classrooms are often implemented and trusted without confirmation or evidence of validity and reliability. Given the importance that public education places on assessment and the expectations held for valid and reliable measures of student learning, it is important for music educators to recognize what information this pilot study has provided about the Model Cornerstone Assessments (MCAs) and how to communicate this to stakeholders, such as administrators. The paradigm shift in measuring student learning in music, described in chapter 1, focuses on assessments that provide relevant and reliable evidence of what students know and are able to do through applied tasks, thoughtfully and flexibly integrated through a music program's curricular content. The purpose of this chapter is to provide a foundation for understanding the concepts of validity and reliability, the extent to which teachers can support using the MCAs as valid and reliable, and how they can communicate a rationale for using the measures in school music curricula. An extensive and rigorous pilot study was administered to investigate the psychometric properties (e.g., validity and reliability) of the National Association for Music Education's Music Model Cornerstone Assessments, described in chapter 2.

Reliability refers to the extent to which assessments are consistent and suggest how well the measurement instruments separate students at various achievement levels. Just as we enjoy having reliable cell phones that we expect to work when we make a call, those who use assessments strive to have reliable scoring devices that are consistent when measuring student learning. Another way to think of reliability is to imagine a scale. The scale is reliable if you weigh something and when you weigh it at another time with the same scale, it should register the same weight unless there has been a change in what is being measured. Statistical analysis of the pilot data provided evidence so that we can have sufficient confidence in the consistency of the rubrics involved in scoring when used by teachers in the field. These rubrics were reliably used by teachers who scored work from other districts and demographics. But we did find that teachers who had not used the rubrics in a classroom did not score student work with the same consistency. So, it is important that whoever uses the rubrics to score student learning has experience teaching the process components of the 2014 National Music Standards and has experience using the MCA rubrics within instruction. Generally, this puts the teachers themselves among the most reliable scorers using the rubrics; there was little, if any, significant difference in scoring between the classroom teachers and peer teachers.

Validity refers to the degree to which evidence and theory support the interpretations of the test scores for intended uses of the assessments. Let's imagine a bathroom scale that consistently tells you that you weigh 130 pounds. The reliability (consistency) of this scale is very good because it reads 130 every time you weigh yourself. The data you have tells you that 130 pounds is how heavy you are; however, it does not tell you how tall you are, so it is only a valid measure of your weight and not of other attributes. Reliability is also all about the data that is gathered and the context in which it is gathered. Without considering the context, the consistency may not be meaningful; for example, if a person stands on the scale with one foot as opposed to two. Since teachers, parents, and school districts make decisions about students based on assessments (such as grades, promotions, and graduation), the validity inferred from the assessments and their contexts is essential—even more crucial than the reliability (Pinellas School District, n.d.).

In reference to validity of the MCAs, *content validity* is the extent to which the content of the test matches the instructional objectives in order that the results can lead to appropriate interpretations. In other words, it is extent to the representativeness to what has been taught and the relevance of the instrument to the task (Messick, 1989). This was accomplished by aligning the MCAs to the 2014 National Music Standards. Alignment was confirmed through mutual agreement between standard writers, practicing music teachers, and content experts. Statistical confirmation was confirmed through Rasch measurement of fit (van der Linden, 1992). This can be seen as a phenomenographic approach (Wesolowski, Parkes, & Burrack, 2017a, 2017b). After a number of revisions and multiple rounds of feedback from the prepilot to the final revisions, content validity was established for all the tested MCAs. *Construct validity* can be seen by how well the criteria work to operationally define the overarching construct being measured. Using separation statistics of scorers, scoring type, and criteria, analyses identified the hierarchy of difficulty across each scored artistic process and measured how closely the raw scores fit the model; the indices of fit provided the evidence of construct validity. Fit statistics within the accepted threshold indicate accuracy and predictability, validity evidence for the construct of the rubrics, and appropriateness for measurement by determining how invariant the measures are (Linacre, 2002b). The findings from the pilot study provided sufficient information to revise components of the rubrics, resulting in strong construct validity.

Developing valid and reliable measures to assess student learning is often not possible because of the time commitment required of a typical music teacher. This is one of the reasons that the Model Cornerstone Assessments, aligned with the 2014 National Standards for Music, have been developed and tested. Given the results of the pilot study, teachers can now integrate these MCAs into their current curricula with reasonable confidence of their fidelity toward the performance standards. This does not negate the importance of assessments of technical proficiency and end-point performance already used in most music programs. The MCAs address the components of the artistic processes, within which the specific skills and techniques are applied. These MCAs enable the music teacher to have a complete picture of student learning, which can guide decisions toward instructional and program improvement. The primary purpose of the MCAs is to allow music teachers to make informed judgments about student learning based upon student development of the process components that comprise creating, performing, and responding.

Chapters 3–9, each pertaining to a specific MCA, provide specific details of the findings related to validity and reliability in a classroom setting. Chapters 10–12 provide details about the rigor of the research supporting the findings. Music teachers should use their understandings of validity and reliability, as described above, along with the findings to support their use of the MCAs in their classrooms. As an example, the following rationale (written by the editors) might be useful:

The Model Cornerstone Assessments were developed and tested through a rigorous process over a period of three years and involved music teachers from across the United States. The final versions have been found to be valid measures of the performance standards in the 2014 National Assessments for Music and can be reliably used in music classrooms across various contexts. They were found to be reliably scored by the music teachers with minimal to no preferential scoring. They are not designed to be used as a measure of effective teaching or determination of the quality of a music program, but are to identify sequential development of the National Standards. They are intended to be one part of a collection of assessments used by a music teacher in a music program, alongside knowledge-, skill-, and technique-based assessments. Together, all assessments provide a thorough picture of student learning across a music program.

Music programs should include a variety of assessments, at least some of which should be aligned across the entire program to permit indications of the progress of student learning across the common developmental learning expectations. Any singular assessment will not be able to appropriately assess student learning in any one course or across a music program. The key is consistency of expected outcomes and in reporting assessment results so they can be useful to the teacher, the program, and district curricular decisions. A reporting process such as this should allow schools and districts to be aligned with statewide outcomes and policy expectations. Each school system will have to determine the nature and content of music assessment in a way that makes sense for those schools.

Assessments should serve the goal of educational accountability by providing data that can be useful for curricular decisions at the school or district level. Effective assessment systems provide teachers with information that enables them to provide better instruction to students. Music supervisors and administrators should work with the music faculty to identify appropriate assessments that meet the goals of educational accountability in music education and that help music teachers better ensure their students' educational achievement. Administrators and school policymakers should support music teachers' efforts to develop appropriate assessments that meet the goals of educational accountability in music education, along with all other core academic subjects, and help music teachers better ensure their students' educational achievement (NAfME, n.d.).

REFERENCES

Linacre, J. M. (2002b). Optimizing rating scale level effectiveness. *Journal of Applied Measurement 3*, 85–106.

Messick, S. (1989). Validity. In R. L. Linn (Ed.), *Educational measurement* (pp. 13–103). Washington, DC: American Council on Education and National Council on Measurement in Education.

National Association for Music Education (NAfME). (n.d.). *Assessment in music education*. Retrieved from https://nafme.org/about/position-statements/assess ment-in-music-education-position-statement/assessment-in-music-education/

Pinellas School District. (n.d.). *Reliability and validity*. Retrieved from https://fcit .usf.edu/assessment/basic/basicc.html

van der Linden, W. J. (1992). IRT in the 1990s—Which models work best. Rasch Research Papers, Explorations & Explanations. Retrieved from http://www.rasch .org/audio/IRT-van-der-Linden-2.mp3

Wesolowski, B., Parkes, K. A., & Burrack, F. (2017a, April). *Phenomenography: Bringing together theory and practice through the process of national standards development and measure construction.* Paper presented at the 6th International Symposium on Assessment in Music Education-Context Matters, Birmingham, UK.

Wesolowski, B., Parkes, K. A., & Burrack, F. (2017b, April). *A phenomenographic approach to music assessment: Leveraging subjectivity to improve objectivity.* Paper presented at the Tenth International Research in Music Education Conference, Bath, UK.

FOURTEEN

Connections to
Higher Education in Music

Phillip Payne and Jeffrey Ward

The 2014 National Coalition for Core Arts Standards (NCCAS) NAfME Music Standards were designed to create a more measurable and flexible set of standards compared to their 1994 predecessors. Shuler, Norgaard, and Blakeslee (2014) stated that the new standards would use the three artistic processes of creating, performing, and responding with 11 anchor standards supporting essential understandings and corresponding essential questions. Once the framework was designed, the standards writers were tasked with translating the process components into measurable activities (i.e., actions of students as they complete activities involving the artistic processes [National Association for Music Education, n.d.]).

During the writing process, an advanced level was established that outlined what should be expected of students who wished to continue studying music at the collegiate level as music majors in tertiary / university-level study. The advanced level of expectation is described by Shuler (2015) as college-level work and comparable to an Advanced Placement Music Theory course delivered in high schools across the United States. Colwell (2006) reported that most music programs only establish a minimum high school GPA and an audition that assures the faculty that the student is musically competent. As a common practice, little other information is gathered on admission to college; therefore, the creation of the new standards and description of the artistic processes could be the first step in establishing a more thorough process of determining qualifications for collegiate admission. The 2014 NCCAS NAfME Music Standards and Model Cornerstone Assessments (MCAs) may provide a better foundation for admissions practices.

Accurate measurement of student learning through artistic processes is the goal of the Model Cornerstone Assessments. The MCAs were developed to provide a valid and reliable set of measures to aid music educators in authentically assessing the described expectations of these standards in their classrooms (National Association for Music Education, n.d.). Researchers and teachers across the United States have recently completed their pilot study testing for reliability, validity, and usefulness of the MCAs across age ranges and disciplines. There are MCAs for each discipline and level of music education, including ensembles, harmonizing instruments, theory/composition, and music technology. There were also five levels of expectation for the four strands of middle and high school music beyond general music based on expected demonstrations of achievement from novice to advanced. Each level (novice, intermediate, proficient, accomplished, advanced) is defined clearly by the criteria provided in the performance standards and documents where students are in their musical development. The advanced level describes what the student should be able to do if he or she wants to pursue a degree in music after graduation from high school (National Association for Music Education, n.d.).

In an effort to connect the newly developed MCAs with collegiate music programs, Ward and Payne (2017) examined the admissions procedures and standards of member institutions of the National Association of Schools of Music (NASM). They found that, other than the required audition, the most common nonaudition tasks required of students studying music in colleges and universities were (1) a music theory assessment, (2) an interview, (3) aural skills assessments, and (4) recommendation letters. None of these tasks were required at more than 54% of the member institutions. Conversely, fewer than 10% of the member institutions required an assessment of composition, improvisation, or music history. In most cases, the assessments administered were diagnostic and not necessarily utilized to measure growth, but merely placement exams. The primary question that emerged from Ward and Payne (2017) was, "How are musical skills and knowledge being assessed or valued at the collegiate level?" The remainder of this chapter contains vignettes that hypothetically describe how students who are considering studying music in college might meet some of the expectations as set forth in the MCAs. These vignettes will be viewed through the lens of the MCAs and the current admissions practices of collegiate music programs to assess how these students might fare in the current admissions process.

IMPRESSIONS FROM THE PILOT STUDY

This epilogue tells the story of three composite students as exemplified at three different levels as defined by the current MCAs. Each vignette was randomly selected for performing group (band, choir, and orchestra) and level of achievement (proficient, advanced, accomplished). The chapter is designed to provide "amalgamations" or "impressionist tales" (Glesne and Peshkin, 1992) of music-classroom experiences commonly shared by those in the profession. Each vignette was constructed after the authors reviewed all the data collected via the pilot study. The aim of the vignettes is to illustrate what a student *might look like* once ready for college/university.

The MCAs were analyzed in light of current research provided in this book and current admission practices of college music programs (Ward & Payne, 2017). Limited connections between the 2014 National Standards (including MCAs) and college admissions practices (included audition procedures) were examined. Therefore, only three composite vignettes were constructed: (a) choir—proficient, (b) band—accomplished, and (c) orchestra—advanced. The vignettes are fictional, but their content is derived from the MCA pilot experiences described by piloting teachers. The school situations in the vignettes are essentially metaphors encapsulating the experiences of those involved in this pilot. Each composite vignette was developed through an extensive review of the results from pre- and postsurveys of the MCA participants, quotes from participants and students, perceptions of the MCAs, and data provided by the pilot study's research advisors (RAs) throughout the process. Vignettes were disseminated for member checking among the RAs to ensure authenticity and consistency with their experiences in working with both the teachers and the students. These vignettes are told from the perspective of the teachers, describing fictitious students.

Choir: John—Proficient Level

John is a senior in high school enrolled for his third year in chorus. As a young male singer, he is developing stability in a comfortable range and consistency at both extremes of his range. Because of John's developing voice, his teacher has assigned him Grade III solo vocal literature. John has considered auditioning for a music scholarship in college, so he has completed the Performing Model Cornerstone Assessment at the proficient level. John began by selecting three contrasting solo selections and completed the MCA "Selecting Music Worksheet: Proficient Level" for each selection. In completing the worksheet, John demonstrated the fact that he met the expectations of a portion of the proficient performance standard: "Explain the criteria used to select a varied repertoire to study based on an understanding of theoretical and structural characteristics of the music, the technical skill of the individual or ensemble, and the purpose or context of the performance" (MU:Pr4.1.E.1a). John's voice needs to continue to mature before he is able to sing with the vocal stability and consistency of the typical incoming college freshman, but the musical selections are in an appropriate tessitura so that he felt comfortable with the choices. Through the music selection assessment, John successfully selected a varied three-selection program, identified the technical challenges and expressive demands, and created goals for preparing the pieces. These skills are vital processes for a potential college music student to develop musical independence as a performer.

Next, John completed the "Analyze, Interpret, Rehearse, Evaluate, and Refine Worksheet" through which he demonstrated how compositional devices influenced and informed his performance (MU:Pr4.2.E.1a). He was able to "develop strategies to address expressive challenges in a varied repertoire of music, and evaluate their success using feedback from ensemble peers and other sources to refine performances" (MU:Pr5.3.E.1a). Through these skills, John demonstrated the ability to analyze musical form and compositional devices and applied this analysis to his artistic decisions and rehearsal plan. Furthermore, John developed self-evaluation skills that will help him identify challenges and create solutions to overcome these challenges.

When John performed, his teacher evaluated him on tone production, rhythm and pulse accuracy, pitch and intonation accuracy, and expressive qualities/stylistic interpretation. This performance was a synthesis of John's work up to this point. Feedback was provided as to what areas need continued growth.

As John was making artistic decisions regarding his solo musical selections, he began listening to recordings of the pieces. John completed the "Responding Worksheet" by identifying the style/genre of each piece and then selected two recordings of one of the selections. For each recording, he identified characteristics and determined which characteristics were common to both pieces. Through identifying these characteristics, John discerned what the performer "intended to express" and identified his "affective response" to each recording. In doing so, John analyzed musical performances and explained and supported his response to these performances based on criteria that he and his teacher determined were important. Furthermore, in completing this analysis, John was able to reconsider his own artistic decisions and apply this analysis to his own performance.

In addition to John's work in performance, his teacher also facilitated creative experiences for the chorus class. John's teacher began by providing information about musical phrases, relating to notation, length, relationships, and harmonic considerations. Musical form was introduced through examples from various genres. Through notations and listening to musical examples, students explored musical motifs resulting in experimentation of improvisatory devices appropriate for a variety of musical styles. Using the solo performance pieces that John selected for the performance MCA and his future college audition, John applied the creative experiences from class by experimenting with various improvisatory devices to determine what is most appropriate for the style of each piece. Using the "Imagine Worksheet—Proficient," he chose particular improvisatory devices for two melodies and recorded his version of the pieces using these devices.

After listening to his recording, John completed the "Plan and Make Worksheet—Proficient," answering the questions "What will I do to improve this improvisation?" and "How do I do this?" John's teacher evaluated the recording of John's improvised melodies and provided feedback based on John's responses to the questions. Based on the evaluation and feedback, John refined his improvisations. He then performed the original and his revised improvisation for his classmates, who provided him feedback using the "Peer Assessment Worksheet." After reviewing the feedback from his classmates, John completed the "Evaluate and Refine Worksheet" to identify what he learned from the feedback and what revisions he would make to his improvisation based on the feedback. Finally, John presented a "final" version of his improvisation to his classmates.

Through this process, John applied various improvisation strategies within specific musical styles and historical genres. Furthermore, John synthesized his own feedback and those of others to refine his improvisation. Although at a "proficient" level, John has demonstrated improvisational techniques and the ability to evaluate and revise his own creative work. These skills can be applied to composition, which can be assessed through the composition MCA, and provide depth to his analysis of musical selections.

Band: Jacquelyn — Accomplished level

Jacquelyn is a high school senior who enjoys playing in the band. She has excelled in many areas, including academics, music, and athletics. She is currently the class president for her school and is the treasurer and an active member of the National Honor Society. Academically, Jacquelyn carries a 3.92 unweighted GPA and has amassed an astonishing 32 hours of dual credits to be applied to her bachelor's degree. Additionally, she excels in basketball and track, where she is an all-district shooting guard and the defending state champion in the discus and javelin. Overall, she is a well-rounded student.

Music is where she finds the greatest enjoyment. She loves to perform, and she loves to make music in a variety of ways. Currently, she is enrolled in band, jazz band, music theory, and pop music lab, the latter because of her infatuation with bluegrass. She wants to learn how to write songs for bands such as Mumford and Sons and the Avett Brothers. One of her goals is to master the instruments and her songwriting prowess. (Currently she plays clarinet, harmonica, ukulele, mandolin, fiddle, bass, and jaw harp). She considered pop music lab as the first step to achieving this goal. Finally, she has a passion for working and making music with others through shared musical experiences.

Her first love is the trombone; she has played since the fourth grade when she heard her first Joe Alessi CD. She currently performs on the trombone with the school's top wind ensemble and is the featured soloist with the jazz ensemble. Furthermore, she is currently a two-year all-state band member and is awaiting the results of the current year's auditions. She is the quintessential band student. Her director describes her as a band-room inhabitant. While she excels in other areas, music is clearly her direction of choice when it comes to selecting a profession. Her director has had ongoing conversations with her about choosing music education as a career and how to prepare. Discussions led to the decision to use the accomplished MCA in ensemble performance. After their initial conversations, they set up a plan to complete the experience and prepare her for music study after high school.

Through an agreement with the theory teacher and the band director, the two teachers set out a plan that would allow Jacquelyn to be successful on this venture. The first order was to select a program to perform. With the varied experiences in high school and home, Jacquelyn quickly narrowed down selections that highlighted her interests and abilities. Among the selections were "Elegy for Mippy II" by Bernstein, an Ewald Brass Quintet, and "I'm Getting Sentimental Over You." Throughout the process, Jacquelyn was detailed in her approach to completing the "Selecting Music Worksheet." Her attention to detail in identifying specific challenges in the pieces and her ability to address these challenges was beyond the capabilities of most students of her age. She was also able to set up a plan for how to address the deficiencies in skills and knowledge to appropriately perform the pieces by concert time. Furthermore, her interpretation of the pieces were veteran in nature due to extensive listening because of spending summers in the band room with her uncle and watching many rehearsals.

From week to week, Jacquelyn met with her director to go over her rehearsal journal and provide updates on her practice sessions. In these meetings, they would discuss problem areas, pedagogical approaches, and musicality of her performance. Jacquelyn's abilities as a technician were apparent throughout this process, and her ability to break tasks down into manageable chunks and then enact a plan was beyond her years as a high school senior. The most impressive part of Jacquelyn's experience was her ability to accurately assess her growth and ability to be self-critical.

Jacquelyn's performance was slated to be interludes between ensembles at the mid-winter concert. She had prepared well, and her performances were stellar. The seamlessness of performance ranging from unaccompanied solo to brass quintet was artfully accomplished. While she had not undertaken the "advanced" level, she was proud of her accomplishments and demonstrated a uniquely deep knowledge of music beyond that of a senior in high school. In following conversations, she began to ask how to connect these experiences to her future endeavors. What she found was that most candidates were asked only to play one instrument (of which she plays many) and sight-read a brief excerpt. How might she demonstrate this wealth of knowledge, skill, and disposition as well as her passion for music and teaching? How might this be measured and considered throughout the audition process?

Orchestra: Maria—Advanced Level

Maria is a high school senior who has played in school string programs since the third grade. Additionally, she plays in a community youth orchestra and *studies privately. Her private teacher has worked with her to develop a 20-minute recital program of varied repertoire with one selection of a Grade V piece. In preparation for this recital, Maria has completed the "Selecting Music Worksheet for Advanced," where she has identified technical challenges and expressive demands of specific sections of her recital repertoire, described her interpretation of the composer's expressive intent, the historical/cultural context, and the formal structure of her repertoire. Additionally, Maria completed the "Analyze, Interpret, Rehearse, Evaluate, and Refine Worksheet," where she developed a rehearsal plan to achieve musical goals based on her analyses of her recital selections. Through this assessment, Maria based her artistic decisions and approaches to technical challenges on research of performance practices and a thoughtful rehearsal plan. The result yielded a fine, research-informed recital and strong repertoire for her music school auditions.*

In Maria's orchestra class at school, she arranged a piece that maintains "the integrity of [an] original composition using similar or other compositional devices" (National Association for Music Education, 2015, p. 8). Using the "Plan and Make Worksheet," Maria created a sketch of her composition that guided her in scoring it for orchestra using traditional notation. Maria and some of her classmates performed her composition for the remainder of the orchestra and received feedback. She revised her composition according to the feedback received from her classmates and her teacher.

As she studied the recital pieces, she listened to recordings of various ensembles performing her recital repertoire. In preparing for college study, Maria completed the responding MCA at a higher level of sophistication. As a part of the advanced MCA, Maria used what was learned from listening to recorded performances to develop criteria to justify her selection of music. Additionally, Maria synthesized varied researched sources to justify her interpretive and expressive intent.

DISCUSSION

Ward and Payne (2017) noted differences between the focus of the 2014 NCCAS NAfME Music Standards and the common admission practices of college music programs. In examining the vignettes above, the researchers have found similar differences between the expected outcomes as demonstrated through the Model Cornerstone Assessments and admission practices. Maria, the string student at the advanced level, demonstrated skills that would be valuable for college music students in analyzing and preparing a piece for performance, creating and refining a composition, and interpreting music through the artistic process of responding. Furthermore, Jacquelyn began to wonder how to demonstrate her competencies when they were rarely (or ever) mentioned in the collegiate audition process. As Ward and Payne (2017) reported, relatively few music college admissions practices assess creative skills, such as composition and improvisation, and even fewer assess a student's ability to evaluate or respond to music.

Audition practices and procedures have been a source of investigation for decades (Brand, 1987; Colwell, 2006; Kelly, 1988; Lehmann, 2014; Motycka, 1969; Royston & Springer, 2015; Shellahamer, 1984). The National Association of Schools of Music (NASM) states, "as a matter of sound educational practice, institutions recruit and admit students only to programs or curricula for which they show aptitudes and prospects for success" (NASM, 2016, p. 68). Without assessing the skills that are intended outcomes of K–12 music education, collegiate music programs are using narrow criteria in determining the admission of students into their programs. Additionally, the information gleaned from a performance audition at the point of admissions is too narrow to provide college music faculty a full picture of a student's potential and prior musical achievements. As collegiate musical curricula include outcomes beyond performance, an admissions process limited to an audition of prepared repertoire does not seem adequate to assess the aptitudes and prospects for success of prospective students. Through examination of MCA results, college music faculty could find the evidence necessary to redevelop baseline expectations for admission while also informing their curricular and admissions practices. In addition to reexamining audition procedures, efforts could also be spent in all areas of curriculum and assessments that document advanced development in the artistic processes throughout the collegiate music programs. Developing curricula that intentionally advance all the artistic processes while including measurable demonstrations of process components could result in higher levels of comprehensive musicianship necessary for success in the 21st century.

As the MCAs and other authentic assessments are increasingly used in elementary and secondary schooling, assessments for college admission may move beyond diagnostic or placement exams toward a mechanism that demonstrates developmental musical growth through process components (such as creating and responding to music in addition to performing music). A focus on artistic literacy through the processes and components may require some adjustments when considering the traditional definitions of adequate preparation for college study. Such considerations may also influence content and instruction within college music programs, and possibly influence the diversity of offerings. While this is exciting, several questions about this topic emerge that must be addressed with research:

1. How might preparation through the 2014 NCCAS NAfME Music Standards affect university or college (including community college) admissions?

a. If students come in with a better understanding and application than before, how does that influence current diagnostic exams?
b. How will it influence course selection?
2. To what extent does the advanced achievement level, as defined in the 2014 NCCAS NAfME Music Standards, indicate readiness for study in a college music curriculum?
a. Do the other levels lend themselves to college study?
b. How will the students who have reached the advanced level of development compete within the current admission process and throughout curriculum at the college level?
3. How will the 2014 NCCAS NAfME Music Standards affect the design and delivery of music-education-teacher preparation programs?
4. How might student preparation through the 2014 NCCAS NAfME Music Standards affect university or college curriculum as recently examined through the College Music Society Report of the Task Force on the Undergraduate Music Major (Campbell et al., 2014)?

As more K–12 public school music programs use the 2014 NCCAS NAfME Music Standards and the Model Cornerstone Assessments associated with these standards, K–12 music teachers will invest more time in the responding and creative processes. This reinvestment of time and effort in precollege students will begin to alter the preparedness of prospective students. As described in the vignettes, how will preparation at a proficient performance level through involvement in choral music influence his or her later music studies? For a student like Jacquelyn, who was multitalented and may choose to vary her experiences through engagement with the artistic processes: While developing a high level of musicality and personal growth, will this experience be considered in a college audition process, or will her prior work be considered? If all these students demonstrate the ability to compose, improvise, and analyze musical styles as related to their performance repertoire and develop strategies to extend their own musical learning, the MCAs could provide college music faculty with information regarding students' musical abilities and prospects for success if considered as a factor in admission into a music program.

REFERENCES

Brand, M. (1987). The best and brightest: Admission requirements for music teachers. *Music Educators Journal, 73*(6), 32–36. doi:10.2307/3400259
Campbell, P. S., Convener, T. F., Sarath, E., Chattah, J., Higgins, L., Levine, V. L., & Rice, T. (2014). *Transforming music study from its foundations: A manifesto for progressive change in the undergraduate preparation of music majors.* Missoula, MT: College Music Society. Retrieved from http://symposium.music.org/index.php

Colwell, R. (2006). Music teacher education in this century: Part II. *Arts Education Policy Review, 108*(2), 17–29.

Glesne, C., & Peshkin, A. (1992). *Becoming qualitative researchers: An introduction.* White Plains, NY: Longman.

Kelly, S. (1988). Marketing your college music program to students. *Music Educators Journal, 75*(3), 27–29. Retrieved from http://www.jstor.org/stable/3398072

Lehmann, A. C. (2014). Using admission assessments to predict final grades in a college music program. *Journal of Research in Music Education, 62*(3), 245.

Motycka, A. (1969). *Music admission policies and practices: The music student enters the NASM accredited institution of higher education.* Retrieved from http://search.proquest.com.er.lib.k-state.edu/docview/64398518?accountid=11789

National Association for Music Education (NAfME). (n.d.). Home page for the National Core Arts Standards in Music. Retrieved from http://www.nafme.org/my-classroom/standards/mcas-information-on-taking-part-in-the-field-testing/

National Association for Music Education. (2015). Ensemble—Creating Model Cornerstone Assessment. Retrieved from http://www.nafme.org/wp-content/files/2014/11/Music_MCA_Ensemble_Creating_2015.pdf

National Association of Schools of Music (NASM). (2016). *Handbook 2016–17.* Reston, VA: National Association of Schools of Music.

Royston, N. S., & Springer, D. G. (2015). Beliefs of applied studio faculty on desirable traits of prospective music education majors: A pilot study. *Journal of Music Teacher Education, 25*(1), 78–94. doi:10.1177/1057083714549467

Shellahamer, B. R. (1984). *Selection and retention criteria in undergraduate music teacher education programs: Survey, analysis, and implications (admission, audition).* (PhD dissertation). Available from ProQuest Dissertations and Theses Global. (303320044).

Shuler, S. C. (2015, February). *Model cornerstone assessments (MCAs): A nationwide initiative.* [Audio podcast] Retrieved from http://www.nafme.org/my-classroom/standards/mcas-information-on-taking-part-in-the-field-testing/

Shuler, S. C., Norgaard, M., & Blakeslee, M. J. (2014). The new national standards for music educators. *Music Educators Journal, 101*(1), 41–49. doi:10.1177/0027432114540120

Ward, J. & Payne, P. (2017, April). *A survey of admission standards and procedures of higher education institutions in the United States in comparison to National Core Music Standards.* Paper presented at the 6th International Symposium on Assessment in Music Education, Birmingham, UK.

FIFTEEN

Curricular and Professional Implications

Frederick Burrack and Kelly A. Parkes

FITTING THE MCAs INTO CURRICULUM

The design of the Model Cornerstone Assessments is focused on student demonstration of each process component, as defined by the criteria in the 2014 National Music Standards (creating, performing, and responding processes). Students demonstrate the process components through tasks that align with the teacher's planned curricular learning sequences. The MCAs are designed for teachers to integrate current curricular content into the models, but music teachers have the option to use the content from the pilot study if they would like to. Whichever their choice, the scoring devices are not content specific; they are designed for consistent scoring of the process components across a variety of content and multiple contexts. The structure of the MCAs enables school curriculum designers, specifically music teachers, to address local instructional issues, relevant content, and desired skill development sequences appropriate for their student populations. Because the MCAs address components of the three artistic processes, it is important to maintain the variety of other assessments for content knowledge and skill development; these are requisite for the tasks but are not specifically assessed in the MCAs. Effective use of multiple assessments requires a shared intention among the music faculty to thoroughly address expectations of learning and a desire to share findings with those whose future instruction is likely to be affected (Mentkowski & Sharkey, 2011).

When the MCAs are used throughout all grade levels of a music program's curriculum, adjustments will have to be made to make the MCAs developmentally appropriate between grades 2, 5, and 8. Curriculum-aligned tasks should be selected that demonstrate the performance standards for the particular grade level. The rubrics from the MCA can be made grade-appropriate by incorporating criteria from the grade-level performance standard, since the National Standards are provided for each. While the performance standards are progressive, the process components and achievement levels remain structured similarly across grade levels.

Student achievement scores should be maintained using an efficient process that allows for analysis within and across each process component to identify learning achievements and to expose deficiencies, which can guide instructional decisions. Technology-based data collection and reporting processes will enable teachers to report individual students' progress as well as the entire class or cohort. The MCAs work well as a summative, one-point-in-time evaluation of achievement, but their strength is also in providing music teachers and their students with indicators of learning within individual components of an artistic process in an educative and formative manner. The scoring devices can expose challenges within an overall process that might hinder further progress. For example, if a student is not achieving a desired level of performance, the performing MCA can make evident a challenge experienced in the process component of (let's say) analyzing, thereby recognizing and informing what needs to be practiced or improved. The inability to identify challenging areas may be what is hindering progress in performance quality, affecting the quality of achievement in the remaining process components. Assessing the final performance product is insufficient to address improvement in the process that leads to the result.

If there is an expectation to document student progress over time, the MCA could be administered at multiple points in an academic year to compare progress in each process component. But in doing this, it is important to note that as students progress through a semester or year, the level of difficulty and complexity of the tasks presented to students often increases as well. This makes comparison of achievement questionable unless the consecutive assessments do not change in difficulty or complexity.

One of the most important findings of the pilot study is in the reliability of teachers assessing their own students. When peer teachers who were experienced with integrating the MCAs into a particular grade level blind-scored the work of other teachers' students as part of the study, we found the consistency of scoring was incredibly high. When expert teachers who had not experienced the measures in a classroom setting were brought in and taught to use the scoring devices, the consistency of scoring was very low. As Driscoll and Wood (2011) note, "it is important to recognize that assessment and the consequent improvement in teaching and learning must remain in the hands of instructors rather than administrators or outside testing agencies" (p. 17). The research resulting from the MCA development suggests that music teachers should be empowered to assess their own students and use the resulting data to guide improvements. The MCAs and professional development must be intimately connected, adequately resourced, and aligned with a school's curricular structure. It is important to note here that teachers using the MCAs, now that the pilot study is complete, will typically not score other teachers' student work or upload student work to be scored by any other individual. However, based on our research, teachers and their administrators should feel confident that the scores given to students by teachers actively engaged in using the National Music Standards and the MCAs are reliable, valid, and to be trusted.

STUDENT OWNERSHIP OF LEARNING

The 2014 National Standards for Music are clearly focused on student experiences with music through developing literacy in three artistic processes. Each process component and the performance standards describe what students do, in contrast to what teachers do through instruction. The enduring understandings and essential questions are also worded to define intended student experiences. Within this experiential paradigm, the MCAs are designed for illustrating student experience and demonstrating all that is defined in the National Standards. Each MCA guides instructional preparation, provides suggestions for the assessment environment, and defines a step-by-step protocol to assist the teacher. Together, these suggestions are designed to help the student learn through the assessment task as it unfolds. The scoring rubrics define what teachers look for *as defined by the performance standards*. Throughout the task, students demonstrate each component of the artistic process. The flexibility designed into each MCA allows students to demonstrate the artistic processes and their component parts in the way most suited to their personal experience with music.

As students internalize the artistic processes through developmental experiences, the possibility they will maintain, continue development, and transfer learning beyond the singular experience may contribute to a lifelong involvement with music. As music educators incorporate and expand on these student-centered learning assessments, the pedagogy of music teaching may also be affected. When school music programs embrace assessments of student learning that allow for the multiple forms of student experience, what defines student achievement will be expanded beyond the current structures of music programs. What used to be considered as alternative forms of musical experience can be embraced alongside traditional products of musical performance. This may also empower future music educators by preparing graduates with the instructional skills and strategies that enable them to take full advantage of the artistic processes and increase their ownership of their music learning.

ENHANCING EXPERIENCES IN SCHOOL MUSIC

As music educators introduce and incorporate the MCAs in their current curricula, they will encounter several instructional considerations. Concerning student performing experiences, music teachers may need to redesign instruction to allow for student preparation of and experiences with each process component. Developmental guidance for students to select appropriate music, analyze and interpret music, and self-regulate their practice skills is often left to chance, or is sometimes dictated by the teacher. Instructional plans for student learning will need to allow for, and guide, student experience through each of the process components.

Music classrooms often embody expectations for students to respond to the music they hear. Intentional instruction of students to listen, analyze, interpret, and evaluate music is often included at elementary levels of instruction. Extending development of responding into ensembles and other musical strands may not initially be recognized as beneficial. Included as a learning component, developing proficiencies in responding may not only enhance performance quality, but can also contribute to lifelong appreciation.

The act of creating music has not been prevalent in many music classrooms. Preparing instruction for students to experience the creating process has often been considered as enrichment beyond traditional music curricula. The creating MCAs can provide valuable guidance to help teachers include this artistic process in all areas of music learning. Professional development for the process of creating can often be found at professional conferences, but the easiest form of guidance can often be found through interactions between music educators in schools or among school districts. The artistic process of creating does not necessarily mean composing. The process components of creating can be attained through a variety of experiences. Such experiences could include improvising a short cadenza based on the melody of a piece to insert into a solo, improvising a new ending to a short piece in a method book, developing a new theme for a theme and variation, creatively editing the expressive decision used in a composition, choosing a pop tune and creating a version or cover, creating a new verse for a song, or mashing a variety of electronic sequences or recorded segments into a new piece. Although composing is often the initial consideration, the artistic process of creating does not specify only the act of *composing*. The act of *creating* music can and should be varied and individualized for students.

The MCAs are not intended to dictate what an artistic experience should look like. This has never been the intent of any MCA tasks. The MCA writers designed the tasks to test the rubrics in ways that were typical or comfortable to most music teachers. Consideration of a typical music classroom (with expert teachers' feedback during the pilot study) influenced decisions with respect to the MCA design. There is no intent to imply that these are the only or preferred ways to apply or assess the standards. Music teachers and their students are encouraged to explore the various ways that students can experience and develop artistic processes. The MCAs are models to assist music teachers, using tested rubrics, that are sufficiently flexible to be applicable in all settings and contexts.

FUTURE RESEARCH OPPORTUNITIES

The pilot research was designed to identify usefulness of the assessment tasks in music classrooms around the United States, the degree to which the scoring rubrics reflect the intent of the standards, and the consistency with which the rubrics could accurately score student work from a variety of contexts. The findings were positive, but certainly not exhaustive of possibilities. It was clear that the scoring rubrics were found to be reflective of the standards. Those that were questionable were revised until content and construct validity were confirmed. The rubrics were consistent in scoring student work among the teachers and blind-peer scorers. Classroom teachers did not score their own students' work with any more severity or leniency than did the peer teachers. Teachers from schools of various sizes and in a variety of economic contexts were found to score consistently using the rubrics. It was found that teachers who were trained in scoring with the rubrics but who had not piloted the MCAs were extremely inconsistent in scoring student work. Consistency of scoring seemed to require the scorer to have implemented and experienced the use of the MCA at the designated grade level in a classroom. The practice of using external scorers to score a teachers' student work with these rubrics is not recommended, in fact, strongly discouraged. Additional confirmation of this finding is suggested for future research. If future studies also find that the most effective scorers of students' work are their classroom teachers and that music educators score their own students as consistently as peer teachers, this will support our finding. The consideration of trusting music teachers to assess their own students when using assessments should be made clear to the profession with replication studies wherever possible.

Replication research on piloted MCAs or validity/reliability research on the MCAs not completed in the pilot provide many opportunities for future research for school music teachers and collaborative researchers. Similar research should include confirming and adapting assessment-task design, refining administration protocols, and enhancing clarity of the scoring devices. Developing alternative task frameworks to which the rubrics might be applied could be a goal of research opportunities. Some researchers (e.g., Beason, 2017) are already taking up the challenge. Testing the rubrics using a variety of curricular content may be an important extension of the current research. Examinations of cultural relevancy or cultural bias are strongly encouraged. Additionally, investigations of the use of the rubrics across socioeconomic status, school size, region, and other relevant demographics could provide valuable information that will inform future use of the MCAs and certainly will uncover issues not yet considered.

REFERENCES

Beason, C. (2017). *A mixed methods design study investigating the use of a music authentic performance assessment tool by high school band directors to measure student musical growth.* (Doctoral dissertation). Texas Wesleyan University, Fort Worth.

Driscoll, A., & Wood, S. (2011). *Developing outcomes-based assessment for learner-centered education: A faculty introduction.* Herndon: Stylus Publishing.

Mentkowski, M., & Sharkey, S. (2011). How we know it when we see it: Conceptualizing and assessing integrative and applied learning-in-use. *New Directions for Institutional Research, 149,* 93–107. doi:10.1002/ir.383

About the Contributors

Dr. Ann Clements researched and led the development and piloting of the MCAs for eighth grade. An active researcher, musician, and pedagogue, Clements has given over 150 presentations throughout the United States and in Australia, Brazil, the Baltics, Canada, Japan, Mexico, New Zealand, and the United Kingdom. She has published in multiple national and international journals including the *Journal of Research in Music Education, Mountain Lake Reader, International Society for Music Education, General Music Today*, and the *Journal of Research for the New Zealand Performing Arts*. Clements is the author, coauthor, and editor of several books in the field of music education, including *The Field Guide to Student Teaching in Music, Alternative Approaches to Music Education: Case Studies from the Field* (editor, Rowman & Littlefield), *Teaching General Music* (chapter author), *Multicultural Perspective in Music Education* (chapter author and editor, Rowman & Littlefield), *Making Music Series* (contributing author), and *The Choral Cookbook* (chapter author).

Dr. Al D. Holcomb is department chair and associate professor of music education at Westminster Choir College of Rider University. He guided the development and piloting of the ensemble MCAs focused on application in choral ensemble classes. Dr. Holcomb regularly presents at national and international conferences on the topics of music assessment, music teacher mentoring and professional development, choral music education, adolescent vocal development, and aural skill development. His articles, papers, and book chapters appear in the *Journal of Research in Music Education*, the *Oxford Handbook of Assessment Policy and Practice in Music Education*, symposia proceedings from International Symposia for Assessment in Music Education, and publications by the National Association for Music Education.

As a Scholar in Residence at the Connecticut State Department of Education, Dr. Holcomb was a leader in development of standards and portfolio assessment for beginning music teachers. As cochair of the Florida Music Assessment Project, he led the development of statewide written tests for music students in grades 8 and 12. Dr. Holcomb served as the choral ensemble research advisor for the development of the 2014 National Core Music Standards and Model Cornerstone Assessments for ensembles. He received his bachelor of music education degree from Texas Christian University and graduate degrees in music education from the Hartt School, University of Hartford.

In addition to teaching middle and high school choral music in Texas and Connecticut, he has conducted various choirs at the Hartt School, University of Central Florida, Singing Boys of Houston, Connecticut Children's Chorus, and honor choirs around the country.

Dr. Daniel C. Johnson took over the pilot for the second grade MCA after the passing of Dr. Carla Maltas. In addition to analyzing data and authoring the chapter for the Second Grade MCA, he also analyzed data and coauthored the chapter for the Harmonizing Instruments MCA. He is a professor of music and music education at the University of North Carolina, Wilmington. A graduate of the New England Conservatory, the University of Arizona, St. Louis Conservatory, and Emory University, he is a distinguished teacher-educator, scholar, researcher, and author. During the past 25 years, Dr. Johnson's teaching experience has spanned the preK–university gamut. A Medici Scholar, he is an international authority on music education pedagogy, having presented teacher education workshops throughout the world, reaching hundreds of teachers and thousands of their students on six continents. Focusing on classroom music instruction, music listening, arts integration, and teachers' professional development, Dr. Johnson regularly receives funding from national- and state-level foundations for his research and outreach projects, including the National Endowment for the Arts, the National Science Foundation, the College Music Society, the North Carolina Arts Council, the American Orff-Schulwerk Association, and Partners of the Americas. His research publications appear in numerous eminent journals including: the *Journal of Research in Music Education*, the *Bulletin of the Council for Research in Music Education*, the *International Journal of Music Education*, *Visions of Research in Music Education*, the *International Journal of Teaching and Learning in Higher Education*, and *Contributions to Music Education*. In addition to the Model Cornerstone Assessment chapters for second-grade learners and harmonizing instruments in this volume, Dr. Johnson has authored a chapter on Orff-Schulwerk Pedagogy in the *Oxford Handbook of Assessment Policy and Practice in Music Education*. His textbook, *Musical Explorations: Fundamentals Through Experience*, is in its sixth edition and published by Kendall Hunt.

Dr. Wendy K. Matthews researched and led the development and piloting of the MCAs for harmonizing instruments. As assistant professor of music at Wayne State University, she teaches courses in music education with emphasis on instrumental music education and conducting. Dr. Matthews holds degrees from the Peabody Conservatory of Music, University of Maryland–College Park, and George Mason University. Dr. Matthews is in demand as guest conductor, clinician, and adjudicator and is the recipient of several teaching awards and research grants. She is also coauthor of *Basic Conducting Techniques* (seventh edition) with Joe Labuta. She has published in numerous journals such as the *Journal of Research in Music Education, Psychology of Music, International Journal of Music Education, Research and Issues in Music Education Journal, Journal of Band Research*, and the *International Journal of Education and the Arts*.

Mary Kate Newell assisted in analysis of the data from the fifth-grade pilot and authoring the chapter. She is a music educator at Chestnut Hill College and the Tatnall School. She is an active performer in the tri-state area and has performed nationally and internationally.

Glenn E. Nierman (BM, Washburn; MM, Cincinnati; DME, Cincinnati), was the researcher assigned to oversee the development and piloting of the ensemble MCAs with instrumental ensembles. He is National Association for Music Education (NAfME) immediate past president for 2016–2018 and is currently Glenn Korff Professor of Music Education at the Glenn Korff School of Music at the University of Nebraska–Lincoln. He teaches graduate courses in curriculum, assessment, and quantitative research methodologies, as well as a non-major popular music guitar class and Introduction to Music Education. His research interests include assessment, instructional strategies, and pre-service music teacher education. Dr. Nierman has authored many journal articles and books; made numerous presentations at NAfME conferences; and given addresses at World Congresses of the International Society of Music Education (ISME) on five continents. His public school teaching experience includes work with middle school general music and choir, as well as high school band and orchestra. Glenn, a past president of both NAfME's North Central Division and the Nebraska Music Educators Association (NMEA), also served his state MEA as chairperson for the following: College/University Affairs, Research, the Council for Music Teacher Education (a NAfME/SMTE state affiliate), and the Coalition for Music Education (the "advocacy arm" of NMEA). He recently completed a term on the ISME executive board and currently chairs NAfME's teacher evaluation task force, which recently completed the publication of second editions of two *Workbooks for Building and Evaluating Effective Music Education—Ensembles and General Music*. His latest scholarly writing includes two chapters in the *Oxford Handbook of Assessment Policy and Practice in Music Education*, edited by Tim Brophy, to be published in 2018.

Denese Odegaard took the lead in development and piloting of the fifth-grade MCAs. She is currently National Association for Music Education (NAfME) president (2016–2018), the Fargo (North Dakota) Public Schools Performing Arts Curriculum Specialist, and has taught orchestra for 33 years. National service includes board member on both the American String Teachers Association (ASTA) and NAfME. While on the ASTA board, she was chair of the Committee on School Orchestra and Strings and received the ASTA Citation for Leadership twice. She was a member of the NCCAS 3rd–5th Grade Writing Team as the Research Advisory. Odegaard authored *Curriculum Writing 101: Assistance with Standards-Based Music Curriculum and Assessment Writing for Band, Choir, Orchestra and General Music*, coauthored the ASTA curriculum (Alfred) and e-Book, *ASTA String curriculum: Assessment Companion*, and has contributed to several GIA, NAfME, ASTA, Alfred, FJH, and Corwin publications.

Dr. Phillip Payne researched and led the development and piloting of the MCA for technology. As associate professor of music education at Kansas State University specializing in instrumental music education, he serves as chair of the music education division and lead advisor for music education. He teaches undergraduate and graduate classes in music education, and supervises student teachers. His contributions for this book were the piloting of the technology MCA and writing the chapter on establishing connections with higher education. His research interests include assessment in music education, technology integration, music education advocacy, music teacher recruiting and retention, personality and instrument choice, and learning strategies for the music classroom. He is an active member of the National Association for Music Education, Society of Music Teacher Education, and Kansas Music Educators Association, where he recently completed six years as the cochair for advocacy. He maintains an active research agenda presenting at international and national symposia. He is also an active adjudicator, clinician, and guest conductor throughout the midwestern United States.

Patricia Riley (priley@uvm.edu), DMA, led the research, development, and piloting of the composition/theory MCAs. She is professor and coordinator of the music education program at the University of Vermont. Prior to this, she taught at the Crane School of Music, State University of New York at Potsdam. Previously, Dr. Riley taught instrumental, general, and choral music for 20 years in the public schools of New Jersey and Vermont; and for five years maintained a woodwind and brass studio at Green Mountain College. Her publishing includes the book *Creating Music: What Children from Around the World Can Teach Us*. She has also published articles in *Music Education Research*; *Research and Issues in Music Education*; *Update: Applications of Research in Music Education*; *Visions of Research in Music Education*; *Journal of Technology in Music Learning*; *College Music Symposium*; *Music Educators Journal*; *Teaching Music*; *General Music Today*; and the *Vermont Music Educator*. In addition to the Model Cornerstone Assessment chapter for composition/theory in this volume, Dr. Riley has contributed numerous chapters to edited books and symposium proceedings including a chapter on composition in international settings in *Composing Our Future: Preparing Music Educators to Teach Composition*. Dr. Riley is a frequent presenter of sessions at international, national, regional, and state conferences. Her research interests include student music composition, cultural studies, technology, and assessment.

Michael J. Ruybalid, PhD, assisted in analysis of data and coauthoring the chapter for the fifth-grade MCAs. He is currently on the faculty of the University of Maryland School of Music where he teaches courses in elementary general music education and supervises music interns. Previously, Dr. Ruybalid was on the faculty of Southeastern Louisiana University, where he taught methods courses in early childhood, elementary, and secondary music education, and supervised student teachers. He earned his PhD in music education from the University of Oklahoma. Prior to beginning his doctoral studies, Dr. Ruybalid taught preK–12th music for eight years in both private and public schools in the San Francisco Bay Area. Dr. Ruybalid has presented conference sessions and workshops at the local, state, and national levels, including sessions on early childhood music for the Early Childhood Music and Movement Association (EC-MMA) and the Organization of American Kodály Educators (OAKE). His research interests include the examination of student intentions regarding school music participation. He has presented his research at state, national, and international research conferences, including the Desert Skies Symposium on Music Education Research and the International Kodály Society (IKS) Symposium. Dr. Ruybalid currently holds Kodály certification (Levels 1–3), Orff-Schulwerk certification (Levels 1–3, Master Class with Chris Judah-Lauder) and Elementary Level 1 certification in Dr. Edwin Gordon's Music Learning Theory.

Dr. Bret Smith led the research, development, and piloting of the ensemble MCAs, focusing on string music education. He is a cellist, conductor, and string teacher/educator who has taught strings and orchestra in a variety of K–12 and private settings as well as university and youth orchestra programs. He is coauthor, with James O. Froseth, of the *Do It! Play Strings* string method series. He has served as an adjudicator, clinician, and program consultant for numerous state and local string programs, and on the editorial committee for several journals in education and psychology including the *String Research Journal* and the *Bulletin of the Council for Research in Music Education*. His research publications have appeared in the *Journal of Research in Music Education*, the *Bulletin of the Council for Research in Music Education*, and *Psychology of Music*. He has contributed chapters to the *MENC Handbook of Research on Music Learning*; *Engaging Musical Practices: A Sourcebook for Instrumental Music* published by Rowman & Littlefield; and two volumes of the Assessment in Music Education series. His chapter on music education assessment policy in the United States will appear in the forthcoming *Oxford Handbook of Assessment Policy and Practice in Music Education*.

His interest in assessment has extended to working with accreditation and assessment issues across higher education applications. He is currently representing Central Washington University's faculty in Washington's state capital as a member of the Council of Faculty, serving as graduate coordinator and interim associate chair of CWU's music department, and coordinating CWU's summer MM program in music education. He also serves as faculty assessment coordinator through CWU's office of the associate provost.

Dr. Smith holds BM and BS degrees in music and systematic musicology from the University of Washington and MM and PhD degrees from the University of Michigan. He is a former member of the faculty of the School of Music at the University of Maryland, College Park.

Dr. Jeffrey Ward assisted in research supporting the connections between the MCAs and collegiate entrance expectations. He has published in national choral and music education journals and presented music education research in Brazil, Canada, China, Germany, Greece, Taiwan, and the United Kingdom and throughout the United States. He is chair of the assessment special research interest group of the National Association for Music Education and a review board member for the International Symposium for Assessment in Music Education. As a conductor, Dr. Ward has previously served as director of music at St. James United Methodist Church in Greenville and artistic director of the Greenville Choral Society. Dr. Ward has also been a guest conductor for county and regional honor choirs. Previously, he has served as the associate dean in the College of Fine Arts and Communication and the associate director of the School of Music at East Carolina University.

Dr. Kristina R. Weimer is an assistant professor of music education at the University of Texas–Rio Grande Valley, specializing in instrumental music education. Weimer's preK–12 teaching experience includes middle school band and general music, elementary general music, early childhood music, and elementary special education (behavior disorders). She has presented at multiple state, national, and international conferences in the United States and Europe. Her research interests include mentoring novice music teachers and professional development for all music teachers. Weimer earned degrees in music education from West Virginia University (BS, MM) and Pennsylvania State University (PhD), and was the 2017 recipient of the A. Peter Costanza PhD in Music Education Outstanding Dissertation Award.

Dr. Brian Wesolowski was the researcher overseeing the Rasch analysis and assisted in the findings discussion. Brian Wesolowski is an assistant professor of music education at the University of Georgia, Hugh Hodgson School of Music, where his teaching focuses on quantitative research design, assessment and policy in music, and psychometrics. He earned his PhD in music education from the University of Miami in Coral Gables, Florida. He holds a bachelor of music degree in music education and jazz performance as well as a master of music education degree from Oberlin College Conservatory of Music. In addition, he holds a master of music degree in jazz studies from the University of North Texas.

His research interests include rater behavior, scale development, policy of educational assessment, and the cognition, action, perception, and expressiveness in improvised jazz and groove-based performances. He has worked closely with multiple state departments of education, the National Coalition for Core Arts Standards (NCCAS), the State Education Agency Directors of Arts Education (SEADAE), the National Board of Professional Teaching Standards, and NAfME's Model Cornerstone Assessment Pilot Study, for which he was responsible for the data analysis of multiple projects. He continues to present research papers internationally and nationally and has articles forthcoming or published in the *Journal of Research in Music Education; Bulletin of the Council for Research in Music Education; Educational Assessment; Research Studies in Music Education; PLOS ONE; Music Perception;* the *Journal of New Music Research; Musicae Scientiae; International Journal of Music Education; Psychology of Music; Psychomusicology: Music, Mind, and Brain; Research Perspectives in Music Education; Music Educators Journal; Saxophone Symposium; Florida Music Director;* and *Georgia Music News.* He has chapters in the *Oxford Handbook of Assessment Policy and Practice in Music Education* and the *SAGE Encyclopedia of Educational Research, Measurement, and Evaluation.*

Dr. Katherine Willow assisted with the pilot and coauthored the chapter for the 8th grade MCAs. She is currently a Doctoral Advisor in the School of Social and Behavioral Sciences at Capella University. Prior to her transition to the University level, she taught choral, instrumental, and general music at the elementary and secondary levels. She holds a Doctor of Musical Arts degree in Music Education from Boston University and degrees in Music Education and Harp Performance from The Boston Conservatory. Dr. Willow's research interests include the role of music education in identity development, boys' identities, and social justice in and through music education, and she has presented on these topics at state, regional, and international conferences. She maintains an active performance career and is co-founder of Gentle Muses, the therapeutic music program at Massachusetts General Hospital.

About the Editors

Dr. Frederick Burrack, PhD, was co-researcher overseeing the MCA development and pilot. Dr. Burrack is director of assessment, chair of graduate studies in music, and distinguished graduate professor at Kansas State University. He is past chair of the National Association for Music Education (NAfME) Society for Research in Music Education (SRME) Assessment Special Research Interest Group (SRIG). He joined the Kansas State music faculty as a music education specialist in fall 2005. He taught instrumental music education at Ball State University from 2002 to 2005 and instrumental music in the Carroll Community School District in Carroll, Iowa, from 1982 to 2002.

He acted as cochair overseeing the national pilot of Model Cornerstone Assessments aligned with the new National Standards for Music Education. Dr. Burrack's research interests include student learning processes and assessment of learning, cross-disciplinary instruction, and instructional thought development in music teachers. He guides professional development seminars across the United States, has numerous publications in music education and assessment journals, and has presented many conference sessions nationally and internationally.

His publications appear in numerous eminent journals including the *Journal of Research in Music Education*; *Music Educators Journal*; *Research and Issues in Music Education*; *Update: Applications of Research in Music Education*; *Academic Intersections*; and *Journal of Technology in Music Learning*. Dr. Burrack has authored chapters in *Teaching Music through Performance in Band*; *Music Assessment Across Cultures and Continents: The Culture of Shared Practice*; *Connecting Practice, Measurement, and Evaluation*; and the *SAGE Encyclopedia of Educational Research, Measurement, and Evaluation*. His latest scholarly writing includes two chapters in the *Oxford Handbook of Assessment Policy and Practice in Music Education*, edited by Tim Brophy, to be published in 2018.

The NAfME honored Dr. Burrack as an exemplary leader in music education as 2017 Lowell Mason Fellow.

Kelly A. Parkes, PhD, was co-researcher overseeing the MCA development and pilot. Dr. Parkes is an associate professor of music and music education at Teachers College, Columbia University, where she directs the student teaching and initial certification program and is the chair of the Teacher Education Policy Committee. Her focus is on conducting quality research and preparing effective music educators and music teacher educators. Dr. Parkes is originally from Australia and has been performing, researching, and teaching in the United States for nearly two decades. Her research interests are in assessment, measuring aspects of music learning and teaching within K–12 schools, and the applied studio. She also examines teaching readiness, professional dispositions, and reflective practices in preservice teachers. She has served as chair of the National Association for Music Education (NAfME) Society for Research in Music Education's (SRME) Assessment Special Research Interest Group (SRIG) and contributed to the Music Teacher Evaluation Workbooks with NAfME. She serves on the editorial committee for the *Journal for Research in Music Education* and is the editor of the *Journal of Research in Music Performance*, in addition to serving on the board of the International Trumpet Guild. Her sustained research activity is found in highly regarded publications such as the *International Journal for Music Education*; the *Journal of Research in Music Education*; the *Journal for Research in Teacher Education*; the *British Journal of Music Education*; the *Bulletin for the Council of Research in Music Education*; *Update: Applications of Research in Music Education*; the *International Journal of Teaching and Learning in Higher Education*; the *International Journal of ePortfolio*; and the *Journal of Technology and Teacher Education*. The NAfME honored Dr. Parkes as an exemplary leader in music education as 2017 Lowell Mason Fellow.

Made in the USA
Middletown, DE
16 August 2024

59219241R00137